Natural by Design

Natural by Design

BEAUTY AND BALANCE
IN SOUTHWEST GARDENS

Judith Phillips

Photographs by
Charles Mann and Judith Phillips

Museum of New Mexico Press
Santa Fe

Manufactured in Korea

Project editor: Mary Wachs
Art director: David Skolkin
Design by: Deborah Fleig
Typography: Set in Bauer Bodoni with Sanvito display on Quark XPress.

Library of Congress cataloguing-in-publication data available.
ISBN *Natural by Design* 0-89013-276-3 (cb); 0-89103-277-1 (pb).
ISBN *Plants for Natural Gardens* 0-89013-281-x (pb).

MUSEUM OF NEW MEXICO PRESS
Post Office Box 2087
Santa Fe, New Mexico 87504

10   9   8   7   6   5   4   3   2

Photograph page ii: An upland meadow of Indian paintbrush and blue flax. CM

Contents

Introduction

NATURAL GARDENING IS A FRESH BREEZE in the world of horticulture. Because its focus is balance rather than control, it is a process that can go on without us but which is richer and more beautiful when we have a hand in it.

Natural by Design applies nature's patterns in developing gardens that reward us with their beauty and ease, despite the extremes of heat and cold, sparse rainfall, poor soils, and blasting winds that defeat less-adapted efforts. It is difficult to give the specific geographical limitations of this book because the ideas and information range from the unbordered realm of human attitudes to the very localized boundries of a street median in Albuquerque. This book applies in spirit to gardening in any difficult dry climate. Specifically, it addresses places in the western United States where:

- elevation ranges between 3,500 and 7,500 feet
- rainfall averages between eight and twenty-five inches annually
- summer high temperatures reach at least ninety degrees F but don't exceed one hundred fifty degrees F
- coldest nighttime winter temperatures drop into the low teens fairly often and may plummet to minus fifteen degrees F on occasion
- day-to-night temperatures fluctuate greatly, commonly thirty to forty degrees daily, occasionally sixty degrees or more within a few hours

A DRIER SOUTHERN UPLAND EXPOSURE FEATURES BAMBOO MUHLY AND LIVE OAK. CM

- soils are frequently alkaline, sometimes saline, and always lacking in organic matter
- strong winds blow virtually year-round

In such places, nature provides solutions for our horticultural woes, if only we know how and where to look. This book is about harmony, about loving where you are on its own terms without surrendering the comforts of home. While *Natural by Design* is about ideas and attitudes, its companion book, *Plants for Natural Gardens*, describes the native and adaptive plants that are the core of natural gardens in the context of how they work in their native ecosystems and how that translates to their use and care in the garden. While each book stands alone, together they are form and content, the map and the fuel for the journey.

All the people who support our landscape design and plant-growing businesses have contributed to the information presented in these pages. Many thanks are due our patrons who take the time to let us know how plants are doing in their gardens so that we can better understand the range of their adaptations (those of the plants and their adoptive parents both). I am lucky to have an occupation (and preoccupation) that is filled with caring people and beautiful places, where every day offers a hundred opportunities to learn something new. Jean and Bill Heflin, Ellen Wilde, and Maggi Caffo have developed truly beautiful gardens by trusting their own instincts. Judy Mandell, Carol Treat, Nancy and Roy Skeens, Russ and Irene Howard, Byron Garner, Gloria and Deneb Teleki, Carol Kinney, and Bob Levin trusted me with their garden challenges and visions and generously agreed to share the results of our collaborations. Thanks to Carol Sutherland, entomologist and director of the Nursery Division of the New Mexico Dept. of Agriculture. I have also been very fortunate to participate in many community projects, including the Albuquerque Police Department xeriscape garden (designed by volunteers including Mil Fleig, George Radnovich, Diane Scena, Robert Squires, Susan Wachter, and myself), Los Padillas Elementary School's outdoor classroom, the Layton Avenue median, and Bosque del Apache National Wildlife Refuge's habitat garden. The descriptions of these gardens, the concerns that shape them, and how they have developed to meet changes in time and space are included not to set them up as models to imitate but to illustrate some ways of applying the ideas to real places. It may all distill down to two words: diversity and flexibility.

I owe special thanks to my partner, Roland Phillips, whose common sense and sense of play keep me buoyant and on course. Thanks to him and to Valda Steele for picking up my considerable slack so that I could focus on writing. These pages would not be nearly as pleasant to peruse without the images of Charles Mann, whose love of plants, gardens, and nature translates so clearly on film. And bouquets to Mary Wachs, my editor, whose job is as easy as herding butterflies, and to David Skolkin, art director, and Deborah Fleig, designer, for smoothing the rough edges.

Natural
by Design

1 A Sense of Place

In the world of horticulture, the degree of difficulty in growing plants—how inappropriate those plants are to their surroundings—has in the past been a measure of their value: the more demanding, the more precious. Only weeds grow like weeds. There's a perverse logic to this reasoning, since a garden at odds with local ecology costs more in labor, fertilizer, water, and pesticides to maintain than does a garden in harmony with its ecological surroundings. In that respect, it is worth more. In the American Southwest, as expanding human populations consume resources beyond our desert's capacity for renewal, we are beginning to reassess those values. Traditional landscapes, accomplishments that they are, lack a connection to place that would make them easier on the environment and the gardener without compromising the beauty that is the impetus for gardening.

This process of attitude adjustment has many faces. Xeriscape, permaculture, natural gardening, habitat gardening, and regional, native, and environmentally responsible landscaping are some of the names given to the effort to make horticulture more responsive to place. Natural gardening is a concept I'm comfortable with because it is broad in scope, with none of the connotations of deprivation that conservation wrongly conjures up. Gardening to enhance a place is, or should be, an honest attempt to cooperate with that place in realizing its potential. In doing so, the gardener cultivates an appreciation of local ecosystems, adapting their essentials for garden use. The result is a beautiful place in balance with the world of which it is an inextricable part.

NATURAL GARDENS RESPOND CREATIVELY TO THE HARSH REALITIES OF HIGH-DESERT CLIMATES. CM

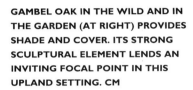

GAMBEL OAK IN THE WILD AND IN THE GARDEN (AT RIGHT) PROVIDES SHADE AND COVER. ITS STRONG SCULPTURAL ELEMENT LENDS AN INVITING FOCAL POINT IN THIS UPLAND SETTING. CM

To truly *know* where we are in the landscape takes time. With an open mind and our senses engaged, we begin to recognize the patterns woven from the interplay of climate, exposures, soils, wind, and inhabitants. Some places are harder to come to terms with than others, and the Southwest deserts are quite stubborn in their demands. There's a world of difference between untended wildness and a natural garden. Wild landscapes are formed by the forces of nature, evolved over time in response to climate, soils, and exposures. Gardens are human domains. Expressions of our creativity, they are places we can be comfortable in nature. When we use natural ecosystems as models to design our gardens, we blend thousands of years of evolutionary fine-tuning with our creative efforts. Reciprocity, balancing what we extract from our local ecosystem with what we contribute to its continued vitality, is the cornerstone of natural design.

In the arid Southwest, natural gardens are water conservative xeriscapes. They are sustainable in the permaculture sense that they do not require constant infusions of resources to survive. They are responsible in that they are based on plant communities able to respond to all the horticultural insults: the meager soils and intense sunlight, baking heat and numbing cold, incessant wind and scarce moisture that the high desert hurls their way. Natural gardens are habitats, not homocentric spaces. These are equal-opportunity affairs where bugs and bacteria are just as essential as trees and flowers, butterflies and birds. We are the hosts at a garden party celebrating the intricate web of interdependence among species.

Natural gardens are the edges where horticulture and wilderness, art and natural history meet. Like the edges where any two ecosystems meet, they are richer and more dynamic than either part by itself. Such gardens are comfortable living spaces for us as well as links in a greenbelt network for wildlife. They are places responsive to the needs of their diverse inhabitants.

While the design and establishment stages of natural gardens can require more effort than conventional landscapes, that same design determines how much and what kind of maintenance will be needed over the long term, as well as how the garden will look and feel. Rather than constantly working to make the garden stay the same, managing a natural garden involves establishing a dynamic equilibrium where desirable plants displace weeds, controlled watering keeps plants healthy, and insect activity is more often welcomed than perceived as a threat. The most important skills needed are keen observation and the finesse to know when to let nature take its course and when to intervene as unobtrusively as possible. Once the balance is struck, the ecogardener trades the drone of the lawn mower for the song of the meadowlark. Who says that conservation demands sacrifice!

Gardens are ultimately about plants. Do we limit ourselves to native plants, and how do we define "native"? The Southwest is a place of contrasts, an ecological mosaic of life zones and plant communities. Mountains rise, sometimes abruptly, above the sweep

APACHE PLUME, ANCHORING THE
SOIL OF AN UPLAND SLOPE, DEFIES
THE EXTREMES OF HEAT AND COLD,
DROUGHT AND DELUGE.

CANYON ROCK FACES WORN
SMOOTH BY CENTURIES OF WIND
AND RAIN SUPPORT A DIVERSITY OF
VEGETATION IN THE CREVICES
WHERE PLANTS CAN SINK ROOTS.

of high-plains grassland and shrub desert. Temperatures, rainfall, and consequently the native plant communities change with the rise and fall of the land. The miles of piñon and juniper, sagebrush, creosotebush, and grasses that seem to roll on until tomorrow give a false impression of emptiness. Southwestern ecosystems are complex communities, fragile because of the harshness of the climate, yet resilient, having evolved in response to that austerity. What we casually observe as acres of sagebrush changes dramatically with the contour of the land, proximity to paved roads, and history of land management. Upslope the sage yields to grasses on the pebbly soils of wind-scoured hilltops. In the washes, desert willows and Apache plume anchor the soil against seasonal flooding. Bush penstemon and chocolate flower line roadside swales, benefiting from the extra water that sheets off the pavement during rainstorms. Each plant community has dominant plants, those that cover vast areas, and an amazing diversity of incidental species that occupy niches within the larger scheme. The aim in natural gardening is to work within the parameters of local conditions but also to explore as broad a range of plant-selection options as the site allows.

In the Southwest, human populations are concentrated in the foothills, desert grasslands, and river valleys where the topography reluctantly entertains farming and ranching and where accidents of natural history or political history built mining boomtowns, railroads, and today's cities. The elevation of human communities ranges mostly between thirty-five hundred and eight thousand feet, with precipitation ranging respectively from three to thirty inches annually. Such are the places southwesterners make their gardens. This book is about gardening in the cold deserts, high plains, and mountain foothills of New Mexico, but while the focus is high desert, many of the concepts discussed will apply in any arid climate, the difference quite literally being one of degree: three degrees F cooler or warmer per five hundred miles north or south, or a thousand feet higher or lower in elevation, being the degree required to shift from one ecozone to the next.

THE DUNES AND VALLEYS OF WHITE SANDS NATIONAL MONUMENT (NEW MEXICO) HARBOR A COMMUNITY OF DESERT PLANTS ADAPTED TO EXTREMES OF HEAT, DROUGHT, AND ABRASIVE WINDS THAT ARE HARSH EVEN BY SOUTHWESTERN STANDARDS.

Changes in elevation and latitude so affect temperatures and rainfall that they determine the makeup of the plant communities that clothe slopes, plains, *playas*, and bottomlands. At low and middle elevations, lack of rainfall, the corresponding low humidity, and high temperatures result in high evaporation rates that vaporize what little moisture is available. Since there is little cloud cover to retain the day's heat, there are great shifts in temperature from day to night. Seesawing forty degrees in eight hours is common. Where rain is more abundant in the uplands both day and nighttime temperatures are cooler. Plants adapted to areas of similar heat, cold, and dryness may be only moderately successful here because they cannot tolerate the drastic shifts in temperature. Mediterranean natives are quite happy with our hot summers, and many can tolerate the cold winters but may be weakened by continued forty degree swings from day to night and finally succumb to the occasional seventy degree plunges we experience in the high desert.

There are equally sharp seasonal distinctions. Spring, usually dry and windy, can sometimes be cool and damp. Temperatures are apt to fluctuate wildly. Last frost might be mid-February in the lowlands or early June at higher elevations. A spell of unusually cool, rainy weather might end abruptly with the onset of record high temperatures. Carpets of wildflowers and soft green grasses brought on by the rain quickly droop and wither away in the scorching heat. Roller-coaster temperatures and drying spring winds followed closely by summer's heat make spring planting a gamble. Begin too early and plants freeze or windburn. Wait too long and they parboil. Plants that have evolved to cope with this climate have a definite advantage. Slow to leaf out, they are rarely teased out of dormancy by an early warm spell. Their fine-textured or waxy leaves are less likely to shred and scorch in the wind. Deeply rooted once they gain a foothold, dryland native plants endure summer's heat waiting for the monsoons to enjoy another spurt of growth.

Often rain is a promise broken. Moisture falling from the clouds evaporates before it reaches the parched soil. When it does come, the soil may be so dry that it repels water, and the precious rain, falling in torrents, runs off, never penetrating to the thirsty roots. Summer is a good season to plant at higher elevations where afternoon clouds and more frequent rains break the heat. The rest of us can use the time to sit in the shade, admiring our gardening successes and assessing our failures, and limit our planting to filling in gaps and working with the heat-loving plants that require warm soils to root out into. Summer monsoons offer windows of opportunity for seeding native grasses or transplanting container-grown shrubs and wildflowers, while the afternoon cloud cover and chance of showers ease the heat. When the shorter cooler days of autumn arrive, they do so with a flourish, bringing a last flush of flowering and rush to seeding. The first frost may come in early September at higher elevations, not until November in the southern deserts, and is more often than not followed by another month of balmy Indian summer. Many trees and shrubs planted in fall will root out through the winter, giving them a substantial advantage when hot weather returns. Smaller plants benefit from early fall planting so that they have six to eight weeks rooting time before hard freezes (twenty-five degrees F or lower). Plants pushing the northern or high-elevation limits of their cold hardiness are better planted in spring, since they are particularly vulnerable to the chance deep freeze their first winter in the garden if they haven't had ample time to root out extensively. In every instance, autumn is the time to quit pampering the garden and ease off watering so that plants harden off in preparation for the cold. High-desert winters are, on average, neither too harsh nor too mild, with temperatures ranging from daytime highs between forty and sixty degrees F and lows in the teens to near zero. Snow may blanket the uplands for weeks without a thaw, while shrub desert and grassland receive only an infrequent dusting of snow that melts within hours. Occasionally polar air masses cause major drops in winter temperatures damaging many otherwise adapted plantings.

These climate and weather conditions bring us back to the question of which plants are ecologically appropriate. If we take a purist stand and use only plants that could occur on the site naturally, true endemic species, we limit ourselves tremendously and, in most cases, unnecessarily. Such an approach is more revegetation than it is gardening and is a narrow view of developing a place's potential. Nevertheless it is nearly a sure thing when it comes to the survival of plants with little input from us.

HIGH-DESERT RAINS CAN BE SO LOCALIZED THAT ONE AREA FLOODS WHILE A MILE AWAY THE SOIL REMAINS PARCHED. WITHOUT DRYLAND PLANTS TO HOLD THE SOIL IN PLACE, INFREQUENT TORRENTIAL RAINS CUT *ARROYOS* THROUGH THE BRITTLE LANDSCAPE.

The main shift in my approach to garden design in the years since my first book, *Southwestern Landscaping with Native Plants*, was published (1987) has been in my attitude toward diversity. I used to think that a landscape would look better and be easier to maintain if the selection of plants was limited to a handful of compatible species: an ode to simplicity, variations on a theme. Looking back at the gardens I've designed over the past decade, efforts to limit the plant palette never really got off the drawing board. Too many good plants begged a place in the sun or shade. Substituting better-adapted plants for those less well suited is still at the core of my designing appropriate landscapes, but there are other important principles that govern natural gardening.

There are patterns in nature, sequences of growth, development, and stability, that when applied to garden design culminate in landscapes that are beautiful and effective, easy to care for and appropriate to their places and the individuals who use them. These patterns have to do with the interrelationships of plants with each other and the soils, exposures and contours of the site, and with insects, birds, mammals, and plants as members of an ecological community. Complexity is the essence of life and a buffer against natural disasters. Creating a natural garden shortcuts evolutionary processes, taking us from bare ground to a stable plant community in a few short years rather than a millennium. Creative thinking, treating problems as opportunities, is basic to all good design. The very features that pose the greatest challenges on a site, such as rock outcroppings, soggy low spots in heavy clay soil, or erosion from storm drainage, can become, respectively, rock gardens, wetland habitats, and dry-streamed pathways, outstanding elements that make a garden unique. Chapter 2 discusses the ways that natural design differs from conventional landscaping and illustrates how a garden may look traditional and still be environmentally sound.

Ecogardens differ from conventional landscapes in some of the techniques and materials used to create them and in having a prolonged establishment stage when fine-tuning with a shovel redresses unforeseen problems. During the first few years after the initial planting has been done, rogue seedling volunteers are relocated, unwanted plants (otherwise known as weeds) are suppressed, and insects are identified and often appreciated as the gardener nudges the place toward equilibrium. Chapter 3, on planting and maintenance, covers this rewarding process of working with nature, reestablishing our focus as human beings in the natural world, and becoming part of the ecosystem ourselves.

The length of the establishment period and the amount of long-term maintenance a garden requires are determined by how responsive the design is to the site and how disturbed the site was initially. With the disturbance of the site to make the garden, the stage is set for the appearance of the primary invaders. Many of the opportunistic plants that flourish as a result of disturbance in nature we view as weeds in the garden. They do their best when conditions are worst. These invaders are often unimpressive to ugly

IN THE UPLANDS, THE GOLDEN DAYS OF AUTUMN MAY DISAPPEAR ABRUPTLY UNDER A BLANKET OF SNOW. CM

9

THE MUTED BLUES, GRAYS, AND
GREENS OF AN UPLAND CANYON
TRANSLATE EASILY AS A GARDEN
ARRANGEMENT OF 'POWIS CASTLE'
ARTEMISIA, THREADLEAF SAGE,
AND DWARF BUTTERFLYBUSH.

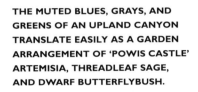

in appearance and always fast growing and prodigious reproducers. The plants most valuable in the garden, whether they are wild or domesticated, are usually slower to establish themselves, longer-lived, less invasive, and attractive for their foliage textures, brilliant flowers, and pleasing form. All in all, the plants we choose for our gardens are rarely the thugs of their native ecosystems. Bringing together a community of plants that is compatible with the site and balanced, in time displacing weedy species, is central to a successful design. The Southwest offers a wealth of possibilities. For landscape purposes we can place them in three plant categories: upland, plains grassland-shrub desert, and oasis communities. Chapters 4, 5, and 6 define each of these ecosystems in general terms and, using gardens that I've designed as examples, illustrate a variety of approaches to working out the problems and capitalizing on the opportunities inherent in each system. Chapter 7, on urban islands, examines natural gardening in the artificial context of the city, creating tame plant communities indirectly related to their natural counterparts. Much of the information in these four chapters is derived from the experiences of gardeners with whom I've worked. Their enthusiasm and hard-won knowledge, to say nothing of their thirst for more experience and greater understanding, make them among the wisest individuals I've ever met. We gossip about plants as if they were good friends, and that is indeed what they become. A selection of plants best adapted to each plant guild is listed by ecosystem. Some will have featured prominently in the gardens illustrated and discussed, while others may be new to cultivation but particularly well suited to specific niches. Since the gardening concepts discussed here apply in general terms throughout arid ecosystems, in some cases low-desert natives are suggested as alternates to broaden the scope of the garden ideas beyond the high-desert ecology that is the focus of this book.

Plants for Natural Gardens, the companion volume to *Natural by Design*, presents detailed descriptions of some two hundred plants, most of which are native to the high-desert Southwest. Some are borrowed from the Great Plains, a few from higher in the mountains. Lists of adaptive plants, some from as far afield as the Pyrenees, the Balkans, and central China, are included to help place those frequently used or newly introduced horticultural cultivars in the context of the ecosystems where they are apt to perform best. The emphasis in the plant profiles is on natives, since they are not well known in gardening circles and are best equipped to handle local conditions. Some of the plants included may take a bit of initiative to find in nurseries. Many native plants with garden potential have yet to be tamed. Many remain untried. This book would have to run thousands of pages in order to cover the wealth of possibilities that exist. I've been told that knowing where to stop is as important as getting started. My hope is to start you looking at wildness as a resource. However, I do not encourage collecting wild plants, which in most cases don't transplant very well anyway. More importantly, their loss may undermine the ecosystem you admire enough to steal from. What I am advocating is observing patterns in nature that can become the seeds of garden design. Information for propagating plants is included in the profiles whenever possible to help you grow the wildland seeds you collect or buy. Grouping the plants by ecosystem, and

THE GILIA AND GRASSES OF THIS HIGH-PLAINS PRAIRIE PROVIDE A MODEL FOR THE SWEEP OF LITTLE BLUESTEM THAT APPROACHES THIS GRASSLAND GARDEN. CM

BROOM DALEA BORDERS SHRUB-DESERT
ARROYOS AS WELL AS THE PATH LEADING
INTO THIS DRYLAND OASIS WHERE THE
ADDITION OF SHADE FROM A RAMADA
AND EVENTUALLY FROM A YOUNG
CHINESE PISTACHE WILL PROVIDE A
COMFORT ZONE.

cross-referencing them where they are more broadly adaptive, reflects the patterns of their adaptations and keeps the planting options in a natural context. The more you consider this context, the more self-regulating the garden ultimately will be.

All the gardens described in this book are potential havens for wildlife, some more obviously so than others. When we open our gates for an interspecies garden party, not all those attending may be equally charming guests. Chapter 8, on habitat gardening, explores some of the joys and frustrations, attitude adjustments and compromises inherent in learning to be gracious hosts.

Chapter 9 covers the long-term management of natural gardens. As you begin the design and development process in your garden, you are writing your own final chapter. Many typical maintenance procedures, such as watering and weeding, done regularly in the establishment stage, diminish in urgency or frequency as a natural balance develops. Many tasks are specific to certain plants, and that is noted in their profiles in the companion volume. Because the design so determines subsequent management, this book is intended to be cycled through, information accumulated and synthesized into a plan that works. The mechanics of plotting a plan on paper are the same regardless of the type of garden being planned and so are left to other authors listed in

Recommended Reading who have already done an admirable job. To most people, the creative process of planning a garden is more compelling than the job of drawing it on paper ever will be. That blank sheet of paper is even more daunting than the tumbleweed wasteland beyond the back door. A landscape plan is simply a map that takes a gardener from an idea to its fulfillment. The more familiar you are with the terrain, the less important it becomes to have a detailed map on paper. While I spend much of my time drawing landscape plans for other people, I am fifteen years into my own garden design with none of it on paper. I've spent a good bit of time transplanting and reworking spaces that, had I thought it out on paper first, may have been avoidable. But I've enjoyed every minute of the time invested and learned a lot in the process.

Learning to appreciate natural complexity is the basis for this book, and that understanding comes over time. The best minds studying ecology today disagree on many issues. Sometimes the single point of consensus is that too little is clearly understood about the interrelationships that bind the natural world together. This book is not about high-desert ecology in any formal sense but uses the natural patterns of select high-desert ecosystems to create gardens that fit their place and purpose. Gardens that are either attempted reconstructions of natural systems or embellishments of them are found at one end of the spectrum. They look very much like the natural ecosystems that surround them, wilder at the perimeters, more restrained in the living spaces. They are arguably the best of the lot since they have a beauty borne of harmony and require the least input to sustain. Gardens whose central focus is water are at the opposite end of the spectrum as they are naturally rare ecosystems in the high desert. They are either well-balanced wetland ecosystems or they are the most difficult and expensive to maintain. Natural gardens can follow a conscious style: cottage, Japanese, California modern, or prairie school. All harken to nature as a model but express widely differing aesthetics.

It requires very little knowledge of plants or ecology to begin gardening naturally. In fact, recognizing that we may never understand why it works, that the more layers of complexity that cloud that understanding the better it may work, is really the lesson we need to learn. We need only be observant and flexible, willing to abandon plants and purposes that prove unproductive and build on those that seem to fit within the larger context. Natural gardens are built on the premises that the goal of gardening isn't the mastery of nature but of self, that the process of learning is as important as the lessons we learn, and that our actions carry responsibility. Our responsibility for a better environment begins in our garden, and that is not a limitation to creativity but an expression of it. The way to a natural garden is often the path of least resistance.

THE RELATIVE ABUNDANCE OF WATER MAKES THE RIBBON OF WOODLAND POSSIBLE ALONG SOUTHWESTERN RIVERS. SHADE AND LUSH VEGETATION ARE HALLMARKS OF OASIS GARDENS.

2　Natural by Design

LANDSCAPE DESIGN IS PART ART, part problem solving. Add the science of ecology to this functional art form, so that art imitates nature, and you have the best of all possible gardens. The artistic side of garden design reflects our standards of unity, harmony, proportion, balance, and color. Our perception of beauty is a complex of inherited and learned values. The sweeping carpets of closely cropped lawn that are so popular have no ecological model south of New England in North America. Lawns evolved from cattle and sheep grazing cool-season grasses in northern Europe and crossed the Atlantic as symbols of affluence and culture, to the manor born. Given the incredible input of water, fertilizer, pesticides, machinery, and labor such lawns require, they are indeed the embodiment of entitlement and conspicuous consumption. As status symbols go, if you want to go Euro, a Volvo has a better return on investment. It's ironic that the American persona is one of the rugged individualist, yet we cling to paradigms of beauty that have nothing to do with us and that are ill-suited to our environment and monotonous to boot. Meanwhile, tourists from across the globe are drawn to the Southwest for the very natural splendor that many gardeners struggle to ignore.

The first task, then, is to define what we consider beautiful in southwestern terms. In the past, people wanting to avoid the work and water of lawn care opted to bury the soil and, optimistically, the weeds with gravel. Add a few die-hard yuccas, a piñon or juniper, and presto: the "southwestern landscape," alternately known as the "rock lawn"—still monotonous but no longer green. Covering the earth with heat-reflecting

IN NATURAL GARDENS, THE EDGE BETWEEN NATURE AND HORTICULTURE MAY BE AS SHARPLY DEFINED AS AN ADOBE WALL OR AS SUBTLE AS DRIFTS OF WILDFLOWERS HUGGING A FLAGSTONE PATH. (TREAT GARDEN, PAGE 90.) CM

15

IN NATURE, DOMINANT PLANT SPECIES
SUCH AS THE CONTRASTING SWEEPS
OF BROOM DALEA AND ONE-SEED
JUNIPER LEND THE LANDSCAPE ITS
VISUAL COHESIVENESS.

screened gravel in the name of gardening pays stylized tribute to the most unattractive desert ecosystems this harsh climate can create. Gardens are about plants and the life they engender; rocks are a construction material that can enhance the appearance and growth of some plants, but a little goes a long way.

How do we arrive at an appropriate southwestern model for beauty in the garden? That depends greatly on where you live, your concept of what a garden should be, and your management priorities. The more you draw on elements of the native plant communities within your range of climate, elevation, and topography, the easier your garden will be to manage. The ecosystem chapters beginning on page 83, and the gardens and plants described in each, cover a range of options from quietly cultivated to unabashedly wild, from minimal maintenance to gardening as an avocation. Exploring nearby natural areas can inspire you further. The challenge is in taming the wild enough to make it comfortable, to make it feel like a garden, without making it totally dependent on your care to survive.

Art in Nature

Art has roots in nature. In natural ecosystems, masses of the dominant plant species lend the landscape its visual cohesiveness, while scattered drifts of plants adapted to

MORE LOCALIZED DRIFTS OF WILD-
FLOWERS AND SHRUBS PROVIDE THE
DIVERSITY THAT MAKES ECOSYSTEMS
STABLE. CM

special niches add the diversity that guarantees ecosystem stability. In a garden, a strong framework of trees and shrubs defines the space, while grasses and wildflowers add the grace notes that make it unique. Unity and variety are complementary parts of the whole. Strong lines and repetition are unifying elements, while a mix of complementary plants keeps things interesting.

Harmony, growing from a sense of place and respect for natural processes, is the essence of ecogardening. It allows for participation in the cycle of the seasons, the comings and goings of birds and insects, the change from leafy canopy to stark skeletons of tree limbs against a usually blue but sometimes brooding sky. It is having places to be idle in the cool shade of a tree or vine canopy and places to bask in the warmth of the mellow winter sun. It is always having a few weeds to pull when pulling hair isn't socially acceptable, but never having so many weeds that they aren't fairly easy to ignore when you want to be in the garden but not *work* in it.

Proportions are a practical matter. Garden features should be sized for the job. In this climate we need shade, but most of the trees commonly used for shade are stream-bank natives of climates much wetter than ours. They become disproportionately large and suffer drought and heat stress for their generosity. The drier the ecosystem, the smaller the trees should be, clustered in groves in basins to catch runoff, as they would occur naturally. Prairie and shrub desert are characterized by their vastness, with little

IN NATURAL GARDENS, FENCES AND WALLS DEFINE SPACES BY EITHER MINIMIZING DIVISIONS OR MORE SHARPLY SIGNALING TRANSITIONS.

A FENCE NEEDED TO LIMIT WILDLIFE BROWSING AND PROVIDE ENCLOSURE IS LESS INTRUSIVE IF STAINED TO MIMIC SURROUNDING VEGETATION.

A RUSTIC POST-AND-WIRE FENCE CAN BOTH DEFINE A BOUNDRY AND MERGE INTO THE GARDEN WHEN PLANTS ARE PLACED TO PARTLY OBSCURE ITS STRUCTURE AND LINES.

interruption between earth and sky. Piñon-juniper woodland and cottonwood *bosque* are more intimate, enclosed ecosystems. In the garden, plants form the walls and ceilings of outdoor spaces. Proportions are key in making gardens evoke a sense of where they are and in making spaces transition to natural areas around them. Boldness and openness are characteristics of the desert that need to be taken advantage of, on the one hand, and made more comfortable on the other. Linking the "great outdoors" to human proportions involves larger spaces than those indoors because outdoor spaces host more expansive activities than do indoor spaces. When a garden is already defined on its far perimeters with walls or fencing, the challenge is to knit the obviously man-made elements into the garden by placing plants to complement or screen the walls or fencing. When the garden space flows into a natural ecosystem with no barriers, the challenge is to merge the two harmoniously. Patios may be stages with grand mountain views or desert panoramas as backdrops. Low walls define their boundaries, serving also as seating areas while keeping vistas open. Higher walls provide enclosure and buffer wind, and small water features attract wildlife while minimizing evaporation. Such courtyard spaces feel as intimate as interior rooms.

Nearly a century ago, Jens Jensen encouraged other midwestern landscape architects to use natural models in their planning. He advocated making sense of large spaces by dividing them into a central expanse with smaller niches tucked along the edges. This approach maintains sweeping views across the expanse while providing more intimate places for socializing at the perimeters. For thousands of years, Japanese gardens have created interest within by keeping part of the garden hidden from view. Both models work in a southwestern context. A meandering path or dry streambed can give definition to a large open space and lead to smaller sitting areas. Jensen's model is particularly well suited for habitat gardens, where a variety of open and enclosed spaces

provides the foraging, basking, roosting, and nesting niches needed by both wildlife and their observers. The smaller the space, or the more urban the context, the more controlled the approach usually becomes. By making definite hard edges between plants and paving, using smaller-scale plants or plants with naturally compact forms, a richly diverse natural garden can be proportioned to fit a city lot's boundaries.

Balance in design is often interpreted as bilateral symmetry, an idea unratified in the nature around us. Landscapes that rely on such ducks-in-a-row measured placement are easy to design and difficult to maintain since plants, like people, are individuals. Some might grow a little taller while others stay a little smaller; some grow dense and twiggy, others spread open and become rangy. Attaining the ideal uniformity requires constant manipulation: pruning, fertilizing, and measured watering. Landscapes dependent upon bilateral symmetry and sheared geometry for their form require constant human interference to remain static. Their appeal lies in their order and control, but their rigid and spartan approach sacrifices individuality and seems lifeless, no more comfortable or imaginative than a gravel landscape. At the other end of the spectrum we find gardens that are plant collections resulting from impulse buys at the nursery, winter blues remedied by diving headlong into the warm gene pool of mail-order catalogs, and the avid gardener's insatiable appetite for yet another new plant. Such gardens are undeniably more vibrant, but in their lack of order lies the seed of discontent. Pleasing as the parts might be, they don't add up to a palpable whole.

HIGH WALLS CREATE COURTYARD SPACES AS INTIMATE AS INDOOR ROOMS.

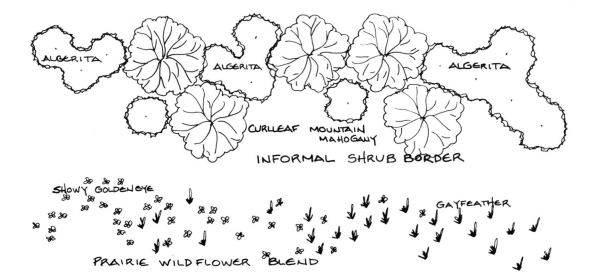

ALGERITA   ALGERITA   ALGERITA

CURLLEAF MOUNTAIN MAHOGANY

INFORMAL SHRUB BORDER

SHOWY GOLDENEYE   GAYFEATHER

PRAIRIE WILDFLOWER BLEND

THE PLACEMENT OF PLANTS MAKES A GARDEN FORMAL OR NATURAL. FEATHERING PLANTS SO THAT THERE IS OVERLAP AND INTER- ACTION BETWEEN SPECIES IS A NATURAL APPROACH TO PLANTING.

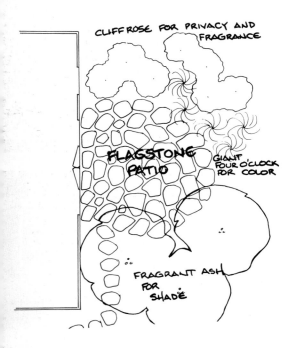

CLIFFROSE FOR PRIVACY AND FRAGRANCE

FLAGSTONE PATIO

GIANT FOUR O'CLOCK FOR COLOR

FRAGRANT ASH FOR SHADE

BALANCE IS ESSENTIAL TO GOOD DESIGN BUT IN NATURAL GARDENS THE BALANCE IS USUALLY ASSYMETRI- CAL—PLANT GROUPINGS OF EQUAL MASS COMPLEMENTING EACH OTHER —RATHER THAN FORMAL.

Natural gardens lie somewhere between the regimented and wild abandon. They look spontaneous but actually require a careful balance of plants and their placement, an understanding of how plants interact as a community, and postplanting fine-tuning until the landscape becomes a self-sufficient ecosystem with the gardener as steward. With fewer hard lines, spaces flow and are naturally defined. Groves of trees, clusters of shrubs, and drifts of wildflowers are the counterpoint to walls, fences, and pathways. The order is nature's order. Different species occupy specific niches in an ecosystem, but a few individual plants may adapt well beyond the normal range of the group. This cre- ates a feathering effect, as one group of plants merges into another with crossovers from each group interrupting the stands of the other. Plants are not spaced at precise dis- tances from each other but are grouped where they will grow best to serve their desig- nated purpose. If each shrub assumes a slightly different size and density based on the available sunlight, water, and nutrients in the soil, all the better. If one should die, we mourn its passing but are glad of the opportunity to try something else in its place. Its absence doesn't create a gaping hole in the symmetry. The balance is one of three desert willows for shade and hummingbirds on one side of the patio with seven Apache plumes used for screening along the other side. If an Apache plume disappears (a long shot, but nature can be unpredictable and accidents happen), there's space to add some threadleaf sage for the scent or a cluster of golden asters for butterflies.

Color is more subtle, not necessarily less vivid, in natural landscapes. The trend in horticulture has been to select and hybridize plants for larger flowers and more color, often at the expense of drought tolerance, pest resistance, and fragrance. Bedding plants, mostly annuals that need replanting each year, are described in terms of color per square foot: big flowers or many flowers covering the surface of the plants to create

a sheet of color. Is the alternative to abandon color? Never! Without red tubular flowers we wouldn't have hummingbirds. Without blue flowers, the bump-and-weave choreography of bumblebees would disappear. Where would butterflies perch and sip? Without color, my job as landscape designer would be more difficult and much less enjoyable. The difference between hybrid flowers and their wildflower ancestors is balance. Brilliant color is contrasted and buffered by green and silver leaves: less brass, more grace—and no loss of genetic diversity that makes a plant community vital, no loss of fragrance that makes an open window on a summer evening an invitation to come out into the garden.

Color and texture can change the feel of a garden. Predominantly hot colors—reds, yellows, some pinks, and oranges—make a space look smaller, while cool blues, purples, and white tend to recede, making a place look larger and more serene. Fine-textured and silver foliage also expand a space. The light texture and open form of southwestern plants make the cover of our wide open spaces seem sparse, belying the biotic diversity that the land supports. Many of the most drought- and heat-tolerant plants have small or finely dissected leaves that reduce their evaporative surfaces. Silver foliage reflects light and makes the plant cooler physically as well as visually. In the garden, silver-leaved and white-flowering plants bordering pathways will literally light up in the moonlight.

APACHE PLUME SEED HEADS GLOW WHEN BLACKLIT (TOP). CM

RICH HUES OF DORMANT WILLOW STEMS AND WINTER-BLEACHED GRASSES PROVIDE WINTER INTEREST. CM

Intense sunlight is a dominant factor in the southwestern landscape. Flowers not adapted to this climate have very brief periods of glory before sun and wind destroy their beauty. Magnolias in high-desert gardens remind me of Scarlett O'Hara returning to Tara after the war: ashes and rags, the sad remains of satins and brocades. But sunlight can also be an enhancer of plant attributes. Blue flax and Indian paintbrush glow in the early morning sun. The feathery seed heads of needle-and-thread grass, Apache plume, and mountain mahogany are equally luminous when backlit by the rising or setting sun. The scarlet and gold leaves of Chinese pistache, sumac, woods rose, amorpha, and cottonwoods blaze warmly against the autumn sky.

Brightly colored flowers are certainly an asset in the garden, but flowers are seasonal. It is the appearance of plants twelve months of the year that is critical. A mostly evergreen landscape will tend to feel somber while an all-deciduous landscape disappears for nearly half the year. Balancing flower color with foliage textures and sculptural plant forms makes a garden reflect the seasons. In native piñon and juniper woodland, grasses and clusters of sumac and chamisa or winterfat effectively contrast the stolid conifers. In grasslands, drifts of wildflowers punctuate seasonal rains, but sand lovegrass and little bluestem are at their ornamental peak September to March when wildflowers are dormant. In *bosque* ecosystems, the sculptural dominance of cottonwoods provides winter interest with little else to distract from their majesty. Depending on the ecosystem model you are using, the ratio of deciduous to evergreen will change, as will your need for screening and wind buffering.

Creating a Functional Design

How the garden looks is usually our first concern, but how well it works is the heart of successful design. Whatever the species, when the plants flourish they fulfill their roles in the landscape with greater impact. While a healthy tumbleweed is no fit substitute for an ailing rosebush, I'll select a cliffrose or fernbush, rugosa or woods rose over most hybrid teas. Until we do the groundwork and decide how spaces will be used, however, we don't have the information we need to make good planting choices.

SPACE AND TRAFFIC PATTERNS

Facing a blank plot plan as the first step in planning a landscape can be discouraging. So much space, so many ideas; so few ideas, no inkling of where to start. The bigger the plot, the more overwhelming the task; the smaller the space, the more critical each choice. Thinking about how space might be used helps to bring it into focus. Make a list of the activities you want to accommodate: outdoor cooking, dining, and entertaining (how many people?); play structures, sandbox, volleyball (sand or grass?) or basketball court (paved?), horseshoes, swimming pool and/or spa; vegetable garden and

composter; clothesline; storage for tools, bicycles, toys, pool equipment, and firewood; wildlife habitat. Be generous, both in listing all the wildest possibilities and in estimating the amount of space each takes (see Appendix of spatial requirements). Block out likely places on the lot or on a plot plan for as many of your options as possible. The smaller the lot, the more selective you'll need to be. You can play volleyball in the park, but the privacy of a spa off the patio and tomatoes that actually taste like tomatoes offer a return well worth the investment in space. You'd love an overflowing perennial cottage garden, but with three preschoolers where would you find the time to tend it? This decade's play yard can evolve into that dream garden. Sort through the options until the spaces are defined, then determine how people will move between those spaces. Jens Jensen had a habit of laying out the use areas and waiting to see where people walked before plotting the pathways. His attitude had more to do with futility than with democracy. What is the point of a lovely meandering walkway if its flow is crisscrossed with ruts and trampled plantings because it doesn't take people where they want to go? Access to utility areas should always be as direct and uncomplicated as possible, since those are the routes used most often, with arms full and attention on the task at hand rather than on the eccentricities of the pavement. A dry streambed leading to a secluded sitting area might ramble less purposefully, since the main task when following it is to

WITH MARKED GRADE CHANGES VARIOUS TYPES OF RETAINING WALLS CAN BE USED TO PREVENT EROSION. THE HARD LINES OF STUCCOED MASONRY WALLS ARE SOFTENED BY CHAMISA, BLANKETFLOWER, AND OTHER WILDFLOWERS DRAPING THE EDGE.

relax and enjoy the garden. Paths should be sized for the traffic they bear and the purpose they serve. They should never be so sinuous that they leave you listening for the conga music, but a few broad curves within the main flow are more inviting than a straight line connecting two points. Paths that bring guests to entryways and gathering places should be generous and well defined, lit in the evening, and well drained to eliminate puddles and icy patches so that the approach is welcoming even when the weather isn't hospitable.

The choice of paving materials balances utility with visual appeal. The walkways in high-traffic areas are often hard-paved for permanence. Concrete is one of the lowest maintenance, longest-lasting paving materials available. Slightly sloped to drain moisture away from buildings and into planted areas, concrete walks and driveways can become part of a rainwater harvesting system. Tinted in earth tones with a textured surface, or scored to resemble tile, concrete can be made to blend into the garden rather than stand apart as a concession to function or economy. Brick pavers and flagstone have a more natural feel and, when set on sand or crusher fines within a mortared or steel border, are permeable. When paving around trees, permeable pavements keep water and oxygen available to the roots. The quality of brick and flagstone varies, and a poor grade of either one will flake away with time and weather. Look for weatherproof bricks and flagstone that show no tendency to splinter.

While masonry requires a level of patience and skill on the part of the amateur or a larger investment in hiring professional contractors, brick and flagstone are beautiful ways to blend architecture with horticulture. Crushed gravel and decomposed granite are more informal paving materials. Permeable like brick and flagstone, fine crushed stone is easy to walk on, available in neutral earth tones, relatively inexpensive, and easy to work with. Applied deeply enough, a minimum of four inches compacted with a roller, gravel is long lasting, requiring resurfacing every three to seven years depending on the traffic and the gravel. The types and sizes of gravels vary locally. Crusher fines, the coarse grit and rock slivers remaining after gravel is crushed and screened, may be light or dark gray, tan, rusty red, and even pale purple depending on the parent rock available locally. If gravel is to be used as mulch or erosion control elsewhere in the garden, using fines of the same rock for paving will help unify the garden. Tan-colored fines blend well with adobe stucco colors while the gray fines have a harder look. Decomposed granite is really granite fines, an intermediate stage of granite rock becoming soil. Foothills sites are often already paved with decomposed granite. One of the advantages of fines over gravels is that fines compact readily, leaving the surface impermeable to weeds, especially when dry.

CONTOURING

Once the landscape space is defined by use and traffic patterns, its contours or lack of them can be considered, reconciling the character of the site with how you want to use it. Ideally, the nature of the site should be considered in the design and placement of the buildings on it. More often the site is remade with a bulldozer to fit a generic ideal, usually flat and barren, a clean slate. Increased potential for weed invasion, erosion by wind and rain, the loss of wildlife habitat, and a sharp rise in the cost of landscaping are the results of this subdivision syncopation. Disturbance is a necessary part of construction. On small urban lots, a clean slate is usually the best that can be expected. On larger suburban or rural sites, a clean slate is the worst prospect. An area twenty feet around the exterior of the future building is needed for access during construction, and if the sewage system includes a septic tank and leach field, more area will be disturbed. But by fencing off the rest of the site and making it clear to the general contractor that any additional disturbance is unacceptable, the character of the site can be preserved and the cost of landscaping may be reduced considerably.

The soil removed to level an area or to create a basin for capturing runoff is called the "cut," and soil added to create berms or level low spots is called "fill." Usually it is more structurally sound and costs less to reshape the soil, using the cut as fill on the same site, than it is to import soil for fill or dump excess cut. In the foothills, cut soil may be used to reduce the steepness of slopes or create level areas of usable space. Coarse decomposed granite can be set aside to use as path paving and mulch. In the valleys where water tables are high, fill is used to raise the floor levels of buildings above the potential flood zone. Foundations are built to extend through the fill to undisturbed subsoil, and the fill is compacted to stabilize construction. Unfortunately, soil compacted enough to support buildings is not the ideal medium for growing plants.

Slopes that rise more than one foot in three feet are potentially erodible. Even flat surfaces stripped of vegetation can erode and will certainly sprout a crop of weeds if not promptly replanted or mulched. Stabilizing the soil is a top priority in most new landscaping projects. If retaining walls are necessary to prevent soil slippage and provide usable level space, they can become an attractive garden feature and a means of making the transition from the more cultivated to the wilder landscape. A transition in building materials from man-made to natural signals a change in the nature of the garden. Stuccoed block or timber retainers and brick or concrete paving might be used in the cultivated landscape area, and dry-stack rock walls and porous paving in the naturalized parts of the garden. Plants draping retaining walls soften the architectural elements and make the walls part of the garden. Plants can be part of the retainer as a rock garden or crowd in on the edges of a stepped walkway. The rough rock surfaces offset the forms and textures of plants such as sedums, penstemon, and veronicas and the plants benefit from the excellent drainage. Where space limits the retainer to a vertical wall, plants may cascade over or grow up in front of the wall. Giant four o'clocks spilling over a wall have both the drainage they prefer and a stage to show off their abundance of foliage and color. Maximilian sunflowers at the base of a north-facing retaining wall will use less moisture since the soil is shaded part of the day, and

BROKEN PIECES OF A FORMER SIDE-WALK ARE RECYCLED AS A LOW RETAINING WALL (TOP).

RAILROAD TIES AND BUFFALOGRASS FORM BROAD PLATFORM STEPS

25

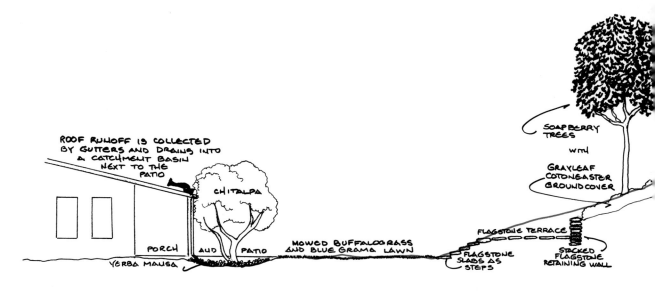

ROOF RUNOFF IS COLLECTED BY GUTTERS AND DRAINS INTO A CATCHMENT BASIN NEXT TO THE PATIO

CHITALPA

SOAPBERRY TREES

wml

GRAYLEAF COTONEASTER GROUNDCOVER

FLAGSTONE TERRACE

PORCH AND PATIO

MOWED BUFFALOGRASS AND BLUE GRAMA LAWN

FLAGSTONE SLABS AS STEPS

STACKED FLAGSTONE RETAINING WALL

YERBA MANSA

ACTUAL GRADE CHANGES OR THE ILLUSION OF CONTOURS CAN TAKE A VARIETY OF FORMS. ABOUT MIDWAY FROM THE STREET, THIS LOT SLOPED SHARPLY TOWARD THE HOUSE. A GROUPING OF LOW SHRUBS CREATES A RISE BETWEEN THE SIDEWALK AND FLAT PRAIRIE. THE HEIGHT OF THE BERM BUILT WITH THE SOIL CUT TO CREATE THE SITTING AREA IS EXAGGERATED BY PLANTING IT WITH TALLER EVERGREEN SHRUBS, WHICH ALSO SERVE AS A SCREEN AND NOISE BUFFER. THE BASIN EAST OF THE BERM AND THE TOE OF THE SLOPE ABOVE THE SITTING AREA COLLECT ENOUGH RUNOFF TO HELP SUSTAIN SMALL TREES THAT SHADE THE TERRACE.

the columns of brilliant daisies will offset the rigid backdrop. Against a south-facing stuccoed wall, Palmer penstemon requires little water to produce a glorious show of delicate flowers and crisp foliage against the grainy wall surface. The relationship between walls and plants is sympathetic and mutually enhancing.

The more extensive the retaining walls are, the larger scale the plants need to be to balance the mass of the walls. A two-foot-high, twenty-foot-long rock wall might be planted in pineleaf penstemon and creeping baby's breath, scarlet globemallow and fringed sage, dwarf chamisa, iceplant, or pussy toes. A five-foot-high, hundred-foot-long rock wall could be planted with Apache plume and prostrate sumac, cliff rose and cliff fendlerbush, mountain mahogany and winterfat, or creosotebush and mariola with an understory of grasses to stabilize the surface while the shrubs provide the deep anchoring. On a less severe slope, the plants alone could provide the desired stability. An imposing vertical wall could be screened from the base with Rocky Mountain junipers, New Mexico olives, and woods roses for a partly evergreen and seasonally colorful distraction. If the wall surface is interesting, leave gaps in the planting and use the contrast between wall and plants to advantage. If the wall is strictly utilitarian, plant more densely to obscure it. The combinations are nearly endless; the important thing is that the choices be complementary.

Grade changes may be made to provide privacy, buffer sound, or create a more interesting surface. Berms—large, rolling earthen mounds—can be used to create enclosed spaces. Planted compatibly, these earth forms immediately muffle noise, becoming even more effective as the plants fill in. Since fill dirt and plants are both relatively inexpensive and can be worked by less skilled hands than carpentry or

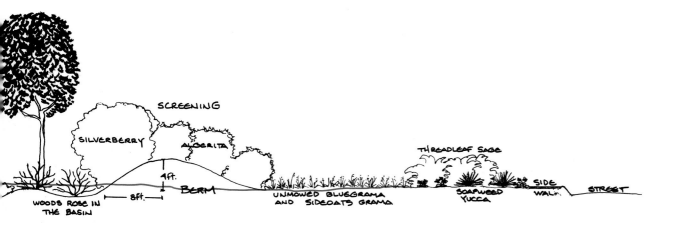

SCREENING

SILVERBERRY

ALGERITA

THREADLEAF SAGE

4ft.

BERM

8ft.

WOODS ROSE IN
THE BASIN

UNMOWED BLUEGRAMA
AND SIDEOATS GRAMA

SOAPWEED
YUCCA

SIDE
WALK

STREET

masonry demand, planted berms not only offer nearly immediate results, they can also cost less. Space is the limiting factor. Nothing looks more contrived, like a pet cemetery, than disproportionately small berms. Steeply sloped berms are difficult to water and create erosion problems. Scale is crucial. The higher the berm, the wider and broader it needs to be with shorter plants at the top. To gain more height, taller plants can be clustered on the sides, the tallest plants near the base. In our climate, the tallest plants always colonize low spots, where moisture is apt to collect. The rapid drainage and greater exposure to wind on slopes have a dwarfing effect on plants in nature. A good rule of thumb is that the slope is never greater than one foot in two feet, so that a three-foot rise has a six-foot base, a six-foot rise, a twelve-foot base.

Where ground surface is limited and immediate screening for privacy is needed, a built barrier is more effective. A lattice screen planted with vines allows air to circulate, an advantage in small south- and west-facing enclosures. Wooden fence panels and latticework usually require more maintenance or rebuilding sooner than brick or stuccoed adobe or block walls do. Graffiti is a problem on accessible flat-surfaced walls and fences. Plants, especially thorny ones, can help protect walls but take time to develop the necessary mass. A noise buffer needs to be a dense deflecting surface, high enough to bounce sound away from or above the area to be protected. Plants used for sound barriers need to be evergreen. Broadleafed evergreens deflect sound more effectively than do needle-leafed conifers.

Gentle contours can make a flat expanse of land more interesting, but when a site is already occupied by a largely undisturbed natural ecosystem, it would seem both arrogant and extravagant to tear out established habitat simply in order to give a little

STACKED FLAGSTONES, NATURAL EXTENSIONS OF THE TERRACE PAVE-MENT, RETAIN THE TERRACE WALL AND FORM STEPS DOWN TO THE LAWN. THE LAWN USES ANY RUNOFF FROM THE SLOPES, PROVIDES PLAY SPACE, AND EXTENDS THE PORCH AND TERRACE ENTERTAINMENT AND SITTING AREAS. A BASIN ALONGSIDE THE PORCH AND EXTENDED PATIO CATCHES RUNOFF FROM THE ROOF AND PAVING TO SUPPORT A SHADING CHITALPA ON THE HOT WESTERN EXPOSURE. SUCH ADJUSTMENTS TO THE TERRAIN MAKE NICHES FOR ADAPTED PLANTS AND SPACES FOR ENJOYING THE GARDEN.

PLANTS NESTLED BETWEEN BOULDERS ALONG
THE EDGES TAKE ADVANTAGE OF THE
EXTRA WATER AVAILABLE

A BED SEVERAL INCHES DEEP OF THREE-
QUARTER INCH CRUSHED STONE PAVES
THE CHANNEL. COARSE GRAVEL AND
BOULDERS REINFORCE BENDS IN THE
PATH AND SHOULD BE SET INTO THE
SOIL FOR STABILITY.

roll to the terrain. Adding drifts of slightly taller compatible plants to the plant community—planting clusters of Apache plume in a stand of threadleaf sage or giant sacaton in a stand of grama—will create a rolling profile without the expense of replanting and watering the whole area and the effort of battling the inevitable invasion of weeds that follows a major disturbance. Those of us lucky enough to acquire a fragment of local ecology do well by embellishing the existing plant community, carving out a niche for our living spaces indoors and out, and thoughtfully increasing the diversity of the surrounding ecosystem without compromising its character. On the other hand, when the land is so changed that preservation is impossible and even reconstruction is inappropriate, where a perennial border is more fitting than prairie and weeds are already gaining ground, reshaping the surface to relieve stark geometry is an attractive option. Contours create ecological niches for plants: yerba mansa or purple ground-cherry might colonize basins, while Santa Fe phlox or skullcap seek the drainage that higher ground affords. Again, a sense of proportion is important: the smaller the space, the more subtle the contours. It should never require a dose of Dramamine to relax in the backyard. (See Appendix on grading.)

WATER HARVESTING

Storm drainage is an important concern in the Southwest since an area receiving only eight inches of rainfall annually may get a third of the year's ration in a few hours. Storm runoff is often considered a threat rather than a resource. There's no denying the power of nature, and respect for that force underlies an ecological approach to gardening. But there's no sense in wasting such a precious resource either. Most subdivisions submit drainage plans to city or state offices as part of the terms of site development. The best plans take natural features into account; the worst ones are set in concrete. Too often, land development profits outweigh quality of life and community safety. On a communitywide scale, dedicating storm drainage easements as open space serves several purposes. A network of natural ecosystems remains intact within the development, giving it a unique character and a regional context. Storm drainage is channeled safely and used to supplement the landscape along its course. The average 360 days of the year when the channel is dry, it serves as a recreational trail system, giving city-bound people access to nature. A greenspace network is maintained for wildlife, keeping local and regional gene pools viable. In contrast, paving runoff channels is a last-ditch safety measure when there hasn't been enough open space dedicated to channel water naturally. The channel will be safer the more absorption potential it has, the more it conforms to preexisting drainage patterns, the wider and more meandering it is, and the greater the diversity of remaining native vegetation. Paved channels can increase the force of the water by increasing its depth and speed, with disastrous results if the system is breached.

CONSTRUCTED WETLANDS USE PLANTS, SUCH AS CATTAILS AND BULRUSHES AS SHOWN HERE, TO PURIFY SEPTIC WASTEWATER.

Compounding the disregard for runoff as a resource, each site within a subdivision is often planned to shunt all runoff quickly and irretrievably into storm drains. Additionally, groundwater levels drop because rainfall and water pumped for irrigation are not returned to the aquifer. If no provision was made for drainage and your plot has potential for receiving major runoff from adjacent lots, you might invest in the advice of an engineer with a reputation for environmentally sensitive planning to avoid costly property damage. But if the drainage patterns are established and the runoff to be dealt with is only what is generated on-site from paving and roof surfaces, a simple system of swales and basins can be used to channel runoff into planted areas, with any over-flow running into the storm drain. Runoff catchments should be placed a safe distance downslope from foundations, at least four feet in sand, ten feet in clay. The larger the volume of water that the basin may catch, the further from walls it should be.

In sand, infiltration is usually fast enough to limit problems of standing water breeding mosquitos. In heavier soils or where a caliche hardpan lies below the surface, a French drain or dry well—a large pit or trench filled with cobbles or other large rocks or rubble—can collect runoff and channel it to planted areas. Catchments should be sized to contain the maximum runoff possible, with overflows at the low points to allow any excess water to drain off the lot into storm drains. Retention ponds that drain very slowly can provide wildlife habitat without breeding mosquitos if they are treated with *bacillus thuringiensis israelensis*, microorganisms that are deadly to mosquito and some fly larvae but do not harm other life-forms.

Although such drainage systems are designed for function, they can be so attractive that they serve as focal points in the landscape. A dry streambed can double as a footpath through the garden when it isn't carrying rainwater to the plants growing along its meander. To serve both functions, the gravel pavement for the base of the channel must be coarse and heavy enough to withstand the periodic washing but fine enough to be comfortable and safe to walk on. Three-quarter-inch crushed stone is a good compromise. The banks of the streambed are reinforced with a mix of coarser grades of the same material, with heavier deposits at the bends in the meander and larger rock of similar parent material as accents and to provide greater stability where needed. All the rock should be similar in color and texture to achieve a natural appearance. Mixing sizes of similar gravels, using the smallest size as the base and overlapping sizes in some places, concentrating the largest gravel below the bends in the meander, imitates the natural sifting and depositing of rock that occurs in nature. The channel itself should be dug eight to eighteen inches below the grade level it drains. Functionally, the narrower the streambed is, the deeper it should be, but it will look best and be most useful as a secondary path through the garden if it is at least four feet wide and eight to twelve inches deep so that after a three- to four-inch layer of gravel mulch is added the channel is still gently concave. Natural *arroyos* are often narrower along the straight runs, broadening at the bends where the water eddies and scours a wider course. Constructed streambeds look more natural if their width varies as well.

Using gravel and plants to keep the runoff clean is important. As water picks up silt it becomes heavier, flows faster, and becomes more difficult to control, scouring the soil and burying the plants it is intended to nourish. Densely twiggy plants that are commonly found growing in *arroyos*, such as desert willow, Apache plume, bush penstemon, threeleaf sumac, and littleleaf sumac, are likely candidates for stabilizing constructed drainage systems.

CONSTRUCTED WETLANDS

The ultimate in recycling wastewater for mutual benefit is building a marsh to do the final cleaning of septic water. Models of this innovative and simple technology are springing up across the country, from municipal systems such as Pintail Marsh, the sewage treatment facility for ShowLow, Arizona, to institutional systems such as the wetland in the outdoor classroom of Los Padillas Elementary School in Albuquerque, New Mexico, to pocket marshes filtering the septic systems of individual households. The size and appearance of constructed wetlands vary with the site and the volume of wastewater being treated, but whether the system features acres of surface water or several square feet of cattails, the process is the same. A balanced community of plants, insects, and microbes purifies the water before returning it to the aquifer, supporting a wealth of wildlife as a by-product.

Whether a pond is intended for water purification or simply as an ornamental feature in the garden, it is an ecosystem and as such requires time in the beginning to establish a balance. Occasionally, heavy rains or greater-than-average evaporation rates resulting from high temperatures and windy conditions may upset the balance, and the pond requires adjustments. In the simplest terms, wetland ecological balance hinges on oxygen-producing plants that absorb carbon dioxide and limit the growth of pond-choking algae. The oxygen also supports fish, which in turn eat insects and their larvae, including mosquitos. The fish add nutrients to the water that support the plants. Like any other type of garden, each pond will react differently depending upon the specific environment it occupies: whether it is in sun or shade, the season of the year, its pH (relative acidity), its surface area in proportion to its depth, and the flow of the water. Ponds are most water efficient if they are deep compared with the surface area and shaded part of the day to reduce evaporation.

Water gardens are the ultimate oases, havens for wildlife and cooling respites for people. While they require more maintenance skill and time than dryland gardens, water features can be designed conservatively. Even a small recirculating basin with a gurgling spill of water becomes a delightfully unexpected focal point in a desert garden.

SOIL TYPES

The type of soil you are working with will influence decisions about reshaping its surface. Heavy clay soils are the least inviting for many dryland plants. Contouring creates well-drained slopes for plants sensitive to compacted soils and reduced oxygen levels. Conversely, swale bottoms provide moist niches for plants requiring more water in sandy soils. Taking the soil into consideration in the design stage sidesteps many future disappointments.

Soils result from the weathering of rock. In the Southwest deserts, sun and wind are the major agents while water and frost are contributing forces. Our soils have a high mineral content unbuffered by organic matter, alkaline in reaction and undesirable from a conventional horticultural perspective. Our soils are geological juveniles, and juvenile delinquents in terms of traditional gardening! It takes little imagination to see the parent rock in the soil we're attempting to garden. Try to break ground and the shovel bounces back, sparks flying. The easiest and most practical way of working these soils is to accept them for what they are and concentrate on plants that prefer them. In the plant profiles found in my companion volume, *Plants for Natural Gardens*, soil preferences are noted for each plant. Some plants are narrowly adapted to blow sand, decomposed granite, or clay while others will grow well in a wide range of soils. Some of the adaptive species grow well in organically amended soil. Those plants usually have more shallow root systems than the others, and the amended soil retains more moisture, or they have nutrient requirements better served by an ample supply of organic matter. Most plants adapted to richly organic soils are unlikely candidates for self-sufficiency in high-desert ecosystems. Those few that are recommended have other characteristics that warrant the extra effort required to grow them.

One facet of ecologically sound landscaping that gets very little attention is that peat moss, the most commonly used horticultural soil amendment, is a strip-mined resource replaced in nature at an average rate of an inch in a century if conditions are favorable. If this wasn't enough of a drawback to consider alternatives, peat moss added to southwestern soils makes the surface dry faster, and once dry repels water, making it difficult to rewet. Meanwhile, hundreds of thousands of tons of organic matter are dumped in our landfills annually. Many communities now have local sources of composted organic matter available at reasonable prices. While the quality is variable depending on the organics being recycled and the season of the year, commercially produced compost is usually less saline than dairy manure, less weedy than horse litter, and less hot than poultry manure. All in all, whether homemade or purchased, compost is the best soil amendment to use when the planting requires it.

The rule of thumb governing soil amendments is that if you can amend most of the soil that the plants will root into, then by all means till in the compost deeply and lavishly. For most of the food-growing portion of your garden, composting is not an option, it's a necessity. For small lawn areas, where uniformity is a prime factor for success, amending the soil to create a uniform base is also necessary. For the cottage-garden style of overflowing perennial borders, where competition between individual plants can lead to the failure of the less aggressive ones, providing a cushy garden soil helps equalize the rivalry. Otherwise, it pays to go with the natural flow and opt for plants that prefer the local venue.

Budget: The Design Bottom Line

Underfunding and the arts are familiar bedfellows, and this extends to flower beds as well. Whether the site is newly developed, renovated, or just new to its present owners, landscaping often appears low on the list of things to do. With building construction and new furnishings a necessary priority of expenditure, there may be little left in the budget for the garden. Good landscaping, like everything of value and many things of doubtful merit, costs more than people expect it to. While few people initially invest the ten percent to fifteen percent of the value of the land and buildings that is recommended, over a period of time at least that much is spent on developing a showplace garden, especially if one considers the value of the water, time, mistakes, and revisions, as well as the actual labor and materials involved.

Because they are complex, natural gardens usually don't cost less to build. Since the whole project takes skill to design and a period of intelligent tinkering to stabilize, an ecologically sound garden may cost more in the first few years than a conventional garden of equal size. If all the work is professionally done you can count on it costing more. On average, payback begins the third year, when watering is reduced, maintenance becomes seasonal, and much of the insect activity becomes self-regulating. The less the site is disturbed initially, the more quickly the balance will be struck. By comparison, from the day they are planted, conventional landscapes of cool-season lawns, foundation plantings, and flower beds carry a fixed high-input level of maintenance. Because the plants aren't as well-adapted as natives, they will regularly use at least forty percent more water than a natural garden does, as well as additional fertilizer, pesticides to control stress-induced attacks by insects and diseases, labor, and lawn equipment used weekly for at least half the year. Replacing annuals in flower beds and failed plants further adds to the annual maintenance costs. An attractive conventional landscape is as expensive to build as a natural garden, and remains expensive to maintain throughout its existence.

In spite of the long-term savings, cost is usually an added incentive, not the primary reason, for going natural. Many people invest in such gardens because it "feels right." Some opt for the ecosystem models of their favorite wild places so that their city spaces connect them to wilderness. Others just want a garden that looks reasonably attractive for extended periods when they haven't time to tend it or a garden that lets them explore the countryside on weekends instead of having to do yard work. Some want to live in harmony with the ecosystem they've bought into. Others want birds and butterflies out the back door.

Whatever the motivation or design philosophy, the cost of a garden is determined by the initial treatment of the site and the final choice of materials. At the beginning of the process, it's better to consider all the possibilities: how spaces will be used, where shade and wind protection are needed, and how large the patio should be, since how much they may cost to build depends on the materials used and the time frame for construction. Budget influences planning both in establishing priorities for building the garden and in choosing materials cost-effectively. The larger the site or less certain its use, the more merit there is in landscaping in stages. An overall master plan can be established with the understanding that as the plan is implemented, it may change to better suit both your increased understanding of site conditions or changes in life-style. The spaces immediately around the buildings are the most intensively used and have the most impact on quality of life, so they have the greatest immediate value. Any changes in contouring have to be done first since they have an impact on everything that follows. Retaining walls are the most expensive way to make grade changes. If the site is steeply sloped and there is little usable level surface for patios or play areas, retaining walls may be necessary to save space and stabilize the construction scars. When a space is important because it is seen from windows or patios, but won't be used otherwise and doesn't threaten to avalanche, it is less expensive to maintain the slope by planting for erosion control and beauty.

Once the grade is set, each project will dictate its own possible stages of development. Weed control, especially of any perennial weeds, takes precedence. Laying the irrigation main lines and low-voltage wiring comes next, followed by any needed construction, be they hard-paved walkways and patios, shade structures, retaining walls, or fences and garden walls. These boundaries are some of the most expensive components in landscaping. Some hardscape materials cost significantly more than others, as noted earlier in the chapter (see "Space and Traffic Patterns"). An area designated as patio or walkway still leaves budget leeway in the choice of paving material. Frost-resistant brick and quality flagstone are more costly than concrete. Gravel and crusher fines are a bargain compared with hard paving but will track grit indoors without a hard surface in between to clean shoes. Skilled labor to set brick or flagstone or to pour and finish concrete adds to the cost of the materials. The amount of use, position as an extension of indoor spaces, and the style of the garden all influence the choice of paving materials. On surfaces that will take a lot of traffic, it will pay in the long run to opt for a more expensive, but long-lived, paving material.

Limiting the hardscaping and dedicating more space to plants increase the importance of a good irrigation system but will still lower the cost of a large project. Enlarging the arid zone of the landscape creates even greater long-term savings. Substituting crushed stone paths for hard paving on secondary paths also reduces cost and is consistent with the feel of a natural garden.

When planting is done in phases, a logical place to begin is with the slowest growing trees and shrubs for shade, screening, and wind protection. Even when perennial weeds are a major problem, such plants are least affected by and don't hamper weed control efforts. Grass or mulched shrub plantings needed to control blowing dust, mud, and annual weed invasion are another priority option. While plants are one of the least expensive elements in a garden, price can vary considerably with how quickly the plant grows and its size. Larger specimens of slower-growing plants such as oaks and mountain mahogany are more expensive than young seedlings of chamisa or broom baccharis that may grow two container sizes in one season. Seeds cost less to cover the same area than transplants do. In a sense, you are really buying time. Since much of an individual plant's ability to thrive under harsh conditions lies in its large root mass compared with its top growth, one of the advantages of dryland adapted plants over conventional nursery stock is that a vigorous young transplant or volunteer seedling will often outgrow a larger, older specimen of a conventional plant. Compromise is the wisest course. So that the landscape looks proportionate initially, use some larger specimens of the slowest

DESERT WILLOWS ARE TAPROOTED, FINE-TEXTURED, SMALL FLOWERING TREES THAT CAN BE USED CLOSE TO WALLS AND FOUNDATIONS TO SHADE WINDOWS AND BRING HUM- MINGBIRDS CLOSE FOR VIEWING. CM

growing plants and plants that form the framework of the landscape. Use a range of smaller transplants for the balance of the plantings that define the garden, and seed large areas with grasses and long-lived perennial wildflowers to stabilize the surface quickly. Add a small percentage of fast-growing annuals for immediate gratification. As the landscape develops, the annuals' role of short-term impact will either be eclipsed by the development of the more permanent plantings or, if they are well suited to the site, they may reseed and establish a niche for themselves.

The most important consideration when developing a garden in stages is the impact each phase will have on those still to come. If the area immediately surrounding the building is done first because it has the most impact on living spaces, keep access open for the later phases of construction and planting. Lay pipe sleeves, two inches or larger in diameter, under paving, through retainers, or under garden-wall foundations so that irrigation and low-voltage wiring can easily be fed through the sleeves later in the project. When a swimming pool is part of the long-term plan, reserve a space at least ten feet larger on each side than the maximum size of the proposed pool for a small front-end loader tractor to access the space.

Hiring skilled labor to do any masonry and irrigation main lines, large tree planting or setting of boulders that require equipment or strength beyond a weekend gardener's means, but doing the balance of the planting and mulching yourself as time and budget allow, is a way to cut the initial cost of the project. Because every customized landscape is a unique blend of variables, there is no realistic way to estimate an average price per square foot. In very general terms, forty percent of the cost may be in hardscaping: paving, shade structures, mulches, and irrigation materials; twenty percent in plants and seeds; and forty percent in labor. While a forty percent do-it-yourself discount is tempting, if your time is very limited or your enthusiasm for gardening is sporadic, and for wielding a pick and shovel entirely lacking, the additional forty percent might be very reasonable. You can participate in the process by overseeing the establishment of the plants, regulating watering, and observing insect activity. If you want to have a hand in the entire process, but your time is limited, planting in stages has a great advantage in reducing the numbers of new transplants being nurtured through the early transition at any given time. Starting small is also a confidence builder for the beginning gardener.

Selecting a landscape contractor that you feel comfortable working with is at least as important as the cost estimate. It pays to shop around. Most communities have insurance and licensing requirements for contractors. Ask for references and look at landscapes the contractor has built. As you move across the spectrum toward a more naturalized style of garden, the number of landscapers familiar with the approach will diminish. The attitude of the contractor toward your plan is critical. Some contractors have a narrow view of landscaping: it includes bluegrass sod or gravel, flower beds, foundation plantings, and fast-growing shade trees. To protect you from yourself, they'll encourage you to abandon your progressive garden ideals in favor of "real" landscaping. At the opposite end of the scale are native landscapers who focus on very wild looking reclamation, scorning a more cultivated style as regressive or "unnatural." Opt for the contractor who is responsive to your needs and shares a vision of the garden you desire. Having a plan on paper is helpful when hiring work out, especially on a complex project. There are too many details involved, too many ways to interpret what seems to be obvious, to operate on verbal communication alone. A signed contract should precede work start-up.

Plant Selection

Natural gardens have soft edges, boundaries made of and blurred by plants. If I had to give one reason for writing this book, it would be to introduce the gardener to a few hundred of my favorite plants. Choosing the right plant for its spot in the garden is doubly important if you expect it to abide there good-naturedly with a minimum of assistance. Plant selection is a three-step process. First, note the kinds of plants that serve your purposes. Trees can provide shade or wind protection, sculptural accent, and bird roosts and nesting. Large shrubs may be needed for screening, separation and enclosure,

THE PORTAL AND AWNING PROVIDE IMMEDIATE SHADE UNTIL ADAPTED TREES GROW LARGE ENOUGH TO COOL THE GARDEN. CM

habitat and ornament. Smaller shrubs are used as an understory layer under trees to suggest separation without blocking views, for color, texture, or fragrance, or for soil stabilization. Wildflowers and grasses are used as ground covers for erosion control, for seasonal interest, and to provide birdseed. Step two: think about the attributes of the plants that would accomplish the desired results in each designated space: evergreen or deciduous; densely twiggy or open and airy; low spreading or compact and mounding; berries in winter; flowers in spring or summer. Finally, consider what the site offers as growing conditions in those spaces, and consult the plant profiles found in the companion volume to make choices based on the roles plants will play in the landscape.

EXPOSURES

The buildings, walls, and fences that form the boundaries of a garden create some protected niches for the less well-adapted plants that we can't seem to live without. The evolution of the garden itself will moderate the climate to some degree, creating still more precious shaded and wind-buffered pockets as tree canopies expand and shrubs fill in. Backing up to the beginning, what will the new plantings have to contend with? Where does the wind scour the soil and deposit sand or litter in eddies? Where is there too much sun for comfort? Which areas dry out the fastest because they are subject to wind and full sun? Are there low spots where water stands after a downpour?

Consider the spaces that are extensions of the house. They will be most comfortable if shaded from the heat and glare of summer's sun but open to the warming low-angle sun of winter. Trees positioned close in for shade should be deeply rooted to preserve foundations and paving, open branched to minimize winter shadows, and should defoliate completely in fall. In the plant profiles and lists of recommended adaptive plants found in the companion volume, these important characteristics are noted to help you make appropriate choices. Plants are rarely perfect in all situations, and some concessions may be called for at times. I like to use desert willows (cold hardy to zero with brief, infrequent drops to minus fifteen degrees F) for shade near windows even though their canopy isn't dense enough to consider them shade trees. They are leafy enough to reduce the glare from reflective walls and paving, have deep roots that will not heave foundations or paving, and bring hummingbirds up close. Their narrow seedpods persist in winter and a multiple trunk form produces shadows, but on a west exposure or placed to frame windows rather than covering them they have little effect on solar gain in winter.

Another advantage of deeply rooted smaller trees is that a broad range of plants grow well beneath them. Concentrating the plantings that require more care in small areas where they will have the most impact limits overall maintenance. The spaces around patios and front entrances are the obvious choices for such emphasis. These are places where a flowering tree canopy contributes color as well as comfort, and an ever-

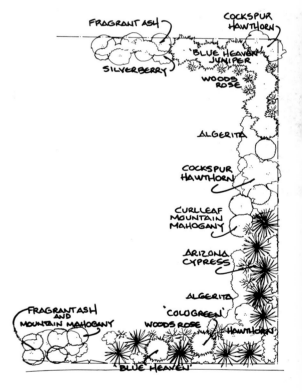

WINDBREAKS ARE MOST ATTRACTIVE AND EFFECTIVE WHEN THEY ARE COMPOSED OF A MIX OF EVERGREEN AND DECIDUOUS PLANTS OF VARYING HEIGHTS PLANTED CLOSELY ENOUGH TO PROVIDE A CONTINUOUS BUFFER.

green ground cover provides winter interest as well as dust control. The relationship is symbiotic. If the trees are well adapted they will never compete so strongly with the plants growing within their root zone that they undermine their growth. The water applied to the understory plants is shared with the trees and allows them to root out into more soil than if the tree was being drip irrigated alone.

The drawback to planting trees for shade is that it takes a few years before a quality tree grows large enough to do the job. Most of the trees planted for shade are fast-growing species such as cottonwoods, true willows, ash, sycamores, maples, and mulberries. These trees are adapted to moist bottomland where they grow large quickly because they have access to a constant supply of shallow groundwater. Moved to higher ground, they lose none of their thirst, and they are more subject to winds that rob their precious moisture and snap their weak limbs. Rather than opting for poorly suited trees when fast shade is a priority, extend a portal roof over part of the patio or build a detached ramada or arbor for immediate relief. Adding vines to drape a shade structure will yield all the leafy cooling advantages of trees until slower growing climate-adapted trees can fill in.

Shaded and wind-protected microclimates along northeast- and east-facing walls moderate conditions enough to simulate higher-elevation ecosystems. At Dog Canyon, south of Alamogordo, New Mexico, there is a classic natural example of this microclimate effect. The path meanders above a stream; as the canyon walls rise higher, dryland shrubs become denser, finally yielding to maidenhair ferns where seeping springs and shade from the canyon wall make conditions too cool and damp for the typical vegetation. Ten feet above the ferns, ocotillo and cactus clothe the crest of the rock outcrop. Such ecological anomalies are surprisingly common and can serve as garden models. The northeast-facing wall of a two-story house can provide a shady niche for aspen, creeping mahonia, kinnikinnick, blue flax, and nodding onion, bordered by a path edged with sage and desert zinnia fifteen feet away in full sun.

Just as sun and shade set boundaries for plant growth, wind sculpts a plant's potential for success. Southwestern plants protect themselves from wind by their fine textured, small, waxy, or down-covered foliage, limber stems, or strong-wooded character that enable them to thrive in conditions that leave their weak-limbed, soft-leafed, temperate-zone brethren in tatters. An advantage to developing a landscape in stages is that introducing more delicate plants can be delayed until a protective framework of trees or shrubs can become established. Whenever wind is a major force on a site, high-profile plants, those that will forever be head and shoulders above the rest, need to be selected for wind resistance. While someone new to the high desert might wonder where in this entire region wind *isn't* a force to reckon with, gardeners working in canyons between mountain ranges from El Paso to Denver will tell you that they have *real* wind problems. Tall buildings in downtown areas have a similar channeling effect, given that velocity increases where a gap narrows. These are not the places to grow hybrid tulips, whose large petals on tall stems shred within an hour of unfolding, or for 'Pacific Giant' delphiniums or gladiolus, which will resemble a sad game of floral pick-up-sticks on a gusty afternoon. Better to build a framework of well-adapted and native plants for shade and wind screening, leaving the icing on the cake for a few years hence when the moderating effect of the trees and shrubs makes planting the tokens to childhood memories or odes to England in the merrie month of May more worth the effort. By the time the basic natural landscaping has moderated the climate enough to grow exotics, gardeners are often so taken with the easy abundance of the well-adapted plants that the delicate aliens remain a pleasant remembrance of other times and other places. If the desire to plant them still burns brightly, the milder environment of the garden is more apt to welcome them.

While arctic blasts in winter and strong spring winds make gardening more difficult and living spaces less inviting, summer breezes are an asset. Windbreaks are most effective when they reduce the force of the wind and direct its flow. Their form is dictated by the function they are designed to serve. A mixed evergreen and deciduous windbreak provides shelter up to five times its height, so that an average twenty-foot-tall planting protects the space on its lee side eighty to one hundred feet from the planting. Many sources of data on windbreak plantings (see Appendix of windbreak plants) also recommend that a windbreak extend fifty feet beyond the buildings it is intended to shelter on either end and that a windbreak be eleven times longer than it is tall. Few residential lots are large enough to meet those requirements but would still benefit by shelterbelt plantings. Common sense prevails. Because very tall trees are alien to the foothills, high-plains grassland, and shrub deserts where wind shapes the landscape, it is more effective to select lower-profile plants and cluster them closely around the garden spaces in need of protection than to try to buffer the entire property with a border of oversize plants. There's an added advantage in creating smaller enclosed spaces, in that frost tends to settle in large openings while small clearings remain significantly warmer. Since any gaps in the windbreak will increase the velocity of wind funneling through them, it is important to keep the planting continuous. Evergreens block wind more completely, but even twiggy bare branches slow winter winds enough to be effective. A combination of the two is more interesting visually and truer to ecological models. From a practical standpoint, a single straight row of one species of plant is less effective in the long term than an irregular combination of several types of plants, some taller, others denser at the base, some evergreen, some with seasonal color. The contrast between the plants is interesting visually, and the eventual loss of an individual here or there over time won't diminish the value of the planting as a whole.

DESIGNING FOR MAINTENANCE

It may seem cart-before-horse to think about maintenance even before deciding what to plant, but who will care for the garden and how much time and other resources they

BUSH PENSTEMON AND CHOCOLATE FLOWER PROVIDE COLOR FOR SEVERAL MONTHS WITH AS LITTLE AS EIGHT TO TEN INCHES OF RAINFALL (TOP).

WINECUPS CLUSTERED IN A BUFFALOGRASS LAWN ADD A DASH OF COLOR AND CAN BE MOWED WITH THE GRASS.

want or can afford to spend there will have a great impact on the final design. A garden with a strong framework of well-adapted and heavily mulched shrubs and trees takes the least amount of ongoing care. If the plants are spaced to accommodate their mature sizes, all the maintenance needed is periodic deep watering and the occasional removal of deadwood. Such a garden can be colorful if the trees and shrubs have showy flowers and interesting leaf textures that change seasonally. Add a midgrass prairie to carpet the open spaces, long-lived wildflowers clustered in drifts, and a minimum of short-term perennials or annuals and the level of maintenance increases a bit, as the grasses require seasonal mowing and flowers need deadheading. On the other hand, the addition of the grass and wildflower understory adds visual depth to the planting and another niche for wildlife that offsets the extra maintenance needed.

The amount and kind of maintenance a garden needs is designed in with the selection of plants and their placement. The more hard-edged the style, the more work it takes to maintain those edges. The more regular the placement, the more obvious it is if something is out of place. The less adapted the plants, the more coddling they'll take to grow. A space that's not tended to some extent is not a garden, since cultivating plants is what gardening is, but you can choose your chores and how much time you want to devote to them. If you're a recreational gardener who enjoys spending your leisure time puttering in the garden, you may always need a bit of open space to try new plants. If you like to prune, growing desert willow, mountain mahogany, and New Mexico olive, with their interesting branching patterns to shape as small sculptural trees, gives opportunities to indulge that creative bent. You might also like mass plantings of chamisa or threadleaf sage, since their greatest ornamental asset is their new growth. Such plants benefit greatly by either cutting them back severely as they begin to grow actively in spring, so that the new growth quickly softens the hard edges of the scalping, or cutting the oldest stems out down to the ground, so the plants stay forever young. A perennial border, kept in its prime by removing the spent flowers, offers still more opportunity to putter. In nature, the seasonal browsing by animals has the same effect, though the intention is a good meal, not a prettier form. Most plants need much less pruning than they receive by overzealous gardeners. If pruning seems like too much work, or dredges up memories of the time as an eight year old when you gave yourself a haircut and had to live with the results, then plan to use plants that look best if left alone, such as Apache plume, fernbush, sumac, junipers, and cotoneasters. Use wildflowers such as giant four o'clock, gayfeather, prairieclover, and butterflyweed that are shrublike in their life span and foolproof in their pruning needs, demanding only that you cut them back to the ground when they go dormant for winter.

If you'd like a lawn, but don't want to mow it every week from May to October, plant buffalograss, blue grama, or a mix of the two and mow once a month instead. Buffalograss, especially some of the new varieties selected for their lower, denser growth habits, might never need mowing. All grasses seem to grow best if the old growth is removed periodically. Most native grasses perform best if mowed high and infrequently. Regular short mowing will thin a stand, leaving gaps for weeds to invade. Any grass that is mowed frequently will need more water and fertilizer to support the regrowth stimulated by clipping. The ideal mowing height for native grasses ranges from four to eight inches. Four inches is the highest blade setting on most conventional mowers. Gas- or electric-powered string-line trimmers that have a hard-blade option are useful for cutting small meadow/prairie plots. If power tools aren't your forte, and mowing in general a task you'd like to avoid, grass areas can be raked to remove old growth in spring. If you enjoy raking leaves in autumn, underplant large trees with a dense herbaceous ground cover such as yerba mansa or creeping lippia, or mulch trees with crusher fines or cobblestones that are easily worked. Underplanted with shrubby ground covers, such as prostrate sumac or lowfast cotoneaster, leaf drop is more difficult to clean up. Remember to match the water requirements of the tree with that of the ground cover. If a tree is taprooted, a deeply rooted shrubby ground cover watered with widely spaced drip emitters will work well, but if the tree roots extensively near the surface, it is better to plant an herbaceous ground cover watered with closely spaced emitters that will support both the tree and ground cover. By choosing small-leaved trees for the canopy, their fallen leaves can sift through the ground cover branches and act as mulch. Leaving leaf litter as a mulch under trees has pros and cons. If the plant shedding leaves is prone to rust or mildew infections when weather conditions are right, the fallen leaves may harbor next season's reinfection. Better to rake up such leaves as they drop or avoid susceptible plants altogether. If the site is very dry and windy, the leaves will collect in pockets and swirl around the garden, more of a problem than a resource. Bark is a good base mulch when planning to let leaves accumulate as mulch. Weed barrier fabric is helpful in preventing reseeding of such weed trees as Siberian elm in shrubby ground covers.

Although it's easy to find gardeners enthusiastic about planting and pruning, raking and even mowing, I've only met a few who have voiced an absolute passion for weeding, and they may have been kidding. Most people, myself included, become increasingly revolted at the prospect of weeding in direct proportion to the magnitude of the area that needs to be tended. Since disturbance breeds weeds, limiting the amount of soil disturbance greatly reduces the scope of weed problems. Weeds will become a minor part of the plant community if most of the landscape is mulched trees and shrubs and long-lived perennial wildflowers and grasses. The less work you intend your garden to be, the less space should be given to short-lived perennials and annuals, and those used should be well-adapted enough to reseed themselves. The following chapter covers weeding and watering options in detail. Developing a stable plant community as part of the design process limits the need for weeding.

How much water you want to use influences design and brings the selection of plants and their placement into sharper focus. Zoned irrigation—grouping plants in the

GLOBEMALLOW AND ONE OF HUNDREDS OF THE YELLOW ARID-ADAPTED SUNFLOWERS THAT THRIVE WITH THE EXTRA MOISTURE THAT CONDENSES ON BOULDER OUTCROPPINGS (TOP). CM

THE INTERPLAY OF SILVER AND YELLOW (WINTERFAT AND RAYED COTA) IS A FAMILIAR THEME IN GRASSLANDS AND DESERTS.

garden according to their water requirements—is a xeriscape concept that has its roots in ecology. In nature, plant communities sort themselves out according to the moisture available. You're more likely to find sideoats grama growing on slopes and screwbean mesquite growing in floodplains, creosotebush growing over a caliche hardpan and broom dalea only on deep blow sands. In each case how the plant responds to water is partly why it grows where it does. The areas close to buildings are logical oases, where the extra water invested cools the living spaces and creates a more inviting environment. The far perimeters of the property might be very low water use as a transition to undeveloped open space beyond or the heat generated by pavement. The parkway strip between sidewalk and street is a logical place for low-water-use plantings, since careful watering is needed to keep runoff from spilling into the gutter, and bordered by paving, such spaces are naturally hot and dry. Middle-ground plantings for privacy screening or wind buffering are moderate in water use since periodic deep watering will be needed to maintain the desired leafiness no matter what the weather.

DEVELOPING THE PLANT COMMUNITY

Once you have an idea of the types of plantings needed and the types of microclimates they will occupy, you can select the individual plant species that will fill the garden spaces and the ecological roles that have evolved through the design process. Plants profiled in the companion volume, *Plants for Natural Gardens*, detail what the plants look like, where they are best adapted, how they may be used in the garden, likely companions, and the best current advice on how to start and manage them in the landscape. In time the garden comes together as a mosaic, a living puzzle. A reminder that plants are living things seems to demand some sort of apology to the thinking gardener, but too often plants fail because they are put where they can't possibly succeed. Usually plants come to be in the wrong place because we imagine they'd look good there. In the cooperative effort between gardener and plants, the success of both depends on looking beyond appearances. While pushing the boundaries of plant adaptations is unwise overall, a little experimentation can be rewarding, especially since many of the plants I am recommending are new to cultivation. Every time we travel to the Sonoran desert, we bring home plants that really don't belong as far north or east as central New Mexico. Every time we travel anywhere, we return with seeds or sprigs of plants too interesting to leave behind. Our souvenirs usually wind up dead, frozen over winter or shriveled over summer. Sometimes, like the Texas ranger I brought north from a nursey near Big Bend, Texas, after several failed attempts to find a suitable microclimate outdoors they get potted in a large tub, summer outdoors and winter in the greenhouse. Sometimes plants, like the skeletonleaf goldeneye I grew from seeds on another trip to southwest Texas, survive several years before a record cold spell sounds their death knell. Occasionally the gamble pays off. Ultimately, the nature of gardens is their transience. Thoughtful design is an attempt on the one hand to limit the uncertainty and instability of gardening in a climate that isn't keen on cultivation and on the other hand to encourage the acceptance of the unpredictable. As gratifying as it is to become skilled gardeners, many garden triumphs remain purely accidental. Thomas Jefferson once observed that the harder we work, the luckier we are likely to be. He was probably out in his garden at the time.

Plants have personalities. There are the meek, like flameflowers, that very rarely inherit the garden, and the bolder blue grama, which may reclaim the West but is generous about sharing the space. The native *artemisia* sages have a rugged windswept demeanor that never looks quite tame regardless of pruning or placement, while *salvia* sages look like garden plants invented for a cottage border. Most daisies, whether coneflowers, blackfoot daisies, zinnias, asters, or perky sue, are both alert and self-assured, the Doris Days of local flora. The closely related sunflowers are bolder, more Aretha Franklin, in their delivery. Saltbush, usually found growing in large stands dominating a basin or slope, has long been known as an indicator of prior human occupation. From a design standpoint that tenacity can mean trouble in a small garden but be just the thing in the most difficult conditions. Drawing together a workable plant community means giving thought to these personalities, which are often visible expressions of adaptability. Bush penstemon and red coneflower, gayfeather and desert zinnia, winecups and buffalograss, giant four o'clock and piñon, silver bluestem and sotol, beargrass and boulders are combinations that play off each other to mutual benefit. Very often the best garden combinations are components of naturally occurring ecosystems. Nature's design ideas are often sage advice.

3 Planting and Early Maintenance

GETTING FROM A PLAN to a finished garden requires a few years of consistent observation and care. Planting time and early maintenance are continuations of the design process, the critical time when a balance is established. While the time of planting and fine-tuning is a time of hard work and uncertainty, it is also a rewarding period of learning to collaborate with nature. Because gardens are processes rather than products, they are never really finished. One beautiful aspect of natural gardens is that they reach a point of dynamic equilibrium when change is slow and the tendency is toward ever greater stability. Armed with a plan, either clearly drawn on paper or loosely formed in the mind, the gardener turns to the site to begin the process of its development. When renovating an older garden, the first order of business is removing all the extraneous elements that don't figure into the new landscape. New construction sites may require immediate soil stabilizing or weed control. In both cases, work begins on the surface.

Site Preparation

The first steps in construction involve making any adjustments needed to the contours, raising berms and hollowing out the drainage basins and swales for water harvesting, defining the traffic patterns that will develop into the hard-paved sidewalks, porous

AS A GARDEN EVOLVES, THE NATURAL AND MANMADE ELEMENTS MERGE TOGETHER. IN THIS GARDEN, THE PLANT COMMUNITY COMPLEMENTS THE DRY STREAMBED PATH THAT IS THE FOCUS.

paved paths, driveway, and any other access needed, and preparing the surface for planting. A new building site that has been recently scraped may regrow some of the original cover. The sage and broom dalea shrub-desert ecosystem can be so resilient that some of what was scraped off the surface may regenerate from the ample roots left intact. You may want to begin developing the landscape immediately surrounding the building, since this area will have more impact on living space, and leave the perimeter alone to see if it will recover somewhat before final decisions are made about replanting.

In *bosque* (wooded) ecosystems, any grade changes around mature cottonwoods should be minimized, since drastically altering soil contours or compacting the soil around older trees will speed their decline. The same is true when working around established trees and shrubs in a landscape renovation. Plant roots require oxygen as well as water to remain vital. As little as eight inches of added soil may bury existing roots deeply enough to smother them. Sometimes trees carefully preserved throughout construction are later undermined during landscaping by altering the growing conditions so drastically that the mature plants can't adjust. There are several options for paving under extant trees, among them using porous materials such as decomposed granite, crusher fines or other gravels, and cinder block pavers especially designed for planting spaces, all of which limit soil compaction in areas that will be driven over regularly. Such surface treatments allow you to use the space without jeopardizing large trees valuable for their cooling, habitat, and link with the history of the place.

Mature trees that are tapping groundwater in an oasis ecosystem may need no provision for supplemental watering. If you are converting a conventional high-water-use landscape to a more ecologically appropriate one, you may choose to leave some of the existing shade trees in place. In order to maintain the health of trees conditioned to sharing water with a bluegrass lawn, new plantings should be clustered throughout the established root zone to maintain the trees' life-support systems. Trees grown in lawns often root shallowly, competing with the grass for water and nutrients. The network of these surface roots will provide strong competition for new transplants. Opportunists such as Siberian elm or mulberry may triple the amount of water needed by the new plants in order to compensate for what the trees syphon off. Mulberries pose the added challenge of producing shade so deep that few plants are adapted to grow within their canopy. If mature trees have been "topped," that is, have had large limbs arbitrarily cut off to drastically reduce their size, they may pose serious hazards. The branches that grow from topped stumps are weakly attached to the tree and very subject to wind breakage. Given the other problems associated with these trees—the weedy self-sowing and beetle plague of the elm and the allergy potential from the pollen of fruitless mulberry—removing the trees may be wiser than trying to salvage them.

SHRUB-DESERT PLANTS ARE SO DEEPLY ROOTED AND RESILIENT THAT THEY WILL OFTEN REGROW AFTER SEVERE DISTURBANCE, BUT RECOVERY TIME IS MEASURED IN YEARS RATHER THAN MONTHS AND IN THE MEANTIME THE EXPOSED SOIL IS OPEN TO BOTH WEED COLONIZING AND EROSION.

When contouring is done on a site, ideally the existing soil can be reshaped without bringing in fill dirt. If added fill is needed, use soil similar to the soil on the site if possible. Contouring with fill that is very different in composition from the base soil creates problems with the infiltration of water and limits the penetration of roots just as amending the soil with compost or peat moss does. In preparation for planting, only amend the soil whose plantings will benefit from the effort and expense: the vegetable garden, small flower beds for exotics, and lawn areas where uniform soil is needed to promote uniform plant growth. Amending the soil for a buffalograss or blue grama lawn may seem to contradict the recommendation to amend only when the root systems will be limited to the amended soil area, since these grasses root much more deeply than the soil could be amended. Any lawn, regardless of the type of grass, is ecologically unsound inasmuch as its governing principle is uniformity rather than diversity, and the best way to grow a dense green lawn is to start with as uniform a seed or sod bed as possible. By gradually increasing the depth of watering and decreasing the frequency, a native-grass lawn can be encouraged to root deeply. The compost is a measure of giving the tender seedlings an easy start.

In nature, grasses grow in mixed stands with other herbaceous plants at densities dictated by rainfall. Competition for space and nutrients is balanced by the enhanced nitrogen made available by soil microorganisms. It is a collaborative situation rather than a strongly competitive one. Lawns, on the other hand, are seeded heavily to exclude weeds; that is, all plants that are not the selected grass. We accept that weeds will always compete initially because newly disturbed soil is their ecological niche. But the problem is compounded by the fact that grasses, the more advanced species in the ecosystem hierarchy, are part of what is called "climax vegetation," the stable, long-term, and *slow*-to-develop plant community. If the site has been disturbed repeatedly, there will be a considerable imbalance between opportunistic weeds and slower grass seedlings, requiring greater seedling densities of the lawn grass and consistent efforts to control the weeds by pulling or mowing, along with incantations and prayers. If the site has a history of minimal disturbance and is being taken from a stand of native vegetation to native lawn, some of the "weeds" that germinate may be the desired grass reseeding itself.

Native grasses respond to organic soil amendments better than most dryland trees, shrubs, and wildflowers. A cubic yard of compost per eighty to one hundred square feet of seeding area, thoroughly tilled six to eight inches into the native soil and raked to a fine crumbly surface, is an ideal seedbed that water and new roots will penetrate easily and uniformly. As the sod develops, the roots that are sloughed off as part of the natural growth process will in time create deeper strata of soil having a greater than

THESE GRAVEL-FILLED PAVING BLOCKS MINIMIZE SOIL COMPACTION AND ALLOW AIR AND WATER TO PENETRATE TO MATURE TREE ROOTS.

average organic content. If the grasses are intended as prairie or filler between shrubs, not amending the surface will result in plant densities similar to what local ecosystems support.

Weed Control

Soil disturbance during construction and landscape site preparation encourages weed invasion. Depending on where you are, the probable interlopers will vary. The first order of business is to define "weed." If it is unwanted and threatens to overrun plants more highly valued, it's a weed. If it has some other nuisance value, such as prickly seed heads that break off easily, or if its pollen greatly contributes to allergies, it also qualifies as a weed. You need to know whether your weeds are annuals or perennials and warm-season (germinate and grow during warm weather) or cool-season (germinate and grow during cool weather) since controls for each category will differ. In most cases, weed control should be undertaken before planting, since a focused initial effort is easier than trying to sort the good guys from the bad after planting is under way. Getting a new planting established to displace weeds as quickly as possible is key to minimizing annual weed recurrences, and the better adapted the landscape plant choices are to the site conditions, the more quickly they will dominate. Since we have both cool- and warm-season pests to contend with, stabilizing the soil quickly prevents new weed-seed sources from developing.

ANNUAL WEEDS

Annual weeds, such as mustards, kochia, tumbleweeds, spotted spurge, pigweed, ambrosia, puncturevine, cheatgrass, and crabgrass, are nature's first line of recovery after a major disturbance. They serve as nurse crops, stabilizing the soil and trapping moisture so that slower-developing perennials can get started. Hard as it may be to consider weeds beneficial, their role in the ecosystem is one of pioneer. Breaking new ground, their roots penetrate quickly and deeply, opening channels for moisture to infiltrate and anchoring the surface to prevent erosion. Deeply rooted, they pull nutrients from lower in the soil profile. As they die, their decay releases nutrients and feeds microorganisms that nourish the developing long-term plant community. Numbers are the deciding factor. Some initial weed cover is helpful. Only when weeds grow so thickly that slower-growing plants are robbed of the light and water they need to develop do they undermine our planting efforts. Annual weeds can usually be suppressed by minimizing any future disturbance, smothering them with mulch, or displacing them with desirable plants.

PERENNIAL WEEDS

Perennial weeds, such as bindweed, Bermuda and Johnson grasses, thistles, and silver nightshade, are more difficult to control because they have the advantage of stored food

AFTER A DAY SPENT WEEDING, RABELAIS NOTED IN HIS GARDEN JOURNAL, "NATURE ABHORS A VACUUM." WEEDS ARE OFTEN THE RESULT OF SOIL DISTURBANCE.

**CLOCKWISE FROM TOP LEFT:
COCKLEBUR, JOHNSON GRASS, KOCHIA,
SILVER NIGHTSHADE, BINDWEED,
AMBROSIA, TUMBLEWEED.**

in the roots and a capacity to regrow from any roots not eliminated. Controlling perennial weeds involves exhausting their food reserves by eliminating as much of the root system as possible and preventing recharge of nutrients by repeatedly eliminating new top growth. Since carbohydrates are transferred from top growth to storage just before flowering and in late summer and fall before dormancy, these are the best times to apply a systemic herbicide. It will move through the roots more extensively, leaving less to regrow. Although I'm not a proponent of herbicide use in general, perennial weed control is nearly impossible without a very consistent effort, sometimes as often as weekly removal for at least one growing season. Once several leaves regrow, perennial weeds are photosynthesizing enough to regain ground. Glyphosate seems to be the most effective and least toxic means of chemical control, especially when applications are timed for maximum effect.

It is possible to weaken a stand of some perennial weeds, particularly grasses other than Bermuda grass, by scalping them close to the ground repeatedly, especially when they are beginning to flower. At that point in the growth cycle, they have exhausted

COCKLEBURS ARE PROLIFIC ON
HEAVY CLAY SOILS, ESPECIALLY
WHERE PERIODIC FLOODING
STIMULATES SEEDS TO SPROUT.

JOHNSON GRASS IS COARSE AND
AGGRESSIVE, SPREADING BY SEEDS
AND ROOT SPROUTS.

KOCHIA, OR RAGWEED, PRODUCES
PRODIGIOUS AMOUNTS OF HIGHLY
IRRITATING WIND-BORNE POLLEN
AND EQUALLY GENEROUS NUMBERS
OF SEEDS THAT GERMINATE AND
GROW WITH VERY LITTLE MOISTURE.

SILVER NIGHTSHADE (HORSENETTLE)
IS PRICKLY AND SPREADS BY SEEDS
ENCLOSED IN ROUND YELLOW
BERRIES AND ALSO BY ITS RHIZOMA-
TOUS ROOTS.

BINDWEED IS A MORNINGGLORY
WITH AN EXTREMELY DEEP AND
EXTENSIVE ROOT SYSTEM. BIRDS
DISPERSE THE SEEDS, AND ROOT
SECTIONS WILL SPROUT AND
CREATE NEW PLANTS.

AMBROSIA MAY BE THE NECTAR OF
THE GODS, BUT ITS IRRITATING
POLLEN AND PRICKLY SEED CAPSULES
MAKE IT THE CURSE OF GARDENERS
ON SANDY DESERT SITES.

TUMBLEWEED IS WIDESPREAD IN
PART BECAUSE OF ITS TUMBLIN'
SEED-DISPERSAL TECHNIQUE.

much of their stored reserves. Removing most of the leaf mass prevents the plants from renewing these reserves. Mowing native-grass lawns too short too often has the same weakening effect.

Valley sites on old agricultural land pose the greatest weed control challenge because years of cultivation, compounded by weed-seed dispersal in irrigation water and by birds, have destroyed natural balances. Mesa and foothills sites, predominantly in newly developed areas, have fewer noxious weeds present, and the likely invaders usually are annuals, which are fairly easy to suppress. Where soil has to be disturbed to seed the desired cover, tilling and watering the seedbed repeatedly will both germinate weed seeds and destroy their seedlings. This is more effective where weed potential is low than it is on valley land where the storehouse of weed seeds is staggering. If the soil is not compacted, very shallow tilling, disturbing only the top inch or two, brings fewer unwanted seeds to light, primed to sprout. If the area is relatively small, soil solarizing is an option. The soil is tilled, thoroughly moistened, then covered with a sheet of clear poly film, the edges weighted with soil so that the area is sealed under the covering. Some weed seeds may sprout as the soil heats up, but as the water in the soil heats to steaming, weed seeds, seedlings, and many soil pathogens and insects will be destroyed. The downside of soil solarizing is that it destroys beneficial microorganisms as well, but since no toxins are used, populations can rebuild quickly. To be effective, solarizing must be done during summer's hottest months.

Afterplanting Controls

The critical period of competition between weeds and new seedlings or transplants is the initial three to nine weeks after planting. In spring, when seedlings have three to five leaves, they can easily be pulled without disturbing the surface much, especially if the soil is damp. Hand weeding a new seedbed also gives you the opportunity to observe its progress closely. Understanding and insight come from careful observation, and tip-toeing across the lawn or prairie, sorting weeds from the desired grasses and wildflowers, is about as close and careful as gardening can get. Two difficulties may arise. If the area is large, hand weeding may be logistically impossible. Also, young seedlings can be difficult to recognize. Tumbleweed sprouts look remarkably like bush penstemon. I once pulled out half the gilia in a seedbed thinking it was mustard before a light bulb went off and I realized my mistake.

In lawns and prairie plantings, after the grass has had a few months to develop, mowing annual weeds to prevent their reseeding is an effective means of tipping the balance in favor of the intended cover. Puncture vine, an annual nuisance because of its sharp seed capsules, spreads out so close to the soil that mowing is ineffective. On otherwise bare ground, a weed-control formulation of horticultural oil spray has been

SEALED UNDER A SHEET OF CLEAR PLASTIC, MOISTENED SOIL HEATS TO STEAMING, KILLING MANY WEED SEEDS, SEEDLINGS, SOIL PATHOGENS, AND INSECTS. TO BE REALLY EFFECTIVE, SOLARIZING HAS TO BE DONE DURING THE HOTTEST SUMMER MONTHS.

used successfully to kill puncture vine, but in plots of mixed seedlings, cutting them out one by one at the soil surface when they start to flower is safer, since the oil spray might also kill tender new grasses and wildflowers. In most cases, if annual weeds are cut off at ground level when they begin to flower, they will not regrow as the plants will have shifted from a vegetative growth stage into a reproductive one. Pulling or hoeing weeds disturbs the soil. Cutting weeds off near the soil surface minimizes disturbance and the opportunity for more weed seed to germinate. Since weeds can set seed as they lie severed and wilted, rather like B-movie monsters that keep rearing up from the grave, it is best to remove the cut weeds to a hot compost pile to be permanently laid to rest.

Using preemergent herbicides in the early stages of developing a garden offers a measure of easy control of annual weeds by keeping their seeds from sprouting. All germination is targeted, however, so you also suppress the germination of wildflowers you might wish to increase, and repeated use may weaken established plants with roots in the treated area. When reading herbicide labeling to determine if a product is safe to use on native plants, you will rarely find any confirmation because until recently these plants weren't considered landscape ornamentals. Herbicides also tend to persist longer in dry soils, prolonging their effectiveness or potential for harm. Preemergents are surface treatments, most effective if they are kept in the top inch of soil; the downside is that this surface treatment increases their potential for blowing or washing into other

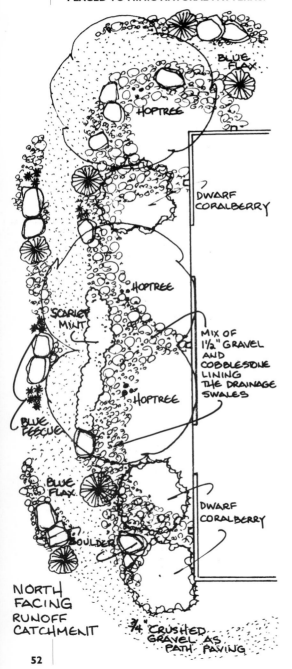

BLUE
FLAX

HOPTREE

DWARF
CORALBERRY

HOPTREE

SCARLET
MINT

MIX OF
1½" GRAVEL
AND
COBBLESTONE
LINING
THE DRAINAGE
SWALES

HOPTREE

BLUE
FESCUE

BLUE
FLAX

DWARF
CORALBERRY

BOULDER

NORTH
FACING
RUNOFF
CATCHMENT

¾" CRUSHED
GRAVEL AS
PATH PAVING

areas. In a habitat garden the preemergent shortcut is not acceptable since it exposes ground-feeding species to toxins.

A wildflower meadow or prairie can be one of the most labor-intensive types of planting to get established. Meadows are not ecosystem models typical of high-desert elevation or climate. They are native to cooler, moister environments. Water enough to support high-elevation meadow plants and weeds respond with enthusiasm while the wildflowers falter in the heat of high-desert summers. Our grassland ecology makes prairie, where warm-season grasses are dominant and wildflowers have more localized habitats, a more practical model to use. The wildflowers that succeed in prairie systems are mostly deeply rooted perennials that compete with grasses because of their longevity and their ability to tap large areas for moisture and nutrients. Annual wildflowers require soil disturbance to persist, as do their ugly stepsister weeds. They might be included in the seed mix only for immediate gratification, something to grow and flower quickly in response to initial gardening efforts. In a year or two, as the perennials develop, the annuals usually disappear, their niche in the plant community filled by more stable plants.

When reclaiming a site that has a weedy history, increasing the seeding rate gives the desired plants a competitive edge. A dense stand of new grasses will support periodic mowing to limit the reseeding of annual weeds. The ideal mowing height for most native bunchgrasses is four to eight inches. Most mowers have a maximum blade height of three to four inches. Frequent short mowing will favor weeds such as crabgrass and spurge and increase the need to water since the soil will be more exposed and dry out faster. Extra watering will increase the need to fertilize, and more water and fertilizer will stimulate the weeds to grow faster. The alternative to this merry-go-round is to establish a balance instead. The day is coming when mowers with broader height adjustments will be widely available because nationwide lawns are shrinking and more diverse plantings requiring less frequent mowing, less watering and fertilizing, and little if any pesticides are gaining ground. Until then, use either a mower with a four-inch blade setting, a brush mower, or a string-line trimmer with a hard-blade attachment for smaller areas. Limit watering and fertilizing to the amount needed to maintain the health of the desired plants. After the first few growing seasons, if the soil has not been disturbed, annual weeds should be reduced to a very minor role in the plant community, manageable on a seasonal basis. When planting an area with groupings of trees and shrubs, limit soil disturbance by scalping annual weeds to stubble without cultivating, and after transplanting apply a generous layer of mulch to suppress the regrowth of the weeds.

Weeds can be an indication of poor water management. Crabgrass develops in native-grass lawn areas when the seedbed is being watered more than the buffalograss and/or blue grama require. The excess watering favors the crabgrass over the seeded grasses. Gradually cutting back on the frequency of irrigation and increasing the depth of watering, and mowing off the crabgrass seed heads or removing the crabgrass by hand using a utility knife to cut it out at ground level, will usually correct the problem. On the opposite end of the scale, prostrate spurge develops in cool-season lawns that are being underwatered. Drought weakens the desired grasses and favors the development of the spurge. Since the spurge is too low-growing to control by mowing, adjusting the irrigation schedule or spray pattern of sprinklers to avoid dry spots can help control spurge problems. Controlling the amount and location of water in the garden is a powerful weed preventative.

Watering

The availability of water determines which plants, both desirable and undesirable, will grow. More garden plants are killed by overwatering than die of thirst, yet there is a misconception that native or drought-tolerant plants don't need to be watered. All plants need some care, especially watering, until they have rooted out extensively enough to tap natural sources of water. The more consistent the care initially, the faster the plants become self-sufficient. Learning to read plant responses is the way to make them grow and prosper and is one of the most confusing lessons of gardening. Every plant is adapted to a specific range of water need. Exposure to sun and wind, the ambient temperature, soil type and contour, and competition with other plants, as well as the genetic predisposition of the plant itself, determine how much and how often a plant will need watering. Plants that are selected for their adaptability to site conditions and spaced according to natural patterns, planted more densely in low areas where moisture collects and more widely spaced on slopes and dry plains, may ultimately require no supplemental water to survive. When plants are spaced more closely to provide shade or screening, buffer wind, or as a dense ground cover; if they must withstand foot traffic, mowing, or are intended to support wildlife; if they are expected to bloom profusely and for an extended period of time, then even the best adapted plants will need occasional watering. The more productive we expect them to be, the more accommodating we need to be.

DROUGHT ADAPTATIONS

Because of all the variables, water use by the same plants will vary from garden to garden. There is no magic formula for determining when and how much to water, but there are general points to consider in managing the amount of water a garden uses. While all the plants discussed in this book and profiled in the companion volume are drought tolerant, they all have somewhat differing needs depending on where and how they are used. The term "drought tolerant" has a range of meanings depending on the context in which it is used. Drought tolerant in many garden catalogs means able to survive short periods without watering. A drought in Georgia is when your leather shoes

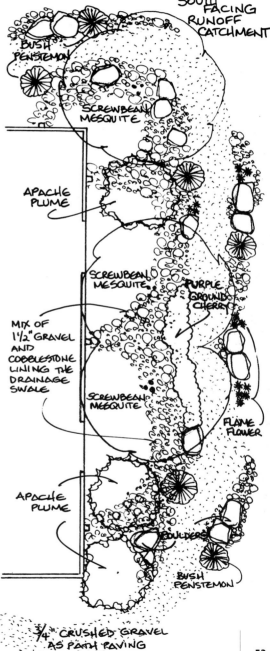

THE PLANTS IN THE SHADED NORTH-FACING CATCHMENT ARE UPLAND NATIVES. SHRUB-DESERT NATIVES WERE CHOSEN FOR THE HOTTER SOUTH-FACING EXPOSURE.

SOUTH FACING RUNOFF CATCHMENT

BUSH PENSTEMON

SCREWBEAN MESQUITE

APACHE PLUME

SCREWBEAN MESQUITE

PURPLE GROUND CHERRY

MIX OF 1½" GRAVEL AND COBBLESTONE LINING THE DRAINAGE SWALE

SCREWBEAN MESQUITE

FLAME FLOWER

APACHE PLUME

BOULDERS

BUSH PENSTEMON

¾" CRUSHED GRAVEL AS PATH PAVING

DROUGHT REQUIRING:
NO SUPPLEMENTAL WATERING ONCE
ESTABLISHED; UNDER HOTTEST, DRIEST
CONDITIONS ONE DEEP MONTHLY
WATERING AT THE MOST.

DROUGHT ENDURING:
DEPENDING ON EXPOSURE AND SOIL,
DEEP WATERING ONCE OR TWICE A
MONTH DURING WARM WEATHER.

DROUGHT EVADING:
WATER ONLY WHEN GROWING AND
BLOOMING.

DROUGHT TOLERANT:
WATER ONCE A WEEK WHEN TEMPERA-
TURES ARE ABOVE NINETY DEGREES F,
EVERY TWO WEEKS WHEN TEMPERA-
TURES ARE ABOVE SEVENTY-FIVE
DEGREES F, MONTHLY THE REST OF
THE YEAR.

mildew from the humidity in your closet but your daisies wilt from a two-week period without four inches of rainfall. In the southwestern deserts, drought can mean months without rain but with no lack of wind, intense sunlight, and heat. True deserts are places where the evaporation rate exceeds average precipitation.

Adaptation to an arid climate takes several forms. Some plants, once they are well established, will thrive without supplemental watering on the harshest sites no matter what the weather. In the garden, at most a monthly deep watering in summer will keep these desert-adapted plants blooming and leafy. Too much extra water will kill them. Stalwarts such as broom dalea, bush penstemon, Mexican oregano, and dune broom are a few of these *drought-requiring* plants. Other plants that root deeply enough to be insulated from the extremes, or have waxy small leaves or silver light-reflective foliage and are compact in form, thus minimizing their evaporative surfaces, will survive under arid conditions but perform best if watered deeply twice a month during the growing season. They will lose leaves, stop flowering, and generally sulk if abandoned when times are tough. These plants are *drought enduring* and comprise the bulk of the wildflowers discussed in this book. Still other plants go dormant when the going gets tough. Their cycle of active growth coincides with cooler temperatures or summer rains. The wildflowers called ephemerals and spring-flowering bulbs, such as species tulips, crocus, and grape hyacinths, are examples of these *drought evaders*. Lastly, there are plants that should receive weekly watering when temperatures are above ninety degrees F. Many of the adaptive species from more temperate climates, such as yarrow and purple coneflower, fall into this *drought-tolerant* category. These plants are capable of surviving short periods without supplemental watering but are adapted to consistent soil moisture or lower average temperatures than are generally found in the Southwest. The hotter and drier the microclimate, the more moisture they require.

SOILS AND WATERING

The soil that the plants were potted in, as well as the soil they are transplanted into, will affect watering greatly. Potting soil, rich in organic matter, actually acts as a hindrance to a plant's effort to root out into the native soil. High desert soils are typically gritty or silty, low in organic matter. When a plant potted in peat humus encounters typical southwestern soils, something has to give. Too often it's the otherwise well-chosen plant that gives its last gasp. The gardener's response is usually to amend the native soil to make it more like the potting soil. If you can't amend most of the potential rooting area, which for many dryland plants would mean amending the soil to a depth of ten feet or more, you are only delaying the time when the plant must bridge the gap between feathers and concrete. Plants in containers smaller than four-inch pots would be almost impossible to grow in native soil, definitely too risky for any nursery that needs to make a profit to stay in business. When transplanting from cell packs or two-inch containers, it is probably better to amend the backfill (soil removed from the planting hole) with one-fourth the volume in compost to ease the transition.

During cool weather you can gently wash most of the peat off the plant roots and plant directly in loosened native soil, avoiding the barriers to rooting that the peat would cause. In the heat of summer it is risky to transplant from small containers no matter what the soil since tender young plants have limited roots for absorbing moisture and the evaporation rate is at its peak. At our nursery on the wind-blasted northern edge of the Chihuahuan desert, we transplant outdoors anytime the temperature is below ninety-five degrees F, covering new transplants with shade cloth to limit evaporation to levels they can tolerate. We lose surprisingly few plants, and those weaklings are better eliminated in the nursery than in the customer's garden anyway. Quart-size containers are the smallest containers we use because they contain enough soil and roots to enable plants to make the transition from nursery to garden with ease. We also use a potting mix that would be a conventional nurseryman's nightmare: equal parts sharp sand, scoria fines, and compost. This mixture meshes well with most of our native soils, and the desert-adapted plants prefer it to spongy peat or gummy bark-based potting soils. This potting mix is not without its ecological cost. Scoria is a renewable resource only where volcanos are active; in our region, luckily, it's been more than a thousand years since local eruptions added to the supply.

Water does not move through different soil strata uniformly. It penetrates sand and decomposed granite more quickly and deeply than it does clay, while clay will retain more moisture than the other soils. Organic matter soaks up moisture like a sponge and holds it well, sometimes too well for plants adapted to desert soils. In using a drip irrigation system, when faced with trying to bridge the gap between organic and native soils, make sure the emitters are directly above the new root ball, so that the water will seep through the lighter soil and eventually penetrate into the native soil. Otherwise, the peat and plant roots may dry out while the soil around the root ball seems damp enough. If hand watering, apply the water slowly or it may run across the outside surface of the root ball and into the surrounding soil, leaving the transplant high and dry. Slow application of water works best no matter what soil you are dealing with, and it can make a life-or-death difference with small plants and when planting on slopes. Hand watering is usually inefficient because people seldom water deeply enough when more than a few plants demand attention. On the other hand, it can be a relaxing way to spend time in the garden getting to know the new transplants. When establishing a new landscape, a combination of both drip and hand watering is best. The plants receive both deep watering and supplements as needed, and in the process the caretaker is drawn into the community.

Any dry soil, regardless of composition, will repel water until the surface tension is broken, allowing moisture to infiltrate. Most dryland plants prefer relatively high

EASILY ERODED BLOW SAND IS TYPICAL OF SHRUB DESERTS (TOP).

DECOMPOSED GRANITE IS TYPICAL OF THE UPLANDS.

HEAVY CLAY SOILS OF VALLEY AND BASIN AREAS ARE SOMETIMES SALTY AS WELL.

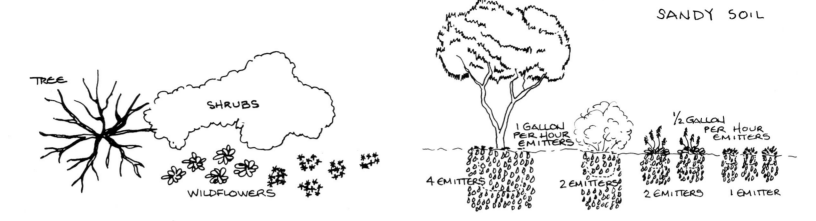

TREE

SHRUBS

WILDFLOWERS

SANDY SOIL

1 GALLON PER HOUR EMITTERS

½ GALLON PER HOUR EMITTERS

4 EMITTERS

2 EMITTERS

2 EMITTERS

1 EMITTER

DRIP IRRIGATION IN DIFFERENT SOIL TYPES. FROM LEFT:

LARGER TREES NEED PROPORTIONATELY MORE WATER. SHRUBS MAY NEED INFREQUENT DEEP WATERING ONCE ESTABLISHED. GRASEES AND WILDFLOWERS MAY NEED LESS WATER MORE OFTEN THAN TREES OR SHRUBS.

IN SAND, WATER MAY PENETRATE TEN TO TWELVE INCHES IN AN HOUR WITH VERY LITTLE HORIZONTAL SPREAD. SAND DRIES OUT RAPIDLY—APPLY LESS WATER MORE FREQUENTLY.

IN DECOMPOSED GRANITE, WATER MAY PENETRATE SIX TO EIGHT INCHES IN AN HOUR WITH SOME HORIZONTAL SPREAD. DECOMPOSED GRANITE RETAINS MOISTURE WELL—APPLY MORE WATER LESS FREQUENTLY.

IN CLAY SOIL, WATER MAY PENETRATE FOUR INCHES IN AN HOUR WITH CONSIDERABLE HORIZONTAL SPREAD. CLAY RETAINS MOISTURE, SOMETIMES TOO WELL—APPLY WATER SLOWLY AND INFREQUENTLY.

oxygen levels in the soil for best growth. As water filters into subsoils, a vacuum is created that pulls air into the soil. In this way soils can be said to breathe. Under frequent flood conditions, the weight of the water compresses the soil and reduces the pore spaces available for the recharge of oxygen. Drip irrigation seems to produce the healthiest plants with the least water, partly because water penetrates gradually without compacting the soil. Still, it takes compromises to design a system that will water new transplants of different sizes adequately, even when the plants are otherwise compatible. Ideally, plants that root more shallowly, and will therefore always need water more frequently, should be placed on irrigation lines separate from those that will root deeply and need longer, less frequent irrigation cycles. Since different soils absorb and retain water differently, a garden with both sandy and clay areas will require different drip lines covering each area. Some compromises can be made by limiting the number of valved zones but adjusting the number and volume of emitters to balance individual water needs with consensus frequency. After the first few years, most drip systems need to be adjusted for the maturing needs of the landscape. Emitters to the drought-requiring plants are plugged or eliminated, and emitters are added to larger trees to support their increasing mass. Shallowly rooted trees, such as fruit trees and streambank natives, can be encouraged to root more extensively by massing water- and shade-tolerant ground covers, such as yerba mansa, creeping lippia, dwarf plumbago, yarrow, or prairie sage, in an extended area around the trees. The water given the ground cover creates a moist zone for the tree roots to grow into.

Gardening in clay soil requires both careful plant selection and careful watering since many plants respond poorly to overwatering in heavy soil. Amending clay to improve drainage is impractical because to do it effectively would involve replacing about seventy percent of the clay with more porous material. Less amendment results

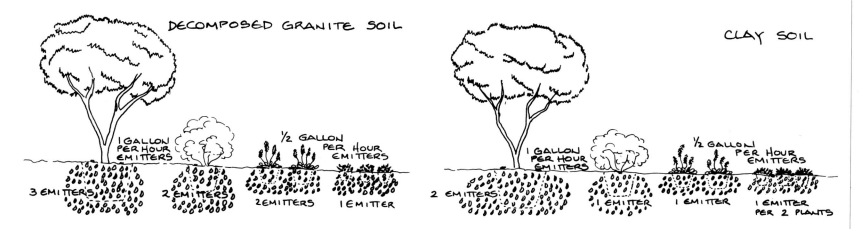

in a soil better suited for making adobe bricks than for growing plants. Sometimes clay layers are superficial, deposited by flooding, and can be dug through to a sandier strata, creating drainage chimneys for plants that require well-drained soils. Because water penetrates different soil types differently, radically changing the soil immediately around new transplants has a containerizing effect. Plants root out into the richly amended soil but are very slow to bridge the gap into the surrounding clay. Since much of a plant's ability to survive harsh conditions is dependent on its extensive root system, limiting its root run undermines its survival.

Soil compaction also limits root development. On new construction sites, much of the area is compacted either intentionally, to meet engineering standards, or inadvertently by subcontractors in the course of their work. Any rainfall during construction only increases the compaction. Counteracting compaction is difficult, but there are solutions. If the final grading is done in late autumn, the compacted soil can be kept damp over winter, and frost heaving will loosen the soil. Another approach is to work potassium fertilizer into the surface and leach it more deeply into the soil profile. Applied at a rate of five pounds per thousand square feet of surface area, potassium causes soil molecules to clump together, creating air spaces in the soil.

WHEN TO WATER

Visible footprints left after walking across cool-season grass lawns and a gray-green cast and brittle texture to native warm-season lawns indicate that it's time to water. Sagging leaves, droopy new growth, and dull leaf color when the soil feels dry a few inches below the surface in sand and decomposed granite are signs that a plant needs water. In clay, the soil may feel damp while the same symptoms of thirst present themselves, owing to the fact that clay soil pulls moisture out of plant tissue to wet itself.

Plants will also wilt and become dull looking when they are overwatered because fungi or bacteria clog the tubes transporting fluids through the plant. It's always better to err on the side of conservation; a plant wilting from too little water can be revived more easily than one rotting from excess.

While heat stress and drought stress are related, extra soil moisture only moderates heat to a limited degree, and keeping the soil saturated around heat-stressed plants can lead to root rot. Heat-loving plants counter extremes with self-shading reflective leaf surfaces and by slowing their metabolisms. Watering excessively when plants are heat or cold dormant will do more harm than good. Expect to lose a few plants along the way, and mark their passing as lessons learned. Much of the information in this book comes of the withered remains of thousands of failed experiments, many of them a direct result of not knowing when to quit watering.

Because of their limited root systems, new transplants need consistent water until they become established. The larger the plant and the root ball, the more water it will take per watering. The smaller and more tender the transplant, the more often it will need water. In warm weather, new transplants might need water every few days for the first two weeks, then twice a week for a few more weeks, with adjustments for soil type and exposure: more often on a sandy, windy site; less water, less often on a sheltered clay site. In autumn through early spring, when evaporation rates are lower, water new transplants thoroughly at planting time, then deeply every few weeks and just enough to keep the soil damp during the coldest weather. Heat-loving, drought-requiring plants transplant better when they are actively growing, early through mid-summer, and will suffer if kept too wet when temperatures are low. On the other hand evergreens, particularly broadleafed evergreens, need monthly watering in winter, since moderate daytime temperatures and freezing winds can dehydrate their leaves.

After the initial weeks of adjusting to the new site, most new transplants should be watered once a week, May through September, the year they are planted. Larger trees and shrubs that are intended for shade, screening, or privacy should be watered regularly until they develop the mass needed to fulfill their intended function. Once mature, well-adapted trees and shrubs can be gradually weaned of the extra water and put on monthly maintenance rations. Visualize the water penetrating the root ball and moving into the surrounding soil. To encourage deep rooting, water enough so that as the plant begins to root down there is moisture available to draw the roots ever deeper. After the initial period of acclimating the new plant to the site, gradually reduce the frequency and increase the depth of watering. The better suited the plants are to the site and each other as a community, the sooner you will be able to relax into a deep-watering schedule. Large riparian trees may never make the transition to minimal watering unless they are growing in shallow groundwater oasis ecosystems. Except in oases, large shade trees may need to be watered regularly throughout their garden lives. Such high-profile trees are alien to most southwestern ecosystems and will rarely flourish without extra water. When temperatures soar and drying winds blow, the evaporation rate is so high that plants not adapted to the high desert aren't able to absorb water fast enough to offset the moisture transpired from leaf and soil surfaces. Sometimes moving an ailing plant to a shadier, more protected spot, such as a north courtyard (or Seattle), will satisfy its needs.

SPRINKLER IRRIGATION

Lawns are the single largest water consumer in the American landscape, but they can be a welcome feature in an ecologically sound garden. They provide valuable play spaces, help cool a patio both visually and physically, and are an icon of civility. How much grass we choose to grow, the type we select, and how we water and maintain it determine just how ecologically sound our lawn will be. Lawns are usually watered with sprinklers that spray water into the air, and therein lies much of the potential for waste. Ideally, the water we spray on the lawn should be used almost exclusively by the grass. Oscillating sprinklers used on the end of garden hoses that arch the water high in the air over much of their cycle are probably the single most inefficient way to apply water. Using low spray-angle heads reduces the evaporation potential. Watering early in the morning when cooler temperatures reduce the evaporation rate further minimizes water loss. Zone the irrigation system to separate areas in the shade much of the day from sunny areas exposed to drying winds, or use lower-volume heads in the shade and higher-volume heads to satisfy the higher water needs of plants growing in full sun. To reduce the amount of runoff generated, avoid planting lawn grass in long narrow strips or on slopes, particularly strips and slopes bordered by hard paving. If grassing a slope is unavoidable, use low-precipitation-rate heads and program the system to cycle on and off for short periods rather than running one long cycle, so that water is applied at a rate that the soil can absorb. Removing thatch and aerating sod so that water penetrates more readily conserves moisture and produces a better-quality lawn. Group runoff-loving plants at the base of the slope to benefit from the inevitable flood of wastewater generated.

Water only as deeply as the grass roots penetrate and only as often as needed to recharge the root zone. Bluegrass roots are concentrated in the top six inches of soil, having evolved in a climate where cooler temperatures and abundant rainfall make deeper roots unnecessary. Deep watering bluegrass is a waste of water. Tall turf-type fescues and the new dwarf fescues will root eighteen inches or deeper. Although native to more temperate climates, the tall fescues are somewhat more heat tolerant than bluegrass and more disease resistant under stress conditions. Buffalograss and blue grama evolved on the dry plains to capture any moisture available; their roots penetrate six feet or deeper to survive months without rain. If these grasses are established by

SPRINKLERS THAT SPRAY A FINE MIST RATHER THAN LARGER DROPLETS WASTE WATER TO EVAPORATION. PLANTINGS SUCH AS LAWNS, GROUND COVERS, AND FLOWER BEDS THAT ARE SPRINKLER IRRIGATED SHOULD BE ON FLAT SURFACES AND SITED AWAY FROM PAVING TO AVOID RUNOFF.

gradually lengthening the watering cycle and decreasing its frequency as they develop from seed to sod, they can be watered much less often and more deeply in time. In cooler weather all grasses require water less often.

An inch of water penetrates clay soil to a depth of four inches, while it penetrates a well-amended loamy soil to six or eight inches and sand to ten or twelve inches. To find out how long it takes to water your lawn grass to meet its needs in your soil, set several shallow containers out on your lawn surface and turn on the sprinklers until there is an inch of water in the containers. If some of the containers are filled much higher than others, the system needs an overhaul. Either some heads are too far apart or their delivery rates differ too greatly. A sprinkler system that delivers an inch of water in fifteen minutes on clay soil will need to run fifteen minutes for bluegrass, a half hour for fescue, and two half-hour cycles a few hours apart for buffalograss and blue grama. On sandy soil it will need to run only half as long, but probably twice as often, since sandy soil dries out faster than clay. Adjust the water cycle seasonally to compensate for the changes in the water needs of the lawn.

Sprinkler systems should provide uniform coverage, so that each nozzle sprays an arc that either completely overlaps or compensates for the spray pattern of adjacent nozzle arcs in order to deliver a uniform amount of water across the entire sprinkler pattern. This is especially important because of the windy conditions prevalent in the high desert. Sprinkler systems that don't cover adequately will be wasteful, since the only way to keep dry spots green is to overwater the rest of the lawn.

DRIP IRRIGATION

Drip irrigation is the most efficient way to apply water to garden areas other than lawns and closely planted spreading ground covers. Because drip is designed to promote deep water penetration, it is particularly well suited to the root systems of dryland plants. Manufacturers of equipment offer guides for designing and installing a drip system that describe the advantages of their equipment and give details for its assembly. The amounts and frequency of watering recommended are primarily for high-water-use plants, so you will need to develop your own schedule based on the conditions and plants in your garden. Though there are many kinds of drip equipment available, they all carry water through larger-dimension main line pipes to smaller-distribution tubing and deliver it out of emitters placed above the root zone of each plant in the garden. Rated in gallons per hour, emitters range in output from one-half to four gph. Compared with conventional watering systems that deliver water in gallons per minute, drip is low volume and low pressure. Water can infiltrate gradually. The actual output of emitters varies depending on the water pressure, number of emitters on a line, and changes in elevation in the garden. Pressure-compensating emitters self-adjust for grade changes, and laying the tubing as a closed circuit with lines running across the slope as much as possible helps equalize distribution. Regardless, plants at the base of

MANY DRYLAND PLANTS ARE TAP-ROOTED, THEIR ROOT MASS FAR EXCEEDING THEIR TOP GROWTH AS THEY BECOME WELL ESTABLISHED IN THE LANDSCAPE. BECAUSE DRIP IRRIGATION IS DESIGNED TO PROMOTE DEEP WATER PENETRATION, IT IS THE IDEAL WATERING SYSTEM FOR DRYLAND PLANTS.

the slope will receive more water because all the water left in the lines above will drain out of the lowest emitters at the end of each watering cycle. This provides a moist niche at the base of slopes for large trees and other plants adapted to such conditions.

Frequency and amount are the two measures to balance when watering. Ideally, plants that root less deeply, and so will need water more often, should be on separate valves from deeply rooted trees, shrubs, and most long-lived dryland wildflowers. As long as all the plants can be watered at the same frequency, differences in how much the individuals require can be accommodated by using fewer or smaller emitters on the low-water users and more or larger emitters on the high-water users. Very low-water users, the drought-requiring plants, should usually have the fewest emitters to begin with and have most of them removed after the plants have rooted down for a growing season. Heavier water users will need more of the highest output emitters and will usually need emitters added after a few growing seasons to accommodate the developing root mass. Another way of compensating for differing water requirements is to put the heaviest water users and more shallowly rooted perennials in the shade, where the evaporation rate is lower. Many garden perennials that are adapted to full sun in more temperate climates perform better in partial or full shade in the high desert.

There are several ways to install a drip system. The most sophisticated, long-lasting, and flexible systems have three-quarter-inch PVC main lines buried twelve to eighteen inches below ground depending on how deeply the soil freezes in winter. At intervals determined by the number and spacing of the plants, half-inch risers off the main lines provide surface outlets for three-eighth- or half-inch flexible poly tubing distribution lines. The emitters are spliced or punched into the distribution lines that wind between and around plants on the soil surface. This surface tubing is either covered with mulch or buried just below the soil surface with the emitters exposed above ground. If the water demand for a tree is six gallons per hour relative to nearby shrubs at two gallons per hour, it is better to use three two-gph emitters evenly spaced above the root ball of the tree and two one-gph emitters on either side of the shrub root balls than to use single higher-volume emitters. Not only is the water distributed more evenly to the root zone but if one of the emitters should clog, the plant will still receive some water until you notice and can correct the problem. The spacing of emitters depends on the spacing of individual plants and the texture of the soil. In coarse sandy soil, emitters may need to be one foot apart to uniformly wet an area, while in medium-textured sandy loam or decomposed granite two-foot spacing may be adequate and in fine silt and clay four-foot spacing may provide similar coverage. Since water always runs downhill, emitters on slopes need to be placed upslope of the area to be irrigated. Having loops of surface tubing running off permanent main lines makes repairs easier and sometimes less expensive. A loop serving a number of plants can be capped off while making repairs and relacing or adding emitters, leaving the rest of the line operable.

The valves that open and close to allow water into each main line are critical in the overall proficiency and longevity of the system. Inexpensive valves can stick open, leaving water running too long. At the very least this can lead to drowned plants and high water bills. At worst, soils may collapse, causing structural damage to walls and paving. The valves are not the place to economize when installing a drip system, particularly an automated one wired to a programmable timer. Each line is assigned a separate station that can be programmed independently of the others. The best timers for natural gardens have a program range from a quarter hour several times daily to several hours every two weeks. The program can then be changed from frequent shallow watering for germinating seeds or easing transplants into new surroundings to deeper, less frequent watering as plants root out and become established. This also allows different stations for lawn sprinklers that operate on a gallons-per-hour, heavy output/short cycle basis. The programming is changed seasonally to compensate for the reduced-moisture demands of the plants in winter and increased demands in summer. An automated system is a convenience, providing consistent water in the gardener's absence, and a conservation tool to avoid overwatering if the watering schedule is changed seasonally and as the planting develops. There is no remote-control garden, especially when the plants are new. A timed drip system can only keep the garden in its prime if it is managed intelligently. Lightning storms can scramble the program, rodents or turtles sometimes chew through tubing, emitters occasionally clog. It's important to walk through the garden on a regular basis when the system is running to make sure it's functioning properly, to look at the plants and see how they are responding to the water they are receiving, and to fine-tune to correct any deficiencies or excesses. The more established the garden becomes, the less frequently the monitoring will need to be done.

An automated system with in-ground main lines is top of the line, cost-effective when the landscaping is extensive and complex and indispensable if many of the plants are not well-adapted to the site. The more self-sustaining a landscape is intended to be once established, the less sophisticated its drip system needs to be. A low-end drip system is made up of only the surface poly distribution lines connected either to a hose or hose bib. The advantage is initial low cost and easy installation. The disadvantage is that since each line is one continuum, any shutdowns for repairs affect all the plants on that line, not just a few on one loop. Timers are also available for this type of system. They are less expensive but have to be replaced more often.

All drip systems have filters to minimize grit in the lines that can clog emitters, pressure reducers to decrease the water pressure in the lines, and back-flow preventers to keep impurities from being syphoned back into drinking water. Early in the development of drip irrigation, clogged emitters were a major problem. Self-flushing emitter designs and filtration devices have minimized repairs and replacement. Careful installation of the system and flushing lines well before putting in the emitters also prevent problems. There are compromises between drip and high-output bubblers that deliver water at lower volumes or split the output of a single bubbler through tubing to four or eight plants. When extremely high mineral content in the water clogs small orifice emitters, higher-output equipment is a useful alternative; however, some of the advantage of slow deep penetration is compromised.

The best way to tell how deeply water is penetrating is to wait several hours after watering and dig down near several plants. Adjustments can then be made in the length of the cycle or number of emitters to balance any inconsistencies or supply more water based on the water profile in the soil. Even when plants are selected to be compatible, differences in the sizes of the transplants and the soil they are potted in may create variables that can't be equalized within the system, regardless of its sophistication. New transplants need regular attention for at least the first few weeks in cooler weather, a month or longer during the hottest weather. Hand watering to supplement the plants that seem to dry out more quickly helps bridge the gap between what the system can supply and what new plants may need. If you are unfamiliar with many of the plants in a small landscape project or are working on a small area of a large landscape, you might opt to hand water at first to become more aware of the plants' preferences before installing the surface distribution drip lines. This will enable you to determine how many emitters each plant needs when the system is assembled.

Seeding

After the drainage and other contours are formed, the main water lines are installed, retaining walls, paving, and shade structures are in place, and steps have been taken to control perennial weeds, it is finally planting time. Whether to start with seeds or transplants depends on the season of the year, the budget, the size and nature of the garden, the nature of the plants themselves, and your confidence as a gardener. Each spring I am completely awestruck at the miracle of seeds. Tiny parcels of garden potential, sprouting seeds can take us from bare earth to blossoms in just a few short months. Still, I worry over the seedbeds at first, poking and prodding and generally making a nuisance of myself until threads of green are plainly visible. Growing plants from seeds takes patience and faith, as well as inside information on the conditions that combine for seedling success. The plant profiles in volume two summarize techniques that have worked reasonably well.

Seeding is most advantageous when the site is large or ultimately is intended to be self-sustaining. Plants that sprout and grow without having their root run interrupted by transplanting are always more self-sufficient. Lawn and prairie plantings are those usually grown from seed. Both use grasses as the primary cover and in the high-desert grasslands are dominant ecosystems. The difference between a cultivated prairie and a

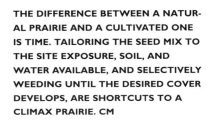

THE DIFFERENCE BETWEEN A NATURAL PRAIRIE AND A CULTIVATED ONE IS TIME. TAILORING THE SEED MIX TO THE SITE EXPOSURE, SOIL, AND WATER AVAILABLE, AND SELECTIVELY WEEDING UNTIL THE DESIRED COVER DEVELOPS, ARE SHORTCUTS TO A CLIMAX PRAIRIE. CM

natural one is time. What it took nature ten thousand years to develop we try to do over the weekend. I don't personally have the patience to think in terms of geological time, but I'm trying to wean myself of the need for immediate gratification when the results are worth the wait. The value of native grasses is their endurance once established. They produce root mass faster than top growth, which gives them an edge in dealing with erratic rainfall and temperatures. Their seedlings are quite fragile for the first few weeks after they germinate. Encouraging faster rooting by creating a soft, friable seedbed makes top growth develop more quickly because roots also develop quickly. In the wild, seeds prompted by rainfall sprout erratically over several months. If the moisture doesn't penetrate deeply enough to provide a reserve for the young seedlings, many of them die. Through the years a renewable stand of grass develops. Ecologically, shrub desert and grassland overlap. In wetter years, grasses dominate. In drier years, grasses recede, leaving the shrubs to maintain the ecosystem. Where drought is prolonged or overgrazing diminishes the grasses beyond their ability to recover, desert shrubs become the climax plant community. Conversely, if precipitation consistently averages more than twelve inches per year and grazing is held to sustainable levels, the grasses will dominate and shrubs will play a relatively minor role in the community. One of the marvels of nature is this ability to successfully manage change. In the garden, we are the managers, providing the seed potential and best possible growing conditions. The majority of seedlings survive and grow relatively quickly. In as little as six months or at most two years, we can produce a climax grassland community.

LAWNS

Native or not, lawns exist on ecologically shaky ground, hence they always take an extra measure of effort to create and more care to maintain. The value of quality seed and a well-prepared seedbed cannot be overstated. Buffalograss and blue grama are the best native lawn grasses for the high desert, each having advantages and limitations. Buffalograss is slower to develop, shorter, and spreads by surface runners to form an even-textured sod, especially on heavier soils. As recently as five years ago, the only cultivars available had been selected for tall coarse growth on rangeland as forage for cattle. In response to the growing demand for better-adapted lawn grasses, new cultivars are being developed that are shorter, denser, and less sensitive to cold so that they green up earlier in spring and stay green later in fall. Buffalograss makes an attractive unmowed ground cover because the fringe of male flower heads never grows more than ankle high above the soft carpet of leaves. Seed averages near ninety percent PLS (Pure Live Seed—the percentage of tested germination) per bulk pound and pretreated seeds germinate within two weeks in warm soil. Seed is pretreated by soaking it in potassium nitrate to soften the woody seed capsules and nudge the embryos out of dormancy. Treated seeds are tinted blue in processing and are readily available though usually significantly more expensive than untreated seeds. Since untreated seeds may take two or three years to germinate, buying the cheaper seed is no bargain. Seeding rates range from four to six pounds per thousand square feet depending on the potential weed competition.

Blue grama is a bunchgrass that offshoots slightly when mowed or grazed. Grass blades reach a foot tall, with seed heads sometimes twice that height. A little finer in texture and faster growing than buffalograss, it usually dominates a mixed seeding at first, especially on lighter soils. Unmowed and unirrigated, it will clump up, leaving gaps for wildflowers in a prairie or weeds in a lawn. Blue grama seems to remain green and soft in extreme heat with less water than buffalograss. Blue grama seeds also germinate best warm, but are chaffy, often less than fifty percent PLS per bulk pound. The chaff acts as a good carrier for the seed, but seeding rates should be based on the PLS, not bulk weight, in estimating coverage: at least two PLS pounds, or four bulk pounds, per thousand square feet to assure a dense stand.

Because buffalograss and blue grama are so similar in color and texture, are compatible in water requirements, and adapt to a range of soils, they are often mixed for lawn seeding. A mix usually covers faster and doesn't develop hummocks as it matures. Although neither grass seems prone to insect attack, and diseases aren't a problem unless they are overwatered and overfertilized, mixing them is more ecologically sound than planting a monoculture. A mixed seeding may be fifty-fifty of each or thirty-seventy buffalograss to blue grama if faster coverage is needed. Neither take well to close cropping, and if consistently mowed shorter than four inches, the stand will thin, inviting weed invasion.

PRAIRIES

Compared with lawns, prairies are stable ecosystems that, once established, take much less care. The differences between a prairie and a meadow are their native elevation, heat tolerance, and water requirement. Prairies consist mainly of warm-season grasses and deeply rooted wildflowers. They naturally occur between three thousand and eight thousand feet in elevation and receive twelve to twenty-four inches of rainfall annually. Meadows are a mix of cool-season grasses and shallow-rooted wildflowers, occur from eight thousand feet to timberline, and soak up at least thirty inches of rain and snow each year. In the high desert, meadows require about the same watering as bluegrass lawns and conventional perennial beds.

Prairies can appear controlled or wild depending on the mix of wildflowers and grasses. In urban settings where weed ordinances may require a tame appearance, the mix should contain species of similar height, water use, and soil preference but with varied texture and seasonal color. The grasses are sown as a blanket overall, and the wildflowers are overseeded in broad sweeps so that they have the greatest seasonal impact and trimming spent seed heads is easier.

Timing is important. Warm-season grasses will germinate best if seeded early May through early August while most of the wildflowers and Indian ricegrass germinate best in either March and April or September and October. Mixing the wildflower seeds with dampened vermiculite or sterile potting soil in polyethylene bags and refrigerating them for a month prior to sowing in early May satisfies the cold requirement of the flowers and accommodates the grasses' need for warmth. If the site isn't ready to seed until midsummer, the grasses can be seeded immediately and the wildflowers overseeded in fall or the following spring. If the site isn't workable until fall or early spring, a temporary cover crop can be used to limit dust and mud, then tilled under in spring, allowing enough time for the cover crop to compost before doing the permanent seeding the following May.

Many high-desert plants either have seed coats that repel water until sufficiently weathered or embryos that remain dormant for different lengths of time after the seed ripens. Ecologically, this is a tremendous asset. A bank of seeds is held in reserve awaiting each new opportunity for growth. In the garden, such erratic behavior is frustrating. Prechilling seeds helps neutralize the climatic defenses. Sometimes acid treatments or abrasion with sandpaper are needed in addition to prechilling. Bush morningglory, which germinates best in warm soils, takes a hot bath to sprout. The various techniques for enhancing germination are outlined in the propagation appendix found in book two,

Plants for Natural Gardens. The best methods and timing for each species are noted as part of the cultural data in the plant profiles, also in book two.

Tree and shrub seeds often take longer prechilling than do wildflowers, and the growth rate is slow initially since the plants build root mass before developing much top growth. Most landscapes are planted with container-grown trees and shrubs. Transplanting trees and shrubs from one- or five-gallon containers already takes faith and patience. Starting a whole landscape from seeds is reclamation rather than gardening. Sometimes a site is so extensive or inaccessible that outlying parts of it are treated as reclamation areas, seeded with a mix of trees, shrubs, wildflowers, and grasses. The more dependent a reclamation seeding is on rainfall to germinate and develop, the more closely the plant selection should match local ecosystems and seeding time coincide with rainfall. There is so little control of the growing conditions in most reclamation projects that it takes much longer for them to develop enough cover to be considered successful. The trade-off is dollars for time.

Transplanting

When working with container-grown stock, it is important to dig generous holes to plant in, loosening the soil so that new roots can penetrate easily. Using an auger to drill holes can save time on big projects, but augers can leave very smooth-sided holes. Even hand-dug holes in clay soil tend to have slick sides that act as a barrier to root development. Rough up the sides of the holes to avoid creating these subsurface clay pots. Planting holes should be sized to suit the type of root system the plant naturally develops. Plants that have deep taproots should have the soil loosened in a space two or three times as wide and once again as deep as their root balls, with the soil in the bottom of the hole tamped down enough so that the plants doesn't settle when watered in. Most arid-adapted trees and shrubs and many wildflowers are such deep-rooted types. Large streamside shade trees and some high-elevation wildflowers develop coarse anchor roots and a more shallow network of fibrous roots that supply the plants with most of their water and nutrients. The soil area loosened for such plants should be up to five times the diameter of, but only as deep as, their roots at planting time. Decomposed granite hardens like concrete when dry but is considerably more permeable and easier to work if the soil is watered a day or two before planting. Holes dug in sandy soil will collapse if not damp enough.

Water the plants several hours before transplanting also, so that both the potting soil and backfill are damp. If the plants are to be drip irrigated, set the unpotted plant in the hole so that the soil level of the root ball matches the surrounding soil. If the plants will be hand watered or flooded, set the plants two to four inches below grade and provide generous basins for watering. As discussed earlier, no amendments are needed for four-inch pots or larger plants in most cases. If the potting soil is a fluffy peat moss mix, you may want to wash most of the foreign soil away from the roots so the plant can root out unhampered. In hot weather, however, such disturbance of the root system can cause problems. Mixing a fourth compost by volume into the backfill creates less of an abrupt change in soil types for new roots to bridge. If the soil mix is gritty, backfill with unamended native soil, tamping gently to collapse any large air pockets. When plants are kept in containers too long they become potbound. If the roots spiral around the edge of the root ball when you unpot the plant, take a sharp knife or pruning shears and slit up the sides of the root mass in three or four places, severing any circling roots. Left uncut, such roots generally continue to spiral, girdling the main stems and impeding root growth. Very often after six months or a year of good care, the plants die. The most important thing to remember when seeding or transplanting is to limit barriers to root growth wherever possible. Thoroughly water plants immediately after transplanting and often enough in the days that follow to prevent serious wilting. A little drooping due to heat stress isn't serious and actually strengthens plants, the same way athletes improve their ability to perform by pushing themselves just beyond their previous endurance. Plants do have a bottom line, however, called the permanent wilting point, and it is just that, a point of no return.

Some plants have a relatively brief period when they transplant most easily, while other plants can be transplanted from containers any time the soil is workable. These preferences are noted in the individual plant profiles in book two to help in planning. Any plant that is being pushed to, or possibly beyond, its limit of cold hardiness is better planted as soon as temperatures stabilize in spring. The more rooting time such plants have, the more likely they are to survive the first winter. As days begin to shorten in fall, plants native to colder areas slow their growth and concentrate sugars in their sap, which acts as an antifreeze. They are slow to reverse the process in spring. Plants native to warmer zones often haven't evolved such defenses, having little need of them. Stimulated by late summer rains, they are liable to continue to grow right up until frost, when they receive the shock of their short lives. When trying to find a warmer micro-climate to winter over less hardy plants, an eastern exposure may be better than a southwestern one. On a southern exposure, stimulated by the warm days, plants may break dormancy and their sap freeze, rupturing cell walls overnight. On an eastern exposure, given the low angle of sun, once the temperature cools down in fall it stays relatively cool all winter. Plants go dormant and stay dormant until spring. Courtyards enclosed with thick walls often maintain temperatures a zone warmer throughout winter and are another good place to attempt to defy geography. An insulating blanket of mulch applied after the temperatures have turned cold can keep the root zone of less hardy plants alive even if top growth dies back.

Mulching

Mulches serve several purposes. Applied four to six inches deep and kept dry, mulch can suppress weeds. It insulates plant roots from both heat and cold, extending periods of active root growth and, hence, enhancing plant growth and vigor. Mulches also make a landscape look more finished at first, unifying spaces until plants can fill in and create continuity. They also prevent soil moisture from evaporating, reducing the overall water demand of the garden.

Different situations call for different mulches. Covering large areas with a gravel mulch is rarely a good solution either for weed control or aesthetics. The hotter the microclimate, the more oppressive a uniform cover of gravel mulch seems. As porous paving and for lining dry streambeds and drainage basins, gravel mulches are ideal. For informal pathways, fine gravel mulches compact and weather well. Gravel fines tend to suppress weeds more effectively than larger gravels because they stay drier and seal over on the surface, providing a better barrier. Oversize gravel, cobblestone, and riprap are useful for stabilizing the surfaces of slopes until plants can root out and bind the soil more deeply. Because of alternate daytime heating and nighttime cooling, moisture condenses around gravels, and the combination of this recycled moisture and a well-aerated surface makes gravel a good growing medium both for some dryland wildflowers and many weeds. Gravels also absorb and reradiate heat, which favors the growth of heat-loving wildflowers. One to two inches of stone mulch can provide favorable growing media for plants that require a well-drained surface to prevent crown rot. Many penstemon and rock garden favorites, such as pussy toes, desert zinnia, sulfur buckwheat, veronicas, and partridge feather, thrive in such niches, even in heavier soils where otherwise they would not.

Like gravel, bark mulch comes in a variety of grades. Medium-size shredded bark, with pieces averaging three inches long and an inch wide, is ideal because it knits together on the surface, staying in place despite the wind. Smaller chipped bark is attractive in small protected areas where wind isn't a factor. Pine needles are similar to shredded bark in their wind resistance but are not readily available unless you have a willing neighbor with pines who can provide a supply. Both these fibrous mulches break down slowly in our dry climate. If the plants they are mulching don't require frequent watering or are being watered with a drip system, they may need renewing only every three to five years. In very windy places where nothing weighing less than fifty pounds stays in place unless rooted or tied down, even pine needles and shredded bark will need replenishing every year or two. Likewise, if the mulched area is being watered frequently, these organic materials will decompose more quickly. When mulch fiber breaks down rapidly, it consumes nitrogen. To avoid nitrogen deficiencies in the adjacent plants, add small amounts of nitrogen fertilizer to the soil.

CHOOSE MULCHES THAT ARE COMPATIBLE WITH BOTH THE APPEARANCE AND THE PLANTS YOU WANT TO CULTIVATE.

Both bark and pine needles are light and will float when they come into contact with a stream of water, so they are a poor choice as mulch where rain sheets off a large roof or paved surface or collects in ponding areas. Both are cooler on the surface than either bare ground or gravel, so low-spreading plants tend to cover more rapidly when mulched with them. Often, by the time the mulch needs refurbishing, it is covered by the maturing plants, and top-dressing the areas between plants is a minor chore.

Bark mulch is a by-product of the logging industry, and as more realistic and sustainable forest management gains ground, or as forests are depleted, fewer trees will be milled and less bark available, and at an increasing cost. The Christmas tree shreddings some communities make available as a by-product of tree recycling programs, and shredded prunings that tree-care companies amass, are alternatives to commercially processed bark. Since these resources vary greatly in content, they may not be as aesthetically pleasing. Using recycled mulch materials as the base and top-dressing with a thin layer of more decorative shredded bark is a good compromise when an attractive or uniform surface is important. When the mulched areas are intended to blend into surrounding piñon–juniper–oak woodland in foothills gardens, shredding the smaller branches of any trees removed or pruned to clear space for construction produces a mulch that looks very much like the existing understory litter.

For naturalized transition areas between the cultivated parts of the garden and the surrounding shrub desert or grassland, baled native-grass hay can offer an alternative to bark mulch with some distinct advantages. Native-grass hay mulch forms a good weed and erosion barrier initially, and as it breaks down the seeds in the hay germinate and fill the open space between plants with grass. (For this same reason such hay is not recommended for use on seedbeds.) It is essential to use clean, weed-free hay of a native grass that is adapted to the site and compatible with the other plants. Of the hay now available, blue grama, alkali sacaton, dropseed, and Indian ricegrass work well on drier sites, little bluestem in wetter areas or at higher elevations. The mulch is applied by pulling two- to three-inch flakes of hay off the bales, laying them side by side like floor tiles, and fanning out the surface straw to knit the sections together. Chopping the hay in a mulcher and blowing it onto larger areas saves time and manpower, but the surface is not nearly as wind resistant, and weeds tend to colonize the bald spots. Mixing the chopped hay with a biodegradable binder—a natural glue manufactured from plantain—two to ten pounds per thousand square feet of surface area, can help reduce wind scouring on large sites. Either way, the stand of grass becomes established without soil disturbance or supplemental watering, thus limiting weed invasion.

Weed barrier fabrics are useful liners under stone and bark mulches where perennial weeds are a problem. Fabrics allow air and water to penetrate but keep seedlings underneath from emerging into the light and weed seedlings on top from rooting readily into the soil. They are no substitute for a concentrated effort to control the weeds or for a deep mulch, since they will not eliminate weeds, only help to slow their progress. Poly sheeting is never a viable option; it greatly limits the air exchange in the soil and eliminates the penetration of rainfall. Plant roots remain at the soil surface seeking oxygen, where they are more susceptible to heat and cold damage. Such shallowly rooted plants are also poorly anchored and prone to blow over in high winds.

Fertilizing

Established adaptive plants that are not watered excessively will rarely need fertilizing unless they are spaced so closely that they are competing for limited resources. Once established, fertilizing can actually be counterproductive. It produces an abundance of tender growth that requires more water to maintain and is more attractive to insects, rabbits, and deer. In the first few years when plants are making the transition to a new site, fertilizing stimulates growth so that the plants fill out and assume their roles in the landscape. A balanced fertilizer applied in early May at half the label-recommended rate is helpful if the site is being relandscaped and has been gardened in the past. If the site is newly developed in a previously undisturbed area, adding one tablespoon of calcium nitrate per foot of growth to new plants the spring after transplanting will encourage a sustainable level of growth. Nitrogen is usually the element lacking in these situations since the soil bacteria that naturally provide nitrogen need time to build up to supportive levels. Once the plants begin to root deeply and tap large soil areas, and soil microorganisms establish mutually beneficial populations in the root zone, fertilizers are unnecessary interruptions in the natural process. Sometimes, because of heat or soil imbalances, new transplants will become iron deficient. Chelated iron or iron sulfate can be applied in summer when the problem is most likely to appear. Iron supplements will green up yellowed leaves without stimulating soft new growth that requires more water. Nitrogen fertilizers shouldn't be used on trees and shrubs after early July because combined with the nitrogen available naturally in rainwater such fertilizers can stimulate new growth too late in the season to harden off sufficiently before hard frosts. Much winter damage to plants is a result of their being too soft from excess fertilizer to weather extreme cold.

Native-grass lawns should be fertilized with one to one and one-half pounds of nitrogen per thousand square feet of area or topdressed with weed-free compost in spring when they begin to green up. A 20–15–10 fertilizer is twenty percent nitrogen by weight, so you would need ten pounds of fertilizer for a two thousand-square-foot lawn. One cubic yard of compost will cover three hundred to five hundred square feet. If the lawn has been mowed and aerated, it is easier to apply fertilizer evenly. Plants should always be watered thoroughly after feeding to wash the fertilizer into the root zone. As the garden matures, and watering decreases, only lawns and closely planted flower beds will need annual fertilizing.

Pest Control

My first insight into alternative thinking about insects happened the first summer that I worked at a retail nursery in Indiana. A gentleman was browsing the insecticide shelves with a frown that I interpreted as indecision. I asked if I could help him find a cure for his pest problem. He assured me that he didn't have a *pest* problem. He was an entomologist at Purdue University with a *pesticide* problem. Eyeing the shelves as if they were the arsenal of the enemy, he explained that broad-spectrum insecticides, indiscriminate in their targets, kill beneficial insects as well as pests, thus destroying natural balances. From that day on, whenever I become intimidated by an insect proliferation, I try to seek the counsel of an entomologist who honors *Hymenoptera* and loves *Lepidoptera*. In more than twenty years I've never found one unwilling to gossip about insects. The Cooperative Extension Service and university entomologists can be tremendous resource people.

Good-intentioned but uninformed caretakers are often the most dangerous garden pests of all. In the United States, homeowners use more pesticides on their lawns and gardens than commercial farmers use to produce the nation's food supply. Recently I saw another dismaying statistic: in 1948, fifteen million pounds of insecticides were used and crop loss to insects was estimated at seven percent; in 1989, one hundred twenty-five million pounds of insecticides were used and crop loss was estimated at thirteen percent. The purpose of pest control should be to protect plant health and promote ecological balance, not to indiscriminately eliminate insects. Since we are outnumbered by zillions, the concept of insect eradication is both arrogant and strategically hopeless.

Learning to balance insect populations so that the ecosystem becomes richer without sacrificing too many plants to the ravages of some pest temporarily out of control is similar to learning the water needs of a new garden: frustrating in the short term but rewarding over time. Suggesting an amnesty program for insects is easy, but how does a person go from not knowing an aphid from an orb weaver to distinguishing beneficial insects from ones that do damage? We don't have to understand in detail the complex of insect activity in our backyards, much less in the ecosystem at large. The insect population will change considerably over the life of a garden anyway. What we do need to understand is that everything is interconnected, that every action we take will ripple through the ecosystem. Even well-considered interference may create changes we cannot anticipate. Walk softly and carry a magnifying glass instead of a spray gun. Go out into the garden and begin to introduce yourself to the throngs of your insect neighbors. If you've never gone looking for insects before, it may be quite appalling at first to realize just how many there are. Most of the creatures you encounter will in some way be beneficial to you as a gardener. Relax, you are among friends.

KNOW YOUR NEIGHBORS. DISTORTIONS IN THE STEM OF SALTBUSH ARE CAUSED BY GALL MIDGES, WHICH IN TURN ARE PREYED UPON BY PARASITIC WASPS.

The first year I grew butterflyweed I learned a hard lesson. As I watered my plants that summer I both admired the monarch butterflies sipping their nectar and simultaneously crushed the black-and-white-striped caterpillars devouring their leaves. The following winter, while browsing through *The Audubon Society Field Guide to North American Butterflies*, I came upon a mug shot of the monarch's larva. It was, of course, the caterpillar I had been saving my plants from. In retrospect, I was more of a threat to the butterflies than their larvae ever were to my plants. That epiphany put an end to my kill first, learn later approach. At our nursery we would never intentionally sell a plant harboring aphids, but we will point out the caterpillars on butterflyweed and rue and let our customers buy or not depending on whether they consider butterflies a bonus and caterpillars tolerable. Often a single plant hosts several insect interrelationships. I never find the big yellow aphids peculiar to butterflyweed on the plants growing at our farm, but after a few days in the city, they sometimes begin to appear. At the farm the plants are patrolled regularly by the large amber-winged tarantula hawk wasp. The absence of the wasp in the city leads to a boom in the aphid population. Rue hosts an interesting balance. Its leaves are fodder for swallowtail butterfly larvae while the ichneumon wasps that parasitize the caterpillars feed on the nectar from rue flowers. As you make a sport of insect watching in the garden, pieces of the puzzle begin to fall into place. Sometimes months after mentally filing away an observation, something you read or a conversation among gardening friends will trigger an "Aha!". If you have more restraint than I did at first, you're less likely to experience the "Oh no!" reaction of realizing you've murdered a friend.

Integrated pest management (IPM) is a systematic approach to pest control. Step one involves the monitoring of insect activity—distinguishing pests from beneficial predators or parasites. The second step is to determine what levels of pest activity are actually damaging to plants. Knowing this, our interference can be limited to spot control of pest populations that have reached damaging levels, working always toward balance. Individual plants and their caretakers have different tolerances. Generally the less adapted plants are to a site, the more prone they are to pest attack because of the stress signals they broadcast. In the evolutionary scheme of things, it is advantageous for insects and diseases to consume the weakest members of a plant community. The remaining individuals are those most able to succeed under local conditions. The larger the number of ill-adapted plants, the larger the pest population grows. When the most susceptible plants are eliminated, the pest population declines. Such is the ebb and flow of life. In the wild, extreme drought or flooding, unusually mild or severe winters, and acid rain and other wind-dispersed pollutants will cause plant stress and a corresponding boom in pest activity. Eventually an equilibrium is reestablished: the strongest plants and low levels of pests remain in balance until the next upset.

HORNWORMS ARE THE VORACIOUS LARVAE OF HAWKMOTHS, WHICH POLLINATE EVENING PRIMROSES, FOUR O'CLOCKS, AND OTHER FRAGRANT NIGHT-BLOOMING WILDFLOWERS. AMNESTY FOR HORNWORMS HELPS GUARANTEE FUTURE FLOWERS.

In the garden, our choice and placement of plants determine whether a dynamic balance is possible and how long it will take to stabilize. Opting to grow ecologically appropriate plants reduces the potential for problems and promotes beneficial insect activity. The more diverse the plant community, the more extended the flowering season; the more ample the supply of nectar and pollen, the more prolific the population of predatory and parasitic insects. Growing predator-friendly plants in the garden is a low-impact way of enhancing natural balances. Many of the parasites of common garden pests such as aphids, scales, and even caterpillars are minute. They rely on plants with shallow flower forms such as mustards, daisies, and the umbels of buckwheats and rue. On the other hand, bordering flower beds, lawns, or prairies with thickets of shrubs and groves of trees will create lacewing habitat. You might notice their tiny beadlike eggs attached to leaves or twigs with silken filaments.

When more active intervention is warranted, supplemental biological controls are the next option. While safer for humans, pets, and wildlife than chemical solutions, biological controls can be just as disruptive to natural balances and must be introduced with care. Praying mantis occur naturally over a very broad range of climate and geography. Indiscriminate predators, they devour both harmful and beneficial insects in quantity and, hence, are a poor choice for introduction to an ecosystem. The best bio-controls are those targeted toward a specific and relatively large pest population. With an ample supply of food to support the predator/parasite relationship, balance overall is maintained.

Nature's solutions to bug control can be supplemented as well. Aphids tend to get an early spring start on pines, golden currants, desert penstemon, and true willows before natural controls such as lady beetles, lacewings, syrphid flies, and gall midges and their larvae are active. The cooler the weather in spring, the longer it will take predator populations to build up to controlling numbers. Check the plants that green up early and the newest transplants in the garden for signs of pest activity, and wash off the aphids periodically to limit pest damage without eliminating predator lunch. As the new growth hardens, the plants will be less appealing to the pest, and beneficial populations will have built up to handle the remaining brood.

While delayed action is sometimes needed to let pest populations build up to levels that will sustain predators, the timing of control measures can be critical. Bacillus thuringiensis is slow acting and should be applied in the early larval stage for best results. Young larvae must consume Bt-contaminated leaves, and it may take several days for them to begin to die. Likewise, the grasshopper parasite, *Nosema locustae*, is more effective on young nymphs than on crusty older generations. A small portion of the population eats the infected bait. As they begin to die, they are consumed by their cannibalistic fellows, who in turn become infected. Over time, the pathogen can significantly diminish the local horde. Horticultural oil is an effective control for scale insects in the crawler stage when they are particularly vulnerable because they lack the moisture-repellent coating they develop once they mature. The oil dissolves their thinner protective coat and the crawlers dry up. The most likely targets for scale in natural gardens are such drought-requiring plants as cactus, saltbushes, broom dalea, some yuccas, and threadleaf sage, especially if they are being watered or fertilized too much.

The pinetip moth is becoming a major pest problem in the Southwest, and its successful control depends on removing larvae-bearing candles, the pine's growing tips, if the plants are few and small enough to manage. (Once most pines are twelve to fifteen feet tall they are usually not attractive to the moth and controls are unnecessary.) If the problem is severe and too extensive for mechanical control, carefully timed spray applications are more effective. Pheromone traps are used to lure targeted pests with an aromatic sex attractant. Spray applications can thus be timed effectively. Treatment is recommended within five to ten days of significant trap catches. Usually there are at least two separate generations of moths annually. Ponderosa pine, a beautiful long-needled pine native to higher elevations throughout the West, seems to be particularly vulnerable to pinetip moths at lower elevations, probably because the pines are already declining from heat stress.

Stressed plants are beacons for insect pests. Flea beetles rarely attack evening primroses until, after a spring of continuous bloom, they begin to flag in the summer doldrums. In the wild, the flea beetles skeletonize the evening primrose, which disappear until the following spring. No harm, no foul. Such an insect rampage in the garden is alarming. Knowing something about the life cycle of flea beetles can help check their damage. The eggs, some larvae, and adults winter over in the soil and leaf litter at the base of primroses, so clipping the plants off at the soil line and raking up any fallen leaves, loosening the soil a little, might expose some of the pests to temperatures cold enough to kill them. Better still, introducing some of the beneficial nematodes that devour beetle eggs and larvae in the soil will seriously reduce the numbers that become active in spring. The 'San Diego' strain of bacillus thuringiensis is effective on flea beetle larvae and other beetle larvae, including lady beetles' progeny. Limit the spray to flea beetle–prone plants when the small greenish-black worms are first noticeable. This targets only the pest without diminishing ladybugs and other beneficials. Furthermore, if you eliminate all of a pest, you starve its predator/parasite as well, leaving a gap in the network that will surely call for further interference after an all too brief interval.

There is a range of options when it comes to pest management. In terms of balancing insect populations so that problems are self-limiting, the most self-defeating endeavor is to engage in or buy a "preventative spray program." Such an approach is costly both in chemicals and their potential for environmental contamination. It is also endless since all it prevents is a natural balance from developing. At the other end of the spectrum is a no-intervention approach, letting nature take its course. If the plants in the garden are diverse and well adapted, and a few plant losses on occasion is acceptable, it is certainly easier than becoming an amateur entomologist. The territory between extermination and capitulation is rich with opportunities to witness the wonders of nature.

DISEASE CONTROL

A similar IPM approach applies to disease-causing microorganisms. The first step is to identify the problem and assess the potential for damage. If controls are warranted, begin with the least disruptive to the ecosystem as a whole. Some plants are more likely pathogen hosts, especially when environmental conditions are favorable. One example is Rocky Mountain penstemon, a relatively carefree plant equally adapted to sun or partial shade. In the wild it may grow in large colonies, but individual plants are widely spaced with grasses and other plants occupying the gaps in between. In the garden, to increase the impact of their spring flower display, we space the plants more closely and, thus, make them more amenable to the dryland fungus called powdery mildew. Group those same plants in the shade near a wall or other obstacle to air circulation and the probability of a mildew problem rises dramatically. Add fertilizer and water frequently and it's a dead certainty. Plants that are especially prone to infection, such as lilacs, coreopsis, and some rose cultivars, sited in open exposures are less likely to develop problems.

Rusts, also wind-borne pathogens, make hosts of serviceberry, sumac, globemallow, roses, and yerba mansa. Close spacing of plants will encourage rusts to spread. Outbreaks are often weather or stress related, favored by cool, damp conditions and excessive watering. Our harsh, dry, and erratic climate usually works to our advantage in limiting the potential for damage. Removing infected leaf litter in fall and smothering spores under a heavy layer of uninfected mulch in spring can reduce the likelihood and extent of reinfection. Keeping serviceberries and junipers, alternate hosts for cedar apple rust, at least five hundred yards apart will help prevent infection. In piñon-juniper woodland or in urban areas where junipers are planted in neighboring gardens, serviceberry might be avoided altogether. The list of plants susceptible, at least under certain circumstances, to leaf spots, root and crown rots, and nematodes would be discouraging if those same plants weren't so hardy and determined to survive. Where diseases limit the usefulness of individual plants, it is noted in their plant profiles found in book two, since the most effective means of avoiding such problems is to use resistant plants and avoid cultural practices such as overcrowding and overwatering.

Disease problems may occur as a result of the supplemental watering and feeding done while establishing new plants. There are low-impact methods of controlling disease problems without upsetting the beginnings of ecosystem equilibrium. Surfactants, the fatty acid salts found in detergents, enhance the wetness of water. Washing infected plants with "wetter water" is sometimes enough to limit the development of spores.

While wetting agents are useful on an occasional basis to spot-treat problems, if they build up in the soil, surfactants can limit the ability of soil to retain water and leach fertilizers out of the root zone of plants. "All things in moderation" seems to be one of the laws of nature. Antitranspirants, temporary latex-based barriers to evaporation used to limit moisture loss from leaves when transplanting, also create barriers to disease infection and spread. A one percent baking soda/two percent light horticultural oil spray mix with water or one-quarter ounce of soda per gallon of water are old remedies for powdery mildew. Given the intensity of our sunlight, any oil spray should be tested on a small area first to make sure that it won't burn sensitive foliage. A one percent household chlorine-bleach solution in water is another old remedy used as a soil drench for root rot. Again, this is an occasional spot treatment since accumulations of chlorine become very effective herbicides. A solution of one part chlorine bleach to ten parts water is a useful seed fungicide and oxygenator, but the seeds must be thoroughly rinsed after treatment or chlorine residues will kill the emerging seedlings.

Even when using relatively nontoxic pesticides, consider the ripple effect on the balance of the garden. As the garden becomes established, if a disease becomes chronic, the plants hosting the pathogen should either be transplanted to a more suitable location or removed and discarded.

Pruning, Deadheading, and Mowing

These categories of garden maintenance make an immediate and obvious difference in the look of a landscape. Two identical plant communities can appear totally different if one is clipped and controlled, the other untamed and untouched. If landscape maintenance is at odds with the design intention, the garden will look out of step with itself. As the garden begins to mature, decisions need to be made about how the plantings look and grow best. While the degree of neatness and order may be subjective, any cutting done to plants should enhance their natural growth patterns. As the garden becomes a tapestry of interwoven plantings, a pleasing harmony emerges. Planning for the mature size of plants eliminates the need for shrink-to-fit pruning. When renovating an older landscape, plants that have outgrown their space to the point of requiring disfiguring pruning should be removed and replaced with smaller-scale plantings. Beyond removing dead or diseased, broken or damaged growth, whether and how plants are cut depends on why they are in the garden and their individual personalities.

TREES AND SHRUBS

Small desert trees often are multitrunked in form, and removing suckers and lower branches as the plants develop enhances their sculptural forms. New trees of such types as desert willow and New Mexico olive can be left to grow unpruned their first few years, so that the natural branching patterns and interesting twists and angles that make them such attractive garden accents begin to develop. When an older landscape is being renovated, overgrown shrubs can be reshaped as small specimen trees (see chapter 9 for tips on pruning). Choose three to five well-formed, well-spaced, strong stems, and begin to eliminate weaker ones at or below the soil line. As these main trunks develop, gradually thin out the smallest lateral branches four or more feet above the ground and remove any branches in the canopy that rub against each other. If this shaping is done annually in early June after the first flush of spring growth, there will be less regrowth of suckers. As the tree form emerges, the plants will take progressively less pruning. To limit suckering and prevent sunscald of tender or previously shaded bark, shaping should be done in stages, removing a third at a time. Trees intended as single-trunk standards, such as pistache, ash, and some oaks, should have the suckers removed each June to direct all the plants' energies to developing their canopies. Trees that might become disproportionately large as they mature, such as valley cottonwood, Arizona sycamore, and many oaks, can be dwarfed in height by training them as multitrunk specimens when they are saplings. Encourage branching by pruning out the dominant terminal bud, then thin out all but three strong shoots to become the trunks. Multitrunk plants share their resources among several terminal buds, and as a result they stay shorter and broader. They become interesting landscape specimens and more expansive shade producers. Many desert-adapted shrubs have naturally dense and mounding forms that require no pruning except the occasional removal of deadwood. Cherry sage can look surprisingly dead in March and leaf out completely by the end of April. Pruning too early in the growing season can induce plants with southern ecological clocks to leaf out too early, only to have the tender shoots frosted off by a typical high-desert late-spring frost. Woody plants should not be pruned from midsummer through to dormancy in autumn to avoid a late flush of growth that depletes their food reserves and leaves them vulnerable to frost damage. Shearing is never a good option in a natural garden because it creates hard lines and contrived forms found nowhere in nature and guarantees a rematch with the shears within the growing season. Sheared plants that lose their leaves in fall look particularly tortured.

WILDFLOWERS AND GRASSES

Deadheading and mowing are techniques that produce similar effects. Deadheading is a more refined approach and refers specifically to removing seed stalks from annual and perennial flowers, either to prolong the bloom cycle or induce a second flowering. Depending on the timing, deadheading may be done to prevent reseeding, to keep enthusiastic self-seeders from running amok, or can be delayed until seed disburses to encourage self-sowing or feed wildlife. Depending on the size of the planting and the coarseness of the plants, deadheading might be done with pruning shears or a string-line trimmer with a hard blade. Plants bordering walks and patios are best hand trimmed to prevent unsightly stubble, while distant drifts of wildflowers can be done more quickly with heavier equipment.

Mowing makes a usable play surface, can actually increase the density of the cover, cleans up old seed heads, and creates a neater appearance. Using a hard blade on a string-line trimmer or a brush mower with a minimum four-inch blade height, mowing is a fast way to tame an overgrown prairie. Native grasses used as lawns, if irrigated conservatively, may need mowing once a month to retain their uniformity. A final mowing after the lawn is dormant in fall looks more formal. Letting the blades grow out to a softer surface before dormancy can be more interesting through winter. If wildflowers are sown in drifts mixed with dryland warm-season grasses as a prairie, a single overall mowing is done in March or April to clean up old growth and open the field for spring's revival. Through the growing season, wildflower areas in the prairie might be mowed selectively to remove spent seed heads so that drying stems don't detract from the current flush of flowers. This can only be done if the wildflowers are purposely seeded in distinct sweeps, so that trimming isn't at the expense of new flowers. When a neat appearance is a neighborhood issue, and the inclination to prune and mow ebbs with the onset of summer (or never existed to begin with), a prairie can be made to look tame with a minimum of trimming by manipulating its content and context. Selecting plants with similar mature heights keeps the surface more uniform. Separating the prairie from sidewalks with a border of moisture-compatible, dense, low-growing, and long-lived perennial wildflowers, such as desert zinia or chocolate flower for a dryland prairie or Mexican evening primrose or yerba mansa for an oasis meadow, can create a tame edge along an infrequently maintained planting. Tall grasses should likewise be separated from low-spreading shrubs so that the grasses don't seed into the shrubs and result in a mangy-dog look that requires regular weeding to correct.

Since the finest show of grass seed heads lasts from August into winter and taller cover provides better habitat, the last mowing is usually done in midsummer to remove the drying stalks of spring and early summer wildflowers. The mowing schedule in habitat areas should coincide with when nests are seasonally abandoned. If you have young children, chances are they'll know where the nesting sites are and when they're occupied, even if you've been too busy to have such inside information.

Garden Diary: Chronicle of Balance

Setting up the long-term management plan is the final step in the design process. It is a combination of realizing the vision of the design and dealing with the exigencies of real life. The best way to set a maintenance schedule is to walk through the new garden with a notebook at least once a month for the first year and seasonally for the next several years. Assess individual plants for their overall appearance: leaf density and color, growth rate, flowering. Assess groups of plants for their combined effectiveness: complementary growth, continuity of interest. Observe insect activity and the comings and goings of other wildlife. Note what satisfies you and where something seems to be missing or out of order. Note any unusual weather: extra rain, hail, extreme heat or cold and wind, or other disturbance, such as dogs digging, rabbits chewing, a neighborhood soccer tournament, that might be having an impact on the garden. As the year progresses, read through your previous notes for reminders and fresh insights. Natural patterns will become more apparent.

With unfamiliar plants, it's hard to know at first what is "normal." Leaves that seemed small and delicate in April may be fully expanded and leathery by June; a blaze of flower color in May may have turned to weathered brown seed stalks by July. The first year, much of the development of the plants will be underground. The inclination is to plant more, fill in the gaps. Luckily budget, lack of time, or the sore muscles that got the garden to this point help temper the urge to overplant. By the end of the second year, the garden and your notes should be developed enough to make any real gaps or deficiencies obvious. Carrying a camera on garden surveys can be useful both in collecting insect mug shots for later identification and for recording the profound changes a new garden undergoes. When browsing seed catalogs in January, a few snapshots of the garden in May, August, and October are a good reminder of where more color might be effective seasonally.

The diary might remind you that the killdeer return to nest in the dry streambed in April, so you'll want to do any cleanup there earlier; by then the prairie looks rangy and dry, in need of mowing or raking. Over the seasons you'll come to realize that in spring the golden currants will have aphids, and by summer it won't matter. The yellow-orange spindle-shaped clusters of eggs on the undersides of the currant leaves are ladybug beetles in the offing. You'll note that the desert willows rarely show any signs of life until late April and that if the giant four o'clocks sprout early the new growth may freeze back and require a second effort. Gayfeather, on the other hand, pushes up a few green shoots like clockwork each March and stays green regardless of the ups and downs of spring. By June you might notice that the chamisas are growing like weeds and the woods roses look puny and yellow. More drip emitters on the roses, fewer on the chamisa might correct both problems. You might also note that the suckers on the desert willow and chitalpa need to be removed and that there is an abundance of delicate-looking dark blue moths with red-and-white spots on their upper bodies, especially around the woodbine and grape vines. In July you may have recorded two weeks of temperatures above one hundred degrees F and daily wind. The buffalo-grass is turning yellow because you've had to water it twice as often. An extra application of fertilizer, a half dose of nitrogen, or, better yet, a label-recommended dose of iron will turn it green again.

Late in July, you've noted, the leaves of the grapes and woodbine are turning brown, a lacework of dried leaf veins, and a few blue-green and yellow caterpillars seem to be the culprits. By September their numbers are legion; make a note to buy some Bt next spring and spray both grapes and woodbine when you notice those pretty blue moths in attendance, since they are the adults of, what else, the grape leaf skeletonizer. As the summer wears on and you spend more and more time deadheading all the wild-flowers you planted for immediate gratification, you start plotting their replacement with fernbush, fendlerbush, flamebush, and Apache plume where space permits, so that you can have flowers but minimize the pruning needed to keep the garden in shape. By the time the Maximilian sunflowers are shouting the last hurrah of autumn, you're planning to add a pistache near the patio for the relief of its shade in summer and its scarlet leaves in fall and silver sage in front of the piñon for winter interest. By the following June the chitalpa near the patio begins to grow in earnest, abuzz with hummingbirds, and you forget the pistache, but winter deep freezes killed the Texas rangers near the piñon, as you half expected, so you replace them with silver sage. In July, the grapes still have their leaves and their first clusters of fruit, thanks to timely applications of Bt. The garden diary is as valuable a tool as any shovel or shears.

4 Upland Gardens

WHEN I FIRST MOVED from Indiana to the Southwest many years ago, I spent as much time as I could in the mountains. Although the plants I found there were unfamiliar, the ecosystem was much closer to what I was used to: thick green carpets of grasses and wildflowers, tall trees and dense brush thickets, and streams running with actual water. To me that was natural, the way things were supposed to be. As deep snow and cold detoured my hiking to the warmer, drier western foothills in winter, I began to open up to the desert. Walking in the rocky *arroyos*, I harked back to Saturday mornings in front of the old black-and-white Zenith, reliving the boulder-strewn landscape that had become familiar through countless episodes of Lone Ranger and Hopalong Cassidy, Sky King and Zorro. I began walking the mesas, lured by the first wildflowers of spring, and found basket-making materials, food, and medicine plants I'd read about in my university days. Though I had learned them out of context, unconnected to place, they, too, were somehow reassuring, familiar. The road from "High-ho Silver!" to anthropology student to native landscaping advocate has led steadily downslope, rooting me firmly in the northern Chihuahuan desert. From the vantage point of my own shrub-desert garden, I can look up to the foothills and down into the Rio Grande Valley. Both are cooler and wetter than our place. On sun-baked summer afternoons, I watch the clouds collect along the mountains, their shadows a distant cool blue. Finally they pile up so high that moisture begins to stream from their bases. Those days I envy foothills

UPLAND ECOSYSTEMS ARE A MOSAIC OF MOIST CANYONS, ROCKY SLOPES, AND OPEN MEADOWS. HERE, GRASSES BLEND WITH PURPLE VERBENA, YELLOW COMPOSITES, AND WHITE PEPPERGRASS. CM

UPLAND EXPOSURES RANGE FROM WIND-SCOURED HILLTOPS TO SHELTERED CANYONS.

gardeners. Uplands catch more monsoon thunderstorms and winter snowfall, twice the seven inches we're likely to average down here.

THE UPLAND MOSAIC

Different as shrub desert and river valley are from foothills and canyon ecosystems, the uplands themselves are a mosaic of microclimates spanning elevations from five thousand to eight thousand feet, with relatively cool north- or east-facing slopes and bottomlands, and drier south- and west-facing slopes. Exposures range from wind-scoured hilltops to sheltered woodland. The southernmost, lowest, driest areas receive at least ten inches of annual precipitation, while the higher, cooler areas receive up to twenty-five inches. Ecologically, the uplands are a mix of piñon-juniper woodlands and juniper savannas merging with high-plains grasslands. Woodland differs from the forests of still higher elevations in the density of the tree cover and the size of individual trees. Because of the greater moisture available and the cloud-cooled temperatures, the higher-elevation woodlands seven thousand to eight hundred feet above sea level support nearly a closed canopy of trees, becoming true forest on north exposures, more open with grassy clearings and shrub thickets on south and west slopes. Further down-slope, between five thousand and sixty-five hundred feet, in response to warmer temperatures and decreased rainfall and snow cover, the tree cover thins to less than half what it is a few thousand feet higher. Savannas are drier still, transitions between

woodland and grassland where junipers are widely spaced and grasses dominate. Finally, in true grassland and shrub desert, junipers are only found in erosion cuts where moisture is channeled and collects to support their growth.

This variety of growing conditions yields a corresponding diversity of plants, some found exclusively in the uplands, others native to forest or desert that find a niche in the foothills. The dominant tree species change with the elevation. Piñon are found throughout the range of upland ecosystems, but they dominate the middle of the wood-land belt. Their numbers increase significantly above six thousand feet, while they are only a minor part of the plant community near four thousand feet. Above seven thousand feet, Rocky Mountain and alligator junipers are more common, and piñon begins to yield to ponderosa pines. Further downslope one-seed, redberry, and Utah juniper share space with dominant piñon, gradually outnumbering the pines as the terrain becomes hotter and drier. Various oaks dominate or play minor supporting roles in the plant community depending on elevation and exposure.

You can read the local landscape by tree cover and height: the taller and closer the trees, the moister or more sheltered the microclimate; the shorter the trees and the more open their spacing, the hotter and drier the exposure. Trees always occupy the wettest areas, grasses and wildflowers colonize intermediate areas, and shrubs populate the hottest, driest exposures where their compact forms, deep roots, and capacity to conserve and store moisture give them an edge. This same pattern applies in the

THE HIGHER RAINFALL AND COOLER
SUMMER TEMPERATURES PROVIDE
LUSHER, MORE DIVERSE AND
COLORFUL PLANT COMMUNITIES. CM

garden. Moist zones are created by the shade of north- and east-facing walls. Paving
and roof surfaces funnel rain and melting snow, increasing the water available to nearby
plants. Runoff catchments near the south and west sides of walls can supplement moisture to small trees needed there for shade. Just as plants are likely to be denser along
arroyos, so may they be more closely planted along walkways and driveways, where the
runoff enhances their growth, and the plants in turn soften and cool the expanses of
paving, making entryways and patios more inviting. Shrubs fit the natural pattern
when used to define lower water-zone boundaries, provide screening and color, and
stabilize slopes. In the foothills, grasslands dominate open, level areas and up to 2:1
slopes. Steeper than 4:1, the grasses are more widely spaced, and the sod formers like
buffalograss and blue grama are replaced by tall bunchgrasses such as sideoats grama

ON SOUTHERLY, MORE EXPOSED, HOTTER, AND DRIER UPLAND SITES THE NATURAL GROUND COVER MAY BE MOSTLY WARM-SEASON GRASSES, SUCH AS BAMBOO MUHLY SHOWN HERE. CM

and needle-and-thread. Taking a cue from natural patterns, our lawns should occupy level ground or, at most, gently sloping contours, making them easier to water and mow. Steeper slopes carpeted with unmowed ornamental grasses and deeply rooted wild-flowers and shrubs are attractive, more stable, and easier to maintain.

Overall, the uplands offer the same challenges of limited rainfall, wind, heat, low humidity, and ungardenlike soils found elsewhere in the desert Southwest, compounded by the sloping terrain, large lot sizes, and an abundance of wildlife browsing at the salad bar. Still, the foothills and canyons are in many ways easier ecosystems to garden compared with shrub desert and grassland. Besides feeling cooler and being moister, the naturally denser vegetation is closer to the coverage most gardeners find attractive. If adapted trees and shrubs are carefully sited to benefit from runoff, the plants that make up the framework of the garden can be largely self-sustaining once they have rooted out extensively. Natural resources such as rock for retaining walls often are a by-product of the garden's development, since there seems to be a boulder just below the surface every time you dig.

Foothills soils are generally rocky, well-drained decomposed granite or gritty limestone sand, but hardpan caliche layers below the surface can create perched water tables where water that percolates from the surface pools on the hardpan, unable to penetrate further. Where moisture is naturally scarce, this rarely creates more than a minor change in the native vegetation, but in a garden where plants are being irrigated, subsurface caliche layers may go undetected until plants begin to die. If caliche layers are thick enough to stop drainage for long periods and too deep to break through, the most practical solution is to compensate for the lack of drainage by adjusting the plant selection to include plants such as chamisa, Apache plume, sumac, prairie sage or grasses that can adapt to a range of soil moisture, and drip irrigate in shorter cycles to avoid underground stagnation. If caliche hardpan is near the surface it can be broken up with a jackhammer to open drainage channels.

One of the major advantages of newly developed foothills areas is that they usually have very limited annual weed problems compared with valley agricultural land, unless large areas have been scraped bare and tumbleweeds, cheatgrass, and kochia have invaded. Even then, weed control is usually a minor concern once the soil is stabilized. There is also the potential for many locally abundant wildflowers and native grasses to volunteer. White-tufted evening primrose, penstemons, globemallows, verbenas, milkwort, needle-and-thread grass, gramas, and Indian ricegrass are just a few of the "good weeds" that might colonize uninvited but not unwelcome. Slow-growing, long-lived, and valuable native trees and shrubs such as piñon, mountain mahogany, and oaks may already populate parts of the property, providing reference points for the landscaping. The rocky foothills soils are actually the preferred growing medium for a wide range of native and adaptive plants.

Although the soil is porous, torrential rainfall on slopes can lead to problems. When the gritty topsoil is very dry, as will be the case on southwest-facing slopes, water will sheet off the surface unless plant roots provide channels for penetration. The rosette forms of many dryland plants act as funnels, breaking the fall of water on their leaf surfaces and directing it to the roots below. Likewise, raindrops roll down the narrow blades of bunchgrasses to the heart of the plant while an extended mass of root fibers soaks up whatever rain hits the soil between the clumps. Shrubs work the same way on a grander scale, putting down deep anchoring roots for stability and a network of fibrous roots to absorb rainfall made more gentle by passing through the canopy of leaves before hitting the ground. Over time, a litter of leaves and twigs collects at the

FOOTHILLS SOILS ARE GENERALLY ROCKY, WELL-DRAINED DECOMPOSED GRANITE, GRITTY LIMESTONE SAND, OR, IN SOME CASES, HARDPAN CALICHE.

BOULDERS HELP KEEP SOIL FROM ERODING WHILE CREATING MOISTURE-CONDENSING NICHES FOR PLANT GROWTH ON UPLAND SLOPES.

base of shrubs that keeps the soil surface softer and more receptive to rain. Gardeners didn't invent mulch, they just recognized and adopted a good idea when they saw one.

On natural slopes, the spaces between plants are often covered with a mix of rock varying from small pebble plating to boulders. Here moisture condenses as the rock cools down in the evening, and a trickle of moisture is harvested for nearby plants. The rock also stabilizes the soil surface and breaks up the flow of water during downpours. One of the challenges faced by upland gardeners is having to deal with unstable slopes that result from the cut and fill sometimes necessary in leveling space for hillside building sites. If the soil is compacted for construction, it is difficult to plant. Uncompacted, it erodes more quickly. The gardener is caught between a rock and a soft spot.

UPLAND STRATEGIES: DEALING WITH SLOPES AND DRAINAGE

Five years ago, the Mandell family moved to the foothills for the views and the sweep of the natural landscape and confronted a potentially dangerous situation. On a lot already sloping one foot in each two to three feet, the builder sited the house near the middle of the hill to reduce the impact that neighboring houses would have on the view. A shelf was cut into the slope that left a ten-foot-high sheer drop-off within fifteen feet of the north wall of the house and a 1:1 south-facing slope five feet from the garden wall enclosing the south courtyard. A few feet from the front gate, a steep, highly erodible slope dropped fifty feet into an arroyo. The house was built on firm ground, but everything around it threatened collapse.

Because most of the roof surface drains into the space between the north wall and the cliff, creating a more gentle contour there was out of the question. To protect the house, the contractor built a railroad-tie retaining wall to support the cliff face and the driveway above it, and a swale was cut along the north wall draining east and eventually down the south slope. As construction was completed in October, it was too late in the year for warm-season grasses to germinate and provide stability. A mix of Indian ricegrass, winterfat, and chamisa, growing wild on the land and likely to germinate and develop roots in fall and early winter, was seeded instead. A riprap of cobblestone was added to provide initial surface stability. The slope was so steep that as the rock was dumped off the top, a timber had to be dragged up the slope on cables, catching the stone and pushing it into the surface. Without the cabled timber, the rock tumbled unimpeded into a heap at the base of the slope. Water was applied from the top with low-precipitation-rate sprinklers.

By spring the cool-season mix dotted the surface with slender silver threads, not much reassurance after six anxious months. As the soil warmed enough for blue and sideoats grama to germinate, their seed was scratched into the surface of still-numerous bare spots. Judy Mandell says, "I felt like a fireman the first year, watering faithfully two or three times a week." Trying to extinguish fear and grow erosion protection, water was added not only faithfully but carefully. If the surface became saturated, the soil on

THE STEEP SLOPE WAS SEEDED WITH CHAMISA AND WINTERFAT AND COBBLESTONES WERE IMBEDDED IN THE SURFACE TO PROVIDE A MEASURE OF STABILITY UNTIL THE PLANTS COULD DEVELOP.

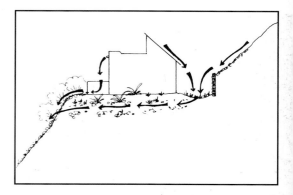

MANDELL SITE.

top would be heavier than the subsoil and create the risk of a mud slide. The wisps of gray and green slowly developed into a dense cover, and after eighteen months the hoses were retired. The only weak spot was a gully formed by the roof drainage on the east end of the slope. Initially it was reinforced with wire over the cobblestone, and Apache plume was planted in the channel, but it continued to erode until old tires were pinned into the deepening gully with steel fence posts to catch sediment and hold larger rock in place. This inelegant but extremely effective approach has stopped the slippage and allowed the plants to develop, obscuring the mechanics and slowing the runoff through the channel. "I feel secure. My hill is stabilized and my house is still standing! I've learned a great respect for the natural flora, and appreciate its earlier slow growth," comments Judy.

Now she faces a new, less intimidating dilemma. For winter safety, the steeply curving south-facing driveway was blacktopped to encourage snow and ice to melt off rapidly. The entry courtyard is concrete paved and drains through weep holes in the courtyard wall. The shrubs in front of the entry courtyard that receive extra runoff from the paved surfaces have grown five feet tall despite the otherwise harsh conditions. They now block the view. Not only have the shrubs grown too tall but they overwhelm the bunchgrasses that dominate the surrounding hillsides. "I guess major pruning is needed now to make it look more like the hills around me," Judy says. In five years the pendulum has swung from an alarming lack of cover to a surfeit. For three and a half years no watering, and for five years no weeding, fertilizing, deadheading, or pest control, was needed. An hour of cleanup seasonally was the only maintenance done. Now it's time to dust of the shears and thin the stand of chamisa and winterfat. Some of the oldest plants will be cut off several inches below ground to leave their roots in place but discourage regrowth. The rest of the oversized specimens will be cut back: the oldest stems removed to the ground, the newest branches cut back to eighteen inches high. How often this procedure will need to be repeated remains to be seen; a safe guess is every three years with average rainfall of fourteen inches, less often during drought cycles, more often after unusually wet years.

Given the severity of the conditions at this site initially, the Mandells were wise to approach their situation as revegetation rather than gardening. While the desire to conform to the surrounding ecosystem began as a philosophical response to the site, it quickly became a functional imperative. Now that the threat of disaster seems remote, soothed by the glow of early morning sun on the ricegrass and the chatter of birds, the desire to blend seamlessly into the hillside has come full circle. Nature herself seems to defer any further embellishment.

In sharp contrast, Carol Treat sought a place to garden intensively, blending long-standing horticultural favorites into the surrounding native plant community. An avid

IN THE TREAT GARDEN THE COURT-
YARD IS INTENSIVELY PLANTED
AROUND THE CAREFULLY PRESERVED
NATIVE LIVE OAK. AN ECLECTIC MIX
OF ORNAMENTALS INCLUDES ROSES,
FRENCH HYBRID LILACS, ASIAN LILIES,
RUSSIAN SAGE, AND PENSTEMON. CM

gardener transplanted to the foothills from forested northern California, she found
herself on gently sloping terrain, at the confluence of several arroyos. The soil is alluvial
decomposed granite mixed with what little organic matter has been flushed off the
surrounding slopes for the past centuries. It is soft, deep, and as easily washed away as
it is workable. The water in the arroyos surges a few feet deep and several feet wide
or not at all. Judging it a force to be accommodated, rather than conquered, Carol has
set about making the arroyo a focus of the natural part of her garden. The drainage
from roof and pavement is diverted and used to water garden plants. A footbridge spans
the arroyo at the front gate and is literally a bridge between nature and horticulture.
Across the footbridge lies a gate that opens into the most densely planted, water-intensive garden.

The first year was spent getting to know the natives on the site, learning the
drainage patterns, shoring up washouts, paving pathways and patios, and building garden
walls and a ramada, complete with an *horno*, a traditional outdoor oven. The aid of Bill
Hays, a landscape architect known for his sensitive blending of architectural elements
into natural settings, was enlisted. A west-facing courtyard overlooks the main arroyo
and a grove of native live oak. A large solitary oak within the courtyard was carefully
protected during construction and is now a focal point of the cultivated garden as well
as a link with the natural landscape outside the walls. The carpeting in the enclosure is

RUNOFF FROM THE *CANALES* (ROOF DRAINS) FOLLOWS A COBBLE-LINED CHANNEL ALONG THE BRICK PATHWAY, SUPPLEMENTING WATER TO A COTTAGE BORDER OF PERENNIALS AND ASPENS. THE BLUE FLOWER SPIKES OF VITEX, SHAPED AS A SMALL TREE, PROVIDE A STRONG CONTRAST TO THE CORAL HONEYSUCKLE SLOWLY DRAPING THE POST-AND-WIRE FENCE. CM

a small fescue lawn, the most water-intensive element in the landscape. Wide shrub-and-perennial borders protect the walls and the oak from excess water. Lilacs and shrub roses combine amicably with fernbush, and penstemon share space with snow-in-summer. Dry-stack rock walls using granite boulders gathered on the site border the beds. An uneven pocket in the otherwise gentle contour of lawn hosts a flower bed that overflows with hybrid lilies and ornamental grasses, each occupying niches where they are best suited.

The garden continues to evolve as a composite of the fancies of its tender and the tolerances of the place. Defining a watering schedule is challenging since some of the earliest transplants are established well enough to be weaned of supplemental watering while new plants are still being added. The long-term plan is eventually to limit the supplemental watering to the courtyard area and to a few exotics in the east garden that are not quite satisfied with supplemental runoff. The east patio, an extension of the kitchen, is a stage for watching sunrises over the nearby mountains and storms in winter. The boldness of nature is balanced by a casual cottage border of herbs and wildflowers, with coral honeysuckle to lure hummingbirds, Russian sage, and artemisias. Runoff is carried to plants in a swale that parallels the patio and cascades along the path. Shaded from the hot afternoon sun, aspens mediate between sharply rising house walls and narrow perennial borders.

As the garden spaces closest to the house become more established, a maintenance strategy is emerging. Wire cages are used to protect new plants from rabbit and deer browsing until they are established, then the cages are removed and reused in another part of the garden. Watering in summer varies from daily to weekly to "as needed," depending on how long the plants have been in place and how well adapted they prove to be. Anything that seems out of step with the surrounding plants is moved to a more suitable location. Weekly spot weeding is done in the cultivated beds. In the natural areas, weeding mostly entails moving plants from one area to another as needed to fill in. Fertilizing is limited to the courtyard in spring. Careful attention is paid to mature sizes at planting time so that plants can develop their own forms without encroaching on each other. "I like the natural look of plants let go," says Carol. Still, the most time is spent deadheading flowers in the cutting beds, about one full day each week in summer: good reason, in such a large garden, to have more of the space be self-sustaining. At this relatively early stage, water use for establishing transplants, combined with the square footage devoted to higher water-use plants, is more than was expected. Smoothing the transition from intensively cultivated higher water-use areas to the surrounding landscape is an ongoing concern. As Carol becomes more familiar with the microclimates in her garden, she has begun to match spaces in her still-evolving natural garden areas with plant communities she finds growing in similar niches on adjacent forest land. Borrowing planting ideas from nature helps accomplish her ideal of "enhancing the natural beauty of this place without changing its essence."

Jean and Bill Heflin's nine-year-old foothills garden occupies the middle ground between revegetation and grand-scale gardening. Though the site is fairly gentle in contour, it is cut by an arroyo and has become a magnet for hungry rabbits. With garden ideas gleaned from experiences as far afield as Canada and the Dominican Republic, a priority of the Heflin garden is color, lots of color. Having gardened in many climates, the Heflins were convinced of the wisdom of working with the site and opted to maintain the arroyo as a dry-streambed focus of the garden. Since it is a relatively quiet channel at its rip-roaring best, the arroyo bed became one of the garden paths and drains into some of the planted areas as it meanders through. To avoid problems of silt-laden water burying the plants during flooding, a dense planting of Apache plume was retained where the arroyo enters the garden. Apache plume slows the flow of the water by filtering out silt. Over time it may be buried repeatedly, always emerging from the sediment with denser growth. A mulch of three-eighths-inch Santa Fe brown gravel was used on the beds and on the main path because it blends with the decomposed granite soil. The level above the arroyo was planted with a postage-stamp-size blue-grass lawn, which is one of the choices they regret making. While the lawn serves as an extension of the patio and any runoff from it is gladly accepted by the rose border, it still uses a disproportionate amount of water and requires more mowing than its care-takers are happy with. As Jean notes, "It looks too green, the wrong kind of green."

There are essentially two kinds of gardens. Some gardens are carefully maintained arrangements of plants and hardscaping, extensions of the architecture, where the need for raking and mowing outdoors are as ritual as dusting and vacuuming indoors. Other landscapes evolve with the interests of their caretakers and the wildlife they support.

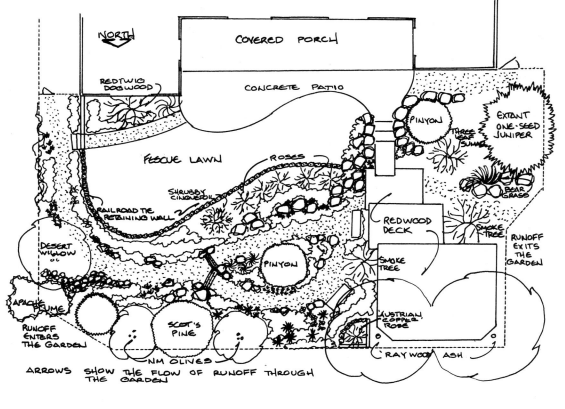

The drawing labels (clockwise/as placed):

NORTH

COVERED PORCH

CONCRETE PATIO

REDTWIG DOGWOOD

PINYON

THREE LEAF SUMAC

EXTANT ONE-SEED JUNIPER

FESCUE LAWN

ROSES

BEAR GRASS

SHRUBBY CINQUEFOIL

RAILROAD TIE RETAINING WALL

REDWOOD DECK

SMOKE TREE

RUNOFF EXITS THE GARDEN

DESERT WILLOW

PINYON

SMOKE TREE

APACHE PLUME

SCOT'S PINE

AUSTRIAN COPPER ROSE

RUNOFF ENTERS THE GARDEN

NM OLIVES

RAYWOOD ASH

ARROWS SHOW THE FLOW OF RUNOFF THROUGH THE GARDEN

THE DRY-STREAMBED PATHWAY MEANDERS BETWEEN DESERT WILLOW (PHOTO BACKGROUND), SCOT'S PINE (LEFT), AND PIÑON (RIGHT). THE WILDFLOWERS INCLUDE GAYFEATHER, ORGAN MOUNTAIN EVENING PRIMROSE, WHITE-TUFTED EVENING PRIMROSE, SCARLET MINT, GLOBEMALLOW, WINECUPS, CHOCOLATE FLOWER, SPIDERWORT, GAURA, BUTTERFLYWEED, CONEFLOWER, BLUE FLAX, FERN VERBENA; PINELEAF, ROCKY MOUNTAIN, SCARLET BUGLER, CARDINAL, DESERT, AND CRANDALL PENSTEMONS; SALVIAS INCLUDE CHERRY SAGE, CULINARY SAGE, PITCHER SAGE, MEALY SAGE, AND CEDAR SAGE; TRADITIONAL GARDEN PERENNIALS INCLUDE VERONICAS, ORIENTAL POPPY, RED VALERIAN, AND CHIVES.

Order is more implied than imposed. They may be less refined but are probably more interesting since they embrace change. Jean's goal from the outset was to have the best of both. By carefully laying out the basic structure of the garden to include in equal measure both carefully maintained areas and those with space to try new plants and color combinations and generally indulge flights of fancy, this goal has been met admirably.

The framework of the garden has evolved to include carefully placed trees, including piñon, Scot's pine, Raywood ash, desert willow, and New Mexico olive, that frame the best mountain view and provide privacy from neighboring houses. The north-facing covered patio is wonderfully cool in summer but too chilly during colder months, so an expansive sunny deck was built to the south bridging the arroyo. From the vantage point of the deck, a whole different garden unfolds. Vistas of distant mountains open and the pattern of the streambed weaves through flower borders bright with penstemon, Mexican hat, salvias, poppies, flax, and paperflower. The further the garden moves away from the house and patio, the less water the plantings require. Along the wooden fence, stained sage gray-green to minimize its presence, grow the most drought tolerant of the lot. The fence is needed to discourage voracious rabbits in the garden. To minimize damage to the garden outside the fence, Jean uses only those plants that the rabbits have ignored.

94

HEFLIN GARDEN ONE YEAR AFTER
PLANTING.

Ellen Wilde's twelve-year-old garden is very much an adolescent. Originally the priorities were water conservation, wind protection, screening for privacy, and minimizing work. Plant choices have consistently been governed by their adaptability to the site, so the net effect is a waterwise garden. Wind continues to be a reason for adding trees and shrubs to the buffer zone surrounding the rock garden and perennial beds. The rock garden wraps around the southeast side of the house, where a two-foot drop in the grade creates an opportunity to showcase, both from inside the house and the patio, the intricate detail of alpine and other compact plants. Blue grama borders interspersed with wildflowers and a gravel path circle the rest of the way around the house. Piñon, both large specimens salvaged during construction and smaller plants added later, as well as Rocky Mountain and one-seed junipers, ponderosa pines, Russian olives, serviceberry, cliffrose, cliff fendlerbush, and chamisa make up the screen and wind buffers. Ellen confesses, "I'm too much in love with plants to let it be little work, and it's becoming less casual than I originally planned. I guess it's my personal nature to want to keep things neat." Mulching the rock garden with fine gravel and the shrub borders and some of the flower beds with bark helps conserve moisture and suppress weeds. The mulches also define space and reinforce the feeling of order. Weeding is an ongoing minor chore, much of it done as seasonal mowing, usually three times in summer,

A LOVE OF PLANTS GIVES THIS MEADOW THE INTENSITY OF AN EXTENDED PERENNIAL BED, EVER CHANGING WITH FLUSHES OF SEASONAL COLOR. IN EARLY SUMMER ROCKY MOUNTAIN PENSTEMON (VIOLET BLUE SPIKES), BLUE FLAX, BLANKET FLOWER (RED AND YELLOW DAISIES), AND INDIAN PAINTBRUSH (ORANGE SPIKES) STEAL THE SHOW. PHOTO BY ELLEN WILDE

GARDEN WALLS AND HARD PAVING DEFINE SPACES BOLDLY. THE OPEN IRON-WORK GATE PROVIDES AN INVITING GLIMPSE OF THE ROCK GARDEN. PLANTS IN THE FOREGROUND INCLUDE SOAPWEED YUCCA AND NEW MEXICO OLIVE HIGHLIGHTED AGAINST THE WALL, WITH PUSSY TOES, PERKY SUE (YELLOW), AND PINE-LEAF PENSTEMON GROUNDCOVERS. PHOTO BY ELLEN WILDE

to keep grasses, including blue grama, from going to seed and encroaching on the rock garden and tumbleweeds from encroaching on the small fenced vegetable garden. The native-grass and wildflower border is mowed in early spring and again in summer.

While most of the trees and shrubs require little pruning, some of the larger piñon have lower branches removed occasionally to allow for the mower, and the new growth on young mugo pines and junipers is pinched back in late spring to make them more compact and dense. The remaining chamisa are cut back to three feet or so each fall, instead of in spring, since the weight of the frequent snow in this higher-elevation garden breaks branches, leaving a sadly flattened mess by spring. The combination of careful plant selection, winter snows that periodically offer welcome insulation from drying winds, and the cooling moisture that accompanies summer monsoons makes watering less of a chore year-round than it would be in a similar garden at lower elevations. May and June are typically the driest months in this high upland garden so drip irrigation for the trees and shrubs makes supplemental watering effortless. Having gradually reduced the size of the wildflower meadow and chamisa screen, the most unruly area in the garden, replacing them with mowed blue grama and mulched perennial borders, Ellen now wishes she had enclosed a garden space with an adobe wall. The longer she gardens in the cold desert uplands, the more she prefers a strong separation between traditional garden plants and wilder natural ones. Not only would a well-placed wall have saved years of wind-whipped, rabbit-consumed frustration, it would satisfy her personal preference for strong definition that the soft lines of plants don't deliver. From a different perspective, this garden, with its quietly cultivated living space and trim native-grass and shrub borders easing into the surrounding piñon-juniper woodland, is a superb example of the understated elegance that natural gardens can embody.

UPLAND STRATEGIES: WALLS AND FENCES

Nancy and Roy Skeens's garden is perched on a rocky hilltop, blasted by canyon winds. The walls of their sunken courtyard reduce the impact of the wind, the road, and neighboring houses. The garden within provides the foreground to a majestic panorama of mountain peaks and canyons. To balance this awe-inspiring view, the courtyard garden aims to charm and invite. A catchment basin was built to contain the runoff from the *canales* that drain into the courtyard. Functionally separate, but visually linked by using the same rock, a small pool reminiscent of a mountain spring gurgles a cooling invitation to birds. A 'Hopa' crabapple shades the pond to minimize evaporation and ease the establishment of the smaller ground cover plants. A border of rugosa roses, dwarf butterflybush, rue, and fernbush lures butterflies. Red yucca, cherry sage, and penstemon bring hummingbirds. Desert penstemon is a favorite for its vigor and gradations of foliage color, as well as its long season of deep rose-pink flowers. Balancing the seasonal color display is a tapestry of leaf colors and textures: the lacy silver "Powis Castle" artemisia, Russian sage, and wooly thyme; soft sage green of curry plant; vibrant chartreuse of golden marjoram; the matted brocade of pussy toes; needle-like greens of rosemary and pineleaf penstemon. The aromas of a half dozen culinary herbs blend with fragrant flowers in a heady bouquet. Since the planting is still in its infancy, much of the tending needed involves observing the development of the plants, dead-heading the spent flowers, cleaning up the pond, and drip irrigating twice a week when temperatures top ninety-five degrees F and otherwise on an as-needed basis. Even in this early balancing stage, no pest control has been necessary. The garden gates keep rabbits out. Beyond the walls, Apache plumes further screen and catch dust from the unpaved road. From the living room windows their feathery seed heads glisten in the sun. Soil disturbance has been kept to a minimum by a conscientious developer who believes his custom homes are greatly enhanced by their natural setting. Native-grass hay mulch was used to revegetate areas where the natural cover was sparse.

UPLAND PLANTS

The challenge of "gardening for place" involves, most centrally, the task of building plant communities. Getting to know the personalities of individual species and how they respond to different exposures and watering schedules aids in blending plants to solve site problems and create beautiful living environments. Invariably my clients fall

A ROCK-LINED SWALE CATCHES RUNOFF FROM THE ROOF AND CHANNELS IT INTO PLANTINGS. THE SMALL SPRINGLIKE POND AT THE TOP OF THE SWALE IS SEPARATE BUT MADE TO LOOK LIKE THE SOURCE OF THE STREAMBED. PLANTS INCLUDE A 'HOPA' CRABAPPLE FOR COLOR AND SHADE, RUGOSA ROSES, ENGLISH LAVENDER, AND DWARF BUTTERFLY-BUSH FOR COLOR AND FRAGRANCE. PINELEAF PENSTEMON, BLUE FESCUE, WOOLY THYME, AND PUSSY TOES ARE TEXTURAL GROUND COVERS.

THE WALLED GARDEN AND ITS MAJESTIC SURROUNDINGS SOON AFTER PLANTING. PHOTO BY ROY SKEENS

A YEAR AFTER PLANTING, THE INTER-PLAY OF COLOR AND TEXTURE IS BEGINNING TO KNIT TOGETHER. AT MATURITY, THIS GARDEN WILL HAVE THE RICHNESS OF BROCADE.

in love with at least a few of the plants in their gardens. There is love at first sight, the early affection for plants that adapt to the site immediately and outshine their companions with their enthusiasm for life. Many penstemon, gayfeather, desert willow, blue mist, cherry sage, and giant four o'clock are among the early favorites. Then there are plants that quietly assume their roles in the garden and after a time earn a large measure of esteem for their constancy and grace under pressure. Threadleaf sage, false indigo, Apache plume, the sumacs, fernbush, the mountain mahoganies, and New Mexico olive are among the many plants that slowly emerge as the heart of the garden because they change with the seasons, are always interesting and attractive in a subdued way, and take so little care. The following list of plants presents many of the best the uplands has to offer the gardener. While they are native to the foothills, many will adapt to the lowlands with ease. Book two, *Plants for Natural Gardens*, offers complete illustrated profiles of the plants listed here.

Upland Plants

Upland · Desert/Grassland · Oasis · ✗ Not Rec. for Urban Gardens · S=Sun, PS=Part-shade, SH=Shade, DR=Drought requiring, DE=Drought enduring, DEV=Drought evading, DT=Drought tolerant

99

TREES

Texas madrone/*Arbutus texana*   DT S/PS

Incense cedar/*Calocedrus decurrens*   DE S/SH

Oklahoma redbud/*Cercis reniformis*   DE S/SH

    Eastern redbud/*C. canadensis*   DT PS/SH

    Western redbud/*C. occidentalis*   DE S/SH

Thornless cockspur hawthorn/*Crataegus crus-galli*

    'Inermis'   DT S/SH

    Russian hawthorn/*C. ambigua*

    Washington hawthorn/*C. phaenopyrum*

Arizona cypress/*Cupressus arizonica*   DE S

Fragrant ash/*Fraxinus cuspidata*   DE S/PS

    Singleleaf ash/*F. anomala*

Texas ash/*Fraxinus texensis*   DE S/PS

Arizona walnut/*Juglans major*   DE S/PS

    Little walnut/*J. microcarpa*

One-seed juniper/*Juniperus monosperma*   DE S

    Utah juniper/*J. osteosperma*

    Redberry juniper/*J. pinchotii*

Rocky Mountain juniper/*Juniperus scopulorum* 'Blue
Heaven', 'Cologreen', 'Table Top' and 'Welchii'   DE S

    Alligator juniper/*J. deppeana*

Bristlecone pine/*Pinus aristata*   DE S

Piñon/*Pinus edulis*   DE S

Quaking aspen/*Populus tremuloides*   DT S/SH

Hoptree/*Ptelea trifoliata*   DE S/SH

Emory oak/*Quercus emoryi*   DE S

    Silverleaf oak/*Q. hypoleucoides*

    Texas red oak/*Q. texana*

Gambel oak/*Quercus gambelii*   DE S

    Arizona white oak/*Q. arizonica*

    Shinoak/*Q. havardii*

    Bur oak/*Q. macrocarpa*

    Chinquapin oak/*Q. muehlenbergii*

    Shrub live oak/*Q. turbinella*

Prairie flameleaf sumac/*Rhus lanceolata*   DE S/PS

    Flameleaf sumac/*R. copallina*

    Smooth sumac/*R. glabra*

    Cutleaf sumac/*R. glabra* var. *cistmontana*

    Evergreen sumacs/*R. sempervirens*
and *R. choriophylla* (hardy to 0 F)

Soapberry/*Sapindus drummondii*   DE S/PS

UPLAND PLANTS

SHRUBS AND VINES

 Utah serviceberry/*Amelanchier utahensis*   DE S/PS

Serviceberry/*A. alnifolia*   DT PS/SH

Pointleaf manzanita/*Arctostaphylos pungens*   DE S/SH

Pinemat manzanita/*A. nevadensis*

Greenleaf manzanita/*A. patula*

Kinnikinnick/*A. uva-ursi*   PS/SH

 Bigleaf sage/*Artemisia tridentata*   DE S

Silver sage/*A. cana*

Black sage/*A. nova*

 Algerita/*Berberis haematocarpa*   DE S/PS

Fremont barberry/*B. fremontii*

Creeping mahonia/*B. repens*   DT PS/SH

 Winterfat/*Ceratoides lanata* syn. *Eurotia lanata*   DE S

Mountain mahogany/*Cercocarpus montanus*   DE S/PS

Mountain mahoganies/*C. brevifolius* and *C. intricatus*

Curlleaf mountain mahogany/*C. ledifolius*

Squawapple/*Periphyllum ramosissimus*

Fernbush/*Chamaebatieria millefolium*   DE S/PS

Mexican star-orange/*Choisysa dumosa*   DE S/PS

 Chamisa, Rabbitbrush/*Chrysothamnus nauseosus*   DR S

Dwarf chamisa/*C. nauseosus* var. *nauseosus*

Douglas rabbitbrush/*C. viscidiflorus*

Rocky Mountain clematis/*Clematis pseudoalpina*   DT PS/SH

Cliffrose/*Cowania mexicana*   DE S

Feather dalea/*Dalea formosa*   DR S

Silver dalea/*D. argyraea* (check hardiness)

Black dalea/*D. frutescens* (check hardiness)

Turpentine bush/*Ericameria laricifolia*   DE S

 Apache plume/*Fallugia paradoxa*   DE S

 Cliff fendlerbush/*Fendlera rupicola*   DE S/PS

Waxflower/*Jamesia americana*   DT PS/SH

Rockspray/*Holodiscus dumosus*   DT PS/SH

Mountain ninebark/*Physocarpus monogynus*

Beargrass/*Nolina texana*   DR S/PS

Beargrasses/*N. microcarpa*

Cholla/*Opuntia imbricata*   DR S

Prickly pears/*O. phaeacantha* and *O. engelmannii*

Littleleaf mockorange/*Philadelphus microcarpa*   DE S/PS

Shrubby cinquefoil/*Potentilla fruticosa* and cultivars   DT S/SH

California buckthorn/*Rhamnus californica*   DE S/SH

Tallhedge/*R. frangula* 'Columnaris'

Threeleaf sumac/*Rhus trilobata*   DE S/SH

Aromatic sumac/*R. aromatica* and *R. aromatica* 'Low Grow'

Prostrate sumac/*R. trilobata* 'Prostrata'

R. trilobata var. *pilosissima*

Snowberry/*Symphoricarpos albus*   DT PS/SH

Coralberry/*S. orbiculatus*

'Hancock' dwarf coralberry/*S. orbiculatus* X *chenaultii*

WILDFLOWERS

 Yarrow/*Achillea lanulosa*   DT S/SH

Greek yarrow/*A. ageratifolia*

Yarrow/*A. millefolium* and *cultivars*

Moonshine yarrow/*A. taygetea*

Wooly yarrow/*A. tomentosa*

Giant hyssop, Bubblegum mint/*Agastache cana*   DE S/PS

Anise hyssop/*A. foeniculum*

Pale hyssop/*A. pallidiflora*

 Nodding onion/*Allium cernuum*   DT PS/SH

Chives/*A. shoenoprasum*

100

Garlic chives/*A. tuberosum*

Allium senescens 'Glaucum'

Pussy toes/*Antennaria parvifolia*   DE S/PS

Harebells/*Campanula rotundifolia*   DT SH

Carpathian harebells/*C. carpatica*

Dalmatian bellflower/*C. portenschlagiana*

Serbian bellflowers/*C. poscharskana*

Roving bellflower/*C. rampunculoides*

Indian paintbrush/*Castilleja integra*   DE S

Indian paintbrush/*C. chromosa, C. indivisa,*

C. linariaefolia, C. purpurea, C. rhexifolia

Sulphur buckwheat/*Eriogonum umbellatum*   DE S/PS

Eriogonum cognatum

Bladderstem/*E. inflatum*

Eriogonum stellatum

Wright buckwheat/*E. wrightii*

Blue bowls/*Gilia rigidula*   DEV S

Red rocket/*Ipomopsis aggregata*   DT

Standing cypress/*I. rubra syn. Gilia coronopifolia*   DT

Perky sue/*Hymenoxys argentea*   DE S

Stemless perky sue/*H. acaulis*

Peppergrass/*Lepidium montanum*   DE S/PS

Baby aster/*Leucelene ericoides*   DE S

Purple aster/*Machaeranthera bigelovii*

Tahoka daisy/*M. tanacetifolia*

Blue flax/*Linum lewisii*   DT S/SH

Fringed puccoon/*Lithospermum incisum*   DE S

Giant four o'clock/*Mirabilis multiflora*   DE S/SH

Angel trumpets/*M. longiflora*

Organ Mountain evening primrose/*Oenothera organensis*   DE S/PS

Missouri evening primrose/*O. missouriensis*

Hummingbird trumpet/*Zauschneria californica*

Scarlet bugler/*Penstemon barbatus* and *cultivars*   DE/DT S/SH

Cardinal penstemon/*P. cardinalis*

Firecracker penstemon/*P. eatonii*

Pineleaf penstemon/*Penstemon pinifolius*   DE/DT S/SH

Mat penstemon/*P. caespitosus*

Crandall penstemon/*P. crandallii* and *P. crandallii* spp. *teucrioides*

Linearleaf penstemon/*P. linaroides*

Rocky Mountain penstemon/*P. strictus* and *P.s.* 'Bandera'   DE/DT S/SH

Alpine penstemon/*P. alpinus*   DE/DT S/SH

Wasatch penstemon/*P. cyananthus*

Wandbloom penstemon/*P. virgatus*

Santa Fe phlox/*Phlox nana*   DE S

Chihuahuan phlox/*P. mesoleuca*

Creeping phlox/*P. subulata*

Milkwort/*Polygala alba*   DE S

Pasqueflower/*Pulsatilla ludoviciana* syn. *Anemone pulsatilla*
DEV/DT S/SH

Scarlet mint, Hedgenettle/*Stachys coccinea*   DT PS/SH

Wooly lamb's ears/*S. lanata* syn. *byzantina*

Cutleaf germander/*Teucrium laciniatum*   DT PS/SH

Greek germander/*T. aroanium*   DE S

Creeping germander/*T. chamadrys*   DT S/SH

GRASSES

Purple threeawn/*Aristida purpurea*   DE S

Sideoats grama/*Bouteloua curtipendula* and cultivars   DE S/PS

Sheep's fescue/*Festuca ovina*   DT S/SH

Blue fescue/*F. ovina* 'Glauca'

Bush muhly/*Muhlenbergia porteri*   DE S

Mountain muhly/*M. montana*

Spike muhly/*M. wrightii*

Needle-and-thread/*Stipa comata*   DE S

Threadgrass/*S. tenuissima*

Upland   Desert/Grassland   Oasis   Not Rec. for Urban Gardens   S=Sun, PS=Part-shade, SH=Shade; DR=Drought requiring, DE=Drought enduring, DEV=Drought evading, DT=Drought tolerant

5 High-Plains Grassland and Shrub-Desert Gardens

IRONICALLY, THE DRIEST ECOSYSTEMS in the Southwest today were once covered by vast inland seas. In the more recent past, at the end of the Ice Age fifteen thousand years ago, what is now high-plains grassland and shrub desert was forested with pine, juniper, and spruce. Within the last five thousand years, woodlands have retreated upslope and the area is again a vast sea, now awash in grasses, filigree desert shrubs, and persistent drought. Because its sweep is so grandly monotonous, it is easy to overlook the essential diversity of grasslands and shrub-desert ecology. Because there are so many similarities in adaptation between grasslands and shrub deserts, I have elected for landscaping purposes to include them in one broad ecological category. This complex of conditions is the most challenging in which to garden. Grassland and shrub desert plant communities offer stubborn resilience, not creature comforts. In terms of gardening, they provide some of the best models for low-input habitats, drier borders, and transition zones between outdoor living spaces and undeveloped wildlands. Building in the amenities of shade and privacy and moderating wind in order to balance human comforts with ecological realities can make prairie and desert gardens as inviting as their upland counterparts.

THE GRASSLAND/SHRUB-DESERT MOSAIC

Just as woodland changes significantly with elevation and exposure, these lower, drier ecosystems undergo subtle variations as they roll and dip across miles of open land. Though there are no hard ecological boundaries, grasslands usually begin to dominate

GRASSES ARE KEY ELEMENTS OF HIGH PLAINS AND SHRUB DESERT, IMPORTANT FUNCTIONALLY BECAUSE THEY STABILIZE THE SOIL AND VISUALLY BECAUSE OF THEIR TEXTURES. BURROGRASS GLOWS SILVER-PINK AFTER SUMMER RAINS.

103

THE NORTH-FACING SLOPES AND BOTTOMS OF DESERT CANYONS ARE ALMOST ALWAYS MARKEDLY GREENER THAN THE HILLTOPS AND SOUTHWESTERN EXPOSURES.

ROCK OUTCROPPINGS TRAP EXTRA MOISTURE, AND THE PLANTS GROWING IN THEIR COMPANY ARE MORE LUXURIANT THAN THE SURROUNDING VEGETATION.

between four thousand and sixty-five hundred feet. Relatively moist northern high plains may exceed fifteen inches of rain and snow annually. Further south, where grassland merges into shrub desert, only six or eight inches of rain may fall. Shade is rare and the wind is relentless. The extent that high evaporation rates determine growing conditions cannot be overstated. Plants adapt by assuming compact growth habits and fine-textured or waxy, resinous leaves. Grass blades roll up, reducing their evaporative surfaces in times of drought. Where conditions are particularly harsh, trees and shrubs may abandon leaves entirely and photosynthesize in their narrow green stems. The life cycles of some wildflowers coincide with the rainy season: no rain, no flowers. Always the root systems penetrate deeply, and often the wispy top growth is scant evidence of the root mass that supports it.

Soils vary greatly, from silty clay sediments in swales and basin floors to deep clay or sandy loams on the plains to gravelly hilltops and rocky ledges and escarpments. Dense stands of prairie grasses or bigleaf sage usually indicate deep friable soils. Creosotebush is an indicator of an underlying hardpan. Feather dalea is found in gravelly soils, but broom dalea only occurs in deep sand. Given the harshness of the environment, choosing plants that prefer the existing soil makes more sense than struggling to maintain ill-adapted cultivars. Expanding upon the natural order is more rewarding than trying to impose an order when nature has other priorities.

On the higher, wetter plains, the density of grasses creates intense competition for resources, resulting in drought by close association. While ninety percent of the plant community may be made up of grasses, many different grass species occur within a relatively small area. Depending on exposure, soil type, and precipitation, the grass community will vary: sideoats grama, needle-and-thread, and purple threeawn are

LAVA FLOWS AND VOLCANIC UPTHRUSTS ARE OTHER PLACES TO FIND THE DIVERSITY ASSOCIATED WITH WATER CATCHMENTS.

JUST AS DESERT *ARROYOS* ARE INTERESTING TRAILS TO FOLLOW IN DRY WEATHER, DRY STREAMBEDS MAKE INVITING PATHWAYS IN DRYLAND GARDENS.

often found on slopes, little bluestem or tobosa in swales. Blue grama, dominant in the shortgrass prairie, is replaced by black grama in the drier shrub desert. For the most part these are warm-season bunchgrasses that begin growth as the soils heat up in spring, may go dormant if moisture is not available during the hottest weeks of summer, and respond quickly to monsoon rains with surprisingly lush growth. Late summer and autumn is the easiest time to try to sort out the complex of grass species. The resplendent flower spikes and seed heads of native grasses are their most distinctive features: the eyebrowlike flags of blue grama; the fuzzy white spikes of Arizona cottontop and sand and silver bluestems; the rosy haze of bush muhly; the lacy amber fountains of sand lovegrass; and the russet fluff of little bluestem. Of the wildflowers associated with high-plains grasses, many are long-lived perennials, such as gayfeather and prairieclover, with root systems comparable to those of shrubs. Their woody or succulent taproots and dense networks of wiry fibrous roots enable these plants to hold their own against the competitive grasses. Wildflowers may be found in great sweeps, seeming to appear suddenly out of nowhere to outshine the grasses for the limited time they bloom, or they may colonize particular niches in swales or on rocky outcrops. Shrubs that occur in grasslands follow similar patterns, occupying areas that are either somewhat wetter or drier where the competition from grasses is less intense

and their individual adaptations give them an edge. We might take a cue from nature when planning our gardens, using a mix of prairie grasses as the overall cover and introducing clusters of shrubs and drifts of wildflowers where, according to their preferences, they are most likely to thrive. Aside from the practical advantage of better growth with less care, there is an easy grace to such places. Groups of shrubs and wildflowers planted in natural patterns have greater visual impact than individual specimens do. Wildflower species selected for seasonal color also can be deadheaded more easily to produce a second flush of blooming or to keep the planting tidy.

Much of the life of the grasslands takes place near or below the ground. Burrowing mammals don't discriminate between the succulent roots of favorite wildflowers and the grubs we find expendable. While they are considered pests in the garden, they perform a task of ecological importance by aerating prairie soil. Without their localized disturbance in these densely populated plant communities, the grasses would decline in vigor and little space would be available for annuals such as sunflowers to colonize and produce crops of nutritious oily seeds to support overwintering birds. The birds, in turn, distribute seeds via passage through their digestive tracts, where they are primed for germination by enzymes that break down impervious seed coats and encase the embryos in a nutrient-rich carrier. Insect activity is also abundant in this ecosystem. The flutter of pollinating moths and butterflies adds to the tapestry of color, while beetles and ants, grasshoppers and crickets contribute to the ecological balance less conspicuously. Their numbers ebb and flow with rainfall and the corresponding variations in plant density. With decreasing precipitation and increasing temperatures, there is a noticeable thinning of plant cover. Shrubs dominate true deserts, places where the evaporation rate is greater than the average precipitation. In addition to the leaf and stem adaptations already mentioned, shrubs are able to store moisture in their tissues. Widely spaced desert shrubs not only have a larger soil area to mine for water and nutrients but additional moisture also condenses on them at night. They harvest water out of thin air. Some grasses that cohabit with dryland shrubs, such as tobosa and burrograss, colonize the basins where water occasionally accumulates. Others, such as the dropseeds and Indian ricegrass, are among the most heat and drought loving. Thready and compact survivors such as bush muhly, black grama, and fluffgrass, round out the list. Often the living ground cover is an extremely efficient but inconspicuous colony of cyanobacteria, a form of blue-green algae related to mosses and lichens that forms a cryptogamic crust on the soil. Cryptogamic soil looks like a thin coating of black dust when the cyanobacteria are dormant. After summer rains the soil is suddenly covered with a rich dark green velvety film resembling moss. The role of cryptogamic crusts in desert ecology is just beginning to be appreciated. The crust is actually a mass of delicate filaments that extends several inches below the surface and absorbs moisture like a sponge. The filaments knit the soil together, helping to resist erosion and fix nitrogen from the air in a form usable by surrounding plants. When this paradoxically tough yet fragile crust is broken by vehicle or foot traffic, dune buggies, dirt bikes, hikers, cattle, or jackrabbits, a highly erodible scar is left in an otherwise stable ecology.

When moisture comes at the right time in the desert, there are many annual and biennial wildflowers that quickly fill in the gaps in the open soil. Annual "weeds" that appear after disturbance might include desert marigolds, spectacle pod, phlox heliotrope, purple mat, and palifoxia, all highly desirable wildflowers, as well as tumbleweeds, puncture vine, and ambrosia. Perennial wildflowers tend to be shrubby and taprooted, spectacular when moisture is available, inconspicuous when times are hard. Most desert wildflowers *require* drought. When planted in a garden, a little extra water is needed to get them started, but too much water, especially in organically amended soil, weakens them, sometimes fatally. Even when the plants are well adapted to local conditions, the difficulty in gardening in the desert is getting the young plants established when sand-laden winds scour the seedlings and life-sustaining water evaporates so quickly. Once the plants are well rooted, limiting watering to just the little needed to sustain flowering will usually make noxious weeds a minor management concern. In this and other ways, the gardening strategies outlined for the uplands apply to high-plains grasslands and shrub deserts. The difference is one of degree: the warmer it is, the more moisture is lost to evaporation. The drier and more exposed the soil is, the more easily it will erode.

Looking out across *playas* and *mesas*, it's easy to imagine that we are looking at the unadorned skeleton of the earth. Precious trees are rare in grasslands and shrub desert, found only in low catchment basins or arroyos that carry snowmelt from the uplands and storm runoff toward the few perennial rivers that cut through these dry environments like seams in a grassy cloak. Arroyo plant communities have great garden potential. Owing to the occasional wealth of water and the wind protection offered by sheltering hills and arroyo walls, plant diversity is greater than that of the surrounding drylands. Small trees provide dappled shade, and relatively dense stands of shrubs stabilize the soil. Plants growing within the drainage channels filter silt from floodwaters, slowing the flow and limiting erosion. In the garden, runoff from roof surfaces and hard paving can be channelled into dry streambeds and used to supplement plants that, in turn, stabilize the soil. Dry streambed arroyos are exciting landscape design devices. They can serve as meandering pathways during dry seasons, and occasionally surprise us with the drama of flowing water. While the grand, sweeping proportions of high-plains grassland and shrub desert are models for treating large landscape areas, arroyo ecosystems are limited in scale compared with the

THE APD XERISCAPE GARDEN WAS DESIGNED AROUND A REMNANT OF THE NATIVE-GRASS PRAIRIE THAT COVERED MUCH OF WHAT IS NOW THE CITY OF ALBUQUERQUE. GIANT FOUR O'CLOCK AND PIÑON WERE ADDED FOR SUMMER COLOR AND WINTER FOLIAGE. CM

THE PATH OF STABILIZED CRUSHER FINES PREVENTS IRRIGATION WATER FROM RUNNING OFF INTO THE STREET, IS WHEELCHAIR ACCESSIBLE, AND ACTS AS A LOW-IMPACT SURFACE FOR JOGGERS WHO RUN THE GARDEN PERIMETERS.

surrounding prairie or desert and can serve as models for the intimate living spaces in dryland gardens. Since walls and paving create heat islands in a landscape, it makes sense to treat our outdoor living spaces and paved approaches to them as arroyo oases. Small dryland trees such as hop tree, redbud, or New Mexico olive in the coldest areas, desert willow where winter lows are above zero degrees F, and acacias, honey mesquite, or palo verde where winters are more moderate, can be grouped to shade patios and entryways. Wide gaps can be left between flagstones and other pavers and planted with desert zinnia, purple groundcherry, lippia, thyme, pussy toes, or veronica to buffer the glare and reduce the heat buildup. The hotter the microclimate, the better it is to keep the underplanting low to allow breezes to circulate under the tree canopy.

GRASSLAND STRATEGIES: CREATING COMFORT ZONES

One of Albuquerque's newer public gardens is a departure from typical park development. The small water-conservative park was created on a site covered with a strong and diverse stand of native grasses, a fragment of the original Albuquerque short-grass prairie now surrounded by homes, offices, and sports facilities. Without much discussion, our team of volunteer planners, landscape architects, and designers determined that grassland ecology would be the focus for what is now the Albuquerque Police Department Xeriscape Garden. Several goals were outlined. With a sampling of the many native and a few adaptive grasses we hoped to inspire a new appreciation for grasses as ground covers and accent plants. We wanted to break the lawn and foundation planting mold, but given its urban surroundings the garden had to be horticulturally as well as ecologically sound. We also wanted to make a place that people would enjoy visiting, with shaded sitting areas buffered from nearby street traffic and a diverse community of plants for color, fragrance, and texture. The park also had to be accessible to as many people as possible, including the neighborhood joggers who had worn a track around the site perimeter when it was a vacant lot. In all, we wanted it to be a comfort zone, a relaxing and familiar garden and a new look at what urbanity has all but displaced.

As the plan developed, the remnant prairie, a mix of black grama, blue grama, sideoats grama, galleta, purple threeawn, fluffgrass and Indian ricegrass, remained in place as the core of the garden, although reduced in size by several unfortunate disturbances while the planning was in progress. A path of soil cement, a mix of crusher fines and stabilizer that is fairly hard but remains more resilient and permeable than concrete, rings the garden as a more formalized version of the original jogging track. It also absorbs any runoff from rain or irrigation, keeping wastewater off the streets. Entering the garden from the west parking lot is a concrete walkway and ramada that will someday house a series of signs describing the xeriscape concepts that the garden demonstrates. Just ahead is a mix of wildflowers including bush penstemon, paperflower, gaillardia, desert zinnia, and evening primroses merging into the prairie; and in beds formed by the walkways, more formal plantings of wildflowers and garden perennials include cherry sage, verbenas, yarrow, and penstemons. The north arm of the path borders the prairie where desert willows and Apache plumes were planted in shallow erosion cuts and on the opposite side of the path form a mixed border with chitalpas, sumacs, chamisa, Spanish broom, and bird of paradise. The south side of the park is divided by a concrete walkway that brings visitors to a ramada that eventually will be shaded by a Chinese pistache and redbuds. A grassy knoll, a mowed-sod mix of buffalograss and blue grama, separates the sitting area from the street. A thick ground cover of unmowed blue grama flanks the mowed native lawn on the west end. An area where mowed blue grama, buffalograss, and galleta were seeded separately to show how each grass performs independently lies across the walk to the east. Blue grama seems to cover more densely and faster while the galleta has developed very slowly, allowing weeds to invade. The buffalograss is noticeably coarser than the blue grama but still fine-textured compared with tall fescue and other lawn grasses. East of the walk from the remnant prairie is a taller grass mix of species not suitable for lawn use. Mowed to four inches in winter, it begins the year as a rather innocuous green carpet.

In spring, little wild yellow asters and white daisy fleabane appear, adding an unplanned grace note early in the season. After many of the spring blooming shrubs and wildflowers have begun to fade out in the mid-June heat, the little "pocket prairie" becomes a wash of pink prairieclover. When the prairieclover fades the blue-bladed sand bluestem starts sending up its fluffy white spikes, followed in early autumn by the russet seed heads of little bluestem. The original seed mix was "contaminated" with Indiangrass, which, aside from being twice as tall as the other grasses, adds yellow and brown plumes of color in the lapse between prairieclover and sand bluestem flowering. After hard freezes, this plot turns a burnished blend of pinks and rust, persisting until winter wear determines the timing of the cleanup/mowing that readies it for spring.

Because the management of the garden would differ significantly from typical park maintenance, the design team met with Parks Management staff to learn their standard operations and discuss how we could meet their needs without sacrificing the ideals we sought to demonstrate. Considering the number of problems that can beset any pioneer activity, we feel lucky to have people tending the garden who are open to setting new standards. In retrospect, one of the things that has made the APD Xeriscape Garden so successful was making management part of the design effort.

GRASSLAND STRATEGIES: THE EDGE BETWEEN UPLANDS AND GRASSLANDS

I met Russ and Irene Howard one gray and blustery winter day on the building site of their new home and garden. They had recently transplanted themselves from the cold Great Basin desert of Reno, Nevada, to the high-plains grassland below the piñon-

THE CONCRETE WALKWAY SEPARATES INFREQUENTLY MOWED GRASS AREAS FROM THE MORE CONTROLLED FLOWER BEDS AND SHRUB BORDERS. CM

BUFFALOGRASS AND BLUE GRAMA ARE USED BOTH AS MOWED LAWN GRASSES (FOREGROUND) AND UNMOWED PRAIRE GROUND COVERS.

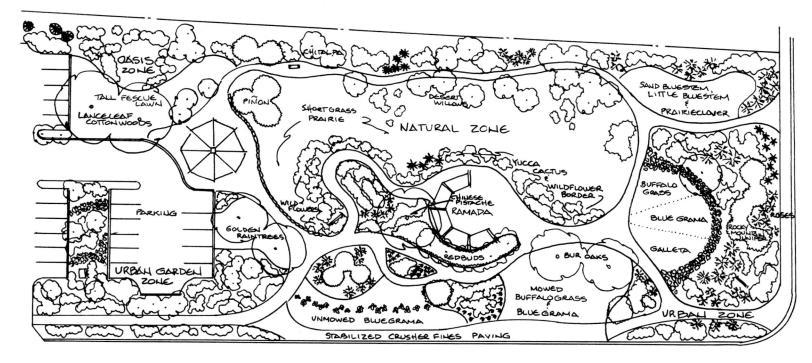

THE APD XERISCAPE GARDEN IS DESIGNED AROUND THREE DISTINCT ZONES:

URBAN GARDEN ZONE PLANTS (MODERATE WATER) INCLUDE GOLDEN RAINTREE, CHINESE PISTACHE, REDBUD, SUMMER BROOM, CHERRY SAGE, DWARF WILLOWLEAF AND GRAYLEAF COTONEASTERS, WESTERN SAND CHERRY, SILVERBERRY, RUGOSA ROSE, RED YUCCA, BLUE MIST, ENGLISH LAVENDER, 'MOONSHINE' YARROW, PINELEAF PENSTEMON, BLUE AVENA, AND 'AUTUMN JOY' SEDUM.

OASIS ZONE PLANTS (HIGH WATER) INCLUDE LANCELEAF COTTONWOOD, NEW MEXICO OLIVE, BLUE WILLOW, COYOTE WILLOW, CHOKECHERRY, FALSE INDIGO, WOODS ROSE, REDTWIG DOGWOOD, CATTAIL, TALL TURF-TYPE FESCUE, AND MAXIMILIAN SUNFLOWER.

juniper belt of the Sandia Mountains near Albuquerque. Their move to a similar ecosystem was deliberate. They enjoy the relatively cool summers of the high desert and the definite change in seasons that these areas share. Having lived in a natural setting near Reno, the Howards again preserved as much of the native vegetation as possible on their new site.

The house was designed to take advantage of panoramic views and provide two distinct outdoor living spaces. Although the house was set as far back from the street as possible, the large windows opening onto the east mountain views, with only scattered cholla cactus, short-grass prairie, and wildflowers in between, left little privacy. A gradual slope away from the street down toward the house is emphasized by a garden wall that also serves as a retaining wall, creating an entry courtyard four feet lower than the grassland it borders. A cluster of New Mexico olives was used to screen the courtyard from the neighbors to the south, feed songbirds in winter, and provide shade in summer. Threeleaf sumac and fernbush are grouped above the wall to further enclose the courtyard without blocking the view of the foothills and mountain peaks. Inside the wall, beds of wildflowers, red yuccas, and curlleaf mountain mahogany provide seasonal color and attract hummingbirds. The paving is rosy brown fine-textured gravel enlarging the concrete entry sidewalk. The porous paving allows heavy rainfalls to soak in where the plantings can absorb it rather than creating a runoff wastewater problem. Windows and a portal on the west side of the house offer a view

IN THE HOWARD GARDEN, THE MAIN ENTRANCE COURTYARD IS ENHANCED WITH CHAMISA, GAYFEATHER, PENSTEMON, AND FERNBUSH. LADY BANK'S ROSE DRAPES THE WALL SIGNALING A TRANSITION TO MORE CULTIVATED PLANTINGS. CM

of sunsets and city lights. Desert willows and chitalpas that straddle the west courtyard wall provide relief from the sun and bring hummingbirds close to the house. Silverberry and grayleaf cotoneaster provide year-round foliage interest and cover for birds in the sun, while cherry sage, lavender, woods rose, and dwarf plumbago underplanted with grape hyacinths supply brilliant seasonal flower color and fragrance in the shade of the west wall. Outside the garden walls, where the natural cover of blue grama, purple threeawn, sideoats grama, galleta, needle-and-thread, fern verbena, and white-tufted evening primrose was left intact, a few piñon, clumps of Apache plume, and threadleaf sage were added to provide roosts and cover for birds. Desert and Rocky Mountain penstemon, gayfeather, chocolate flower, prairie sage, and gaillardia add color to the grass mix.

The landscape was intended to be low maintenance, requiring a general cleanup each spring and fall. Weeding is still needed four times a summer to remove the mare's tail and tumbleweeds that colonized the disturbed areas along the driveway and where utility lines were installed. To keep them from overwhelming new plantings, naturally occurring thistles are also removed periodically from areas that are being watered regularly, but most outside the irrigated zone are left for nectar for butterflies and nesting down for goldfinches. One of the piñons that suffered in transplanting is recovering slowly with the help of light applications of fertilizer. Once established, the rest of the

NATURAL ZONE PLANTS (LOW WATER) INCLUDE DESERT WILLOW, CHITALPA, CUTLEAF SUMAC, ROCKY MOUNTAIN JUNIPER, PIÑON, CURL-LEAF MOUNTAIN MAHOGANY, BIRD OF PARADISE, CREOSOTEBUSH, CLIFFROSE, BUSH PENSTEMON, PALM YUCCA, SOAPTREE YUCCA, SOTOL, SOAPWEED, PARRY AGAVE, FERNBUSH, SPANISH BROOM, APACHE PLUME, CHAMISA, PROS-TRATE SUMAC, THREELEAF SUMAC, PAPERFLOWER, ROCKY MOUNTAIN PENSTEMON, VERBENA, BLANKET FLOWER, CHOCOLATE FLOWER, GAYFEATHER, DESERT ZINNIA, WHITE-TUFTED EVENING PRIMROSE, GIANT FOUR O'CLOCK, PALMER PEN-STEMON, DESERT PENSTEMON, BLUE FLAX, CONEFLOWER, BUFFALO-GRASS, BLUE GRAMA, LITTLE BLUESTEM, SIDEOATS GRAMA, SAND BLUESTEM, AND GALLETA.

plantings have not needed supplemental feeding. Irene also takes several hours a week in spring and summer to deadhead spent flowers, wash aphids off soft new growth, and check on the progress of new transplants and volunteer seedlings. New plants are protected until they have developed enough to outgrow rabbit browsing. Irene is one of the few gardeners I know whose sympathies lie with the cottontails. She is apt to spend a few hours a day working in her garden. Some of this tending is needed to produce the more refined look she prefers, but some of the time spent simply satisfies a personal love of gardening, being part of the process from seed to nectar to seed again.

Russ oversees the drip system that runs a weekly ninety-nine-minute cycle from April through October and monthly from November through March. Emitter output varies from one gallon per hour to four gallons per hour depending on the size and needs of individual plants. In retrospect, a more elaborate system with three separate lines may have been more appropriate: one for the native trees and shrubs, which would be run longer and less often; one for the adaptive shrubs so that they could be watered deeply but more often than the natives; and one for the wildflowers, which need water most often in summer and currently determine the frequency of the entire watering schedule. It wasn't until the third growing season after most of the planting was done that the landscape began to meet its gardeners' expectations. Time, additions of wild-flowers from gardening friends, and anonymous donations of seeds left by visiting wildlife have resulted in an increasingly complex landscape that becomes more interesting and enjoyable as it matures.

GRASSLAND STRATEGIES: GARDENS AND PERSONAL GROWTH

To landscape her home in the Southwest, Maggi Caffo had to rethink much of what she learned in her Maryland gardens. She began her first high-plains garden with the advantage of an open mind and the desire to develop a native garden that reflected her new surroundings. Unfamiliar with local plants, she was forced to grow along with her garden. She built her garden on intuition, observations she made while walking open-space areas near her home, information gleaned from reading and talking to other gardeners, and plants salvaged from neighborhood construction sites and purchased from local native-plant nurseries.

After six years Maggi finally considers her garden finished, but only because she and her husband are building a new home nearby and she has a clean slate to begin working on. Long before the house plans were complete, Maggi was assessing the successes and shortcomings of the old garden as a first step in planning the new one. "I overplanted and didn't pay enough attention to how the plants look in winter." (Easy to do in grassland where individual plants are often rather nondescript, their collective sweep being their splendor.) The old garden focused on large perennial beds overflowing with an ever-broadening collection of wildflowers. The flowers are left to go to seed to attract birds to the garden. The garden is a wash of color from May to November and attracts a variety of birds, but seasonal thinning of volunteer seedlings and trimming of dried seed stalks are major chores that involve working over the whole garden several times each year. In addition, Maggi works about two hours each week in the garden "to not get behind too much." Watering has been on an as-needed basis. About half the plants need deep watering weekly during hot weather to bloom profusely.

Gardening near the mouth of a canyon has meant learning to cope with powerful east winds. "One thing we found is that no matter how awful the winds are, the local native plants are just fine. They are truly amazing to live with, water thrifty with glorious flowers in the hottest garden!" says Maggi.

Devoting more of the garden space at the new house to native trees and flowering shrubs, some with evergreen leaves, interesting stem color, or dried seed heads in winter, will provide more habitat by layering the canopy and will limit the cleanup to smaller wildflower areas. Maggi now has the advantage of hundreds of hours of intensive high-plains ecology study in her garden and hiking in natural areas to draw on in selecting plants for the new garden. "No rabbitbrush where it would get much water" was an early lesson. That Spanish broom supports a hearty population of aphids was another. As the walls of the new house rise above their foundations, the new garden takes shape on paper. It won't be long before Russian sage and mountain mahogany, fernbush and cliffrose, fendlerbush, blue fescue, and an array of penstemons, chocolate flower, and perhaps a few cotoneaster are the new kids on the block.

SHRUB-DESERT STRATEGIES: LESS WORK, MORE TIME TO PLAY

After so many years as landscape designer, I was pretty smug about having seen or heard it all. When Byron Garner asked me to design his backyard around a scale model railroad, that delusion evaporated like rain in the desert. He graciously supplied me with magazines that offered all kinds of hands-on information. A native of the south-

THE RENOVATION OF THE FRONT BEGAN WITH REMOVAL OF A BLUE-GRASS LAWN AND ASH TREE. THE RUSSIAN OLIVE, WOODBINE, PIÑON, AND MUGO PINE REMAINED. NEW MEXICO OLIVE, APACHE PLUME, SILVER GROUNDSEL, SOAPWEED YUCCA, PRICKLY PEAR, GOLDEN ASTER, AND BLUE SPURGE ADD SEASONAL COLOR, TEXTURE, AND BIRDSEED.

WILDFLOWERS BLOOM PROLIFICALLY AND ARE LEFT TO PRODUCE SEEDS. THE BEDS REQUIRE REPEATED REMOVAL OF DRIED SEED STALKS FOR TIDINESS.

113

THREADLEAF SAGE (FOREGROUND) AND
BROOM DALEA ARE TRUE NATIVES IN
THIS GARDEN. ORIGINALLY THE BUF-
FALOGRASS AND BLUE GRAMA WERE
INTENDED TO BE A MOWED LAWN BUT
THEIR SOFT ROLLING TEXTURE HAS
KEPT MOWING TO A MINIMUM. TOP CM

eastern U.S., he wanted southwestern native plants as the core of the garden. Byron seemed more concerned with the problem of growing plants on the sand dunes that came with the house (and into the house with every gust of wind), and with having the landscape be low maintenance than he was about the design elements. That, after all, was why he hired a professional. He wanted a plan that he could build himself, along with the hundreds of hand-milled railroad ties and trestle timbers and the locomotive engine that would be assembled as a functioning railroad.

The front yard needed to blend into a neighborhood of bluegrass lawns or gravel-scapes, and a three-foot slope in fifteen feet of horizontal space made runoff a problem. The postage-stamp-size, blue grama lawn covers the most level area, and any runoff drains across the sidewalk into New Mexico olives in the parkway that will offer some shade and provide a complement to the proportions of the house without undermining the pavement or producing a lot of leaf litter. The shrub border includes piñon, silver-berry, and cotoneasters as evergreens, chamisa and red yucca, Apache plume, threadleaf sage, English lavender, and a broom dalea that grew back from roots left after total site upheaval during construction. Desert zinnia, globemallow, and Mexican evening primroses were added for more flower color. Although a half-and-half mix of buffalograss and blue grama was seeded, the blue grama has become dominant. Since Byron likes the soft rolling texture of the grass unmowed, what was intended as a token lawn has become ground cover.

The steep slopes in the backyard were retained minimally with boulders, used mostly to form the pathway to an upper deck, and accented with bush penstemon, narrowleaf penstemon, blue spurge, and Indian ricegrass. Threadleaf sage and broom dalea were added to bolster the stand of those that grew back after construction, with bush morningglory and dune broom added as soil stabilizers and for their color or tex-ture. Cliffrose, chamisa, vitex, and 'Hillspire' junipers were planted for screening along the south-facing garden wall and curlleaf mountain mahogany along the two-story north-facing wall. Cherry sage and chocolate flower provide a long season of color, and plants with small leaves and compact forms such as rosemary, fringed sage, desert zinnia, pineleaf penstemon, and blue fescue were used to landscape the railroad right-of-way.

Maintenance involves very occasional weeding and pruning, taking an average of one hour monthly. There has been no need for fertilizer or pest control. Watering is done with a drip system programmed to water a half-hour three days a week or an hour once a week. Emitter rates vary from one-half gallon to two gallons per hour. Like the Howards, Byron would opt to have more zones so that he could control better and not have to overwater some plants to meet the greater needs of others. What seems cost-effective at construction time sometimes proves inefficient over the long term. Although forty-five species of plants seem like a diverse plant community on seven thousand square feet of planting space, every year a few new species are added "for variety and interest." He offers words of wisdom to do-it-yourselfers: "I would suggest hiring help for the heavier and more labor-intensive work—the stone setting, path building, and ground sculpting." Derailed by laborious garden construction, it took Byron longer to get his train running down the track.

SHRUB-DESERT STRATEGIES: SAND, WIND, AND COMMITMENT

Anticipating the move from the Chicago area to central New Mexico, Gloria and Deneb Teleki began their search for an architect, building contractor, and landscape designer when they found a site that swept them off their feet: a 270-degree panorama of mountains, river valley, and shrub desert. Building a home and garden that reflected that quiet grandeur was foremost in their planning. They were leaving a deeply shaded woodland garden where lack of light limited plant diversity and an abundance of rainfall supported lush growth. They could have relocated to the moon and not been much further afield than on their new site. They approached me with a well-considered list of preferences and concerns, including the desire for an abundance of colorful flowers. Deneb's agronomy background made him well aware of the impact of climate on plants, and Gloria's regard for regional style prompted her to think native. Sometimes it seems the only real common denominator that characterizes the diverse group of individuals that I am fortunate to work with is their remarkable common sense, which isn't nearly as common among the general population as it ought to be.

Because the Telekis were developing what they hope will be the home and garden that they spend the rest of their lives enjoying, and because they both suffer physical limitations that will grow more restrictive over the long term, access to and through the garden was a primary concern. Preserving the views while providing privacy, buffering the wind, and merging the walled garden with the desert beyond were other priorities. Though the list of favorite plants they hoped to find a place for in their new garden was limited to lilies, peonies, spring bulbs, a few fruit trees, and echinacea specifically, their general wish list included lots of diversity: plants to attract birds, plants for color, texture, and seasonal interest, and, most importantly, plants that are well adapted. Given the nature of the site, a generous plot of blow sand atop an escarpment peninsula open to winds from every direction, native and adaptive plants made perfect sense.

The final materials and specifications list included ninety-nine plant species, forty-seven of them native. The numbers of individuals plants per species varied, but in some cases the initial quantities of the nonnative species were bolstered to cover losses within their ranks during the early period of establishment even though they were carefully chosen and many were placed in more protected niches created by the house and garden walls. Hard-paved walkways approach the front entrance, lead to garden gates,

PROPORTIONS ARE IMPORTANT IN ANY LANDSCAPE, BUT IN THIS PART OF THE GARDEN THE SCALE IS SET BY A MODEL RAILROAD.

IN THE PROTECTION OF A *LATILLA* FENCE STAINED TO MATCH THE WOOD TRIM OF THE HOUSE, CHERRY SAGE, PURPLE CONEFLOWER, MORNINGGLORY, AND YELLOW ICEPLANT ARE AN OASIS OF COLOR. CM

GRAVEL-LINED DRAINAGE SWALES CARRY RUNOFF FROM THE ROOF AND PAVING TO BASINS WHERE DESERT WILLOW, DWARF BUTTERFLYBUSH, BUSH PENSTEMON, CHOCOLATE FLOWER, AND EVENING PRIMROSE FLOURISH. CM

and meander through the large back and side gardens, creating a series of large planting beds and islands. Although the site is fairly flat in contour, the minor changes in elevation are made with ramps rather than steps, and a fine exposed aggregate surface reduces glare and improves traction. Because of the amount of paving, thirty-one trees of fourteen species, including Chinese pistache, smoketree, crabapples, and desert willows, were planted to shade the walkways. Bristlecone, border, and piñon pines, two species of juniper, Oklahoma redbud, and a heritage apricot grown in a village nearby since early pioneer days shade the walls, reducing the reflected heat. Small blue grama and buffalograss lawns extend off the portal to stabilize the sand and provide a green foreground for the shrub and flower borders. All the planted areas except for a cactus garden and planting of broom dalea and threadleaf sage that mirrors the desert beyond the wall are heavily mulched to conserve soil moisture, reduce heat and glare, and stifle weeds. Gravel-lined drainage swales carry runoff from the roof and paving to basins where shrubs and wildflowers flourish. Shredded bark covers the rest of the beds, and a polypropylene silt fence (similar to snow fencing in northern climates) borders the unwalled front garden to keep the sand from neighboring building sites that have been scraped bare of vegetation from burying the mulch and plantings. On some spring afternoons, inches of sand crest across the driveway. One dune reached eighteen inches before the wind subsided. Tumbleweed-laden sand blown into the mulches has increased the early weed problem. Once all the lots are built on and landscaped, the marching dunes will be relegated to the file of gardening stories that are as amusing in retrospect as they are horrifying to witness.

"Under extreme conditions, natives do better," say the Telekis. "Sand-laden winds have taken their toll on the pantywaists," shredding the leaves of some of the adaptive plants, even those protected by walls. Even the natives took their licks. The lawns had to be reseeded twice due to the combined misfortunes of weather and inexperience on the part of the landscape contractor. The prickly poppy has never become established, despite several seeding and planting attempts, because greedy doves and quail unearth the seeds and finish off any sprouts that manage to emerge. While rabbits are walled out of the back garden, quail have systematically reduced to stubble the yellow iceplant. The desert penstemon refuses to grow where it's wanted even though the drainage is excellent, the exposure is typical of its natural preferences, and the appropriate gods have been petitioned. There's no reason for it to fail except that the color would be perfect against the blue-gray coyote fence. Aspiring to perfection is probably the operative curse.

"This garden has been a commitment," the Telekis concur, "and everything will not do well. You can plant three identical-looking plants and they each develop at different rates." There are many more birds and fewer insect problems here than in their Illinois garden. Cyclical booms of grasshoppers and flea beetles have been tolerated until damage levels became too high. Populations were then reduced with biological controls. Aphids are being controlled systemically on the roses and ignored or washed off the red yucca bloom stalks. The bark mulch may be providing habitat for centipedes, spiders, and scorpions. Some chemical pesticides are also used. Aside from gluttonous hordes of doves and quail, killdeer nest in one of the drainage basins, road-runners entertain with their antics, kestrels soar overhead, and many songbirds visit seasonally. As the tree canopy develops and the shrubs fill in, the layers of habitat will invite more diversity.

In a garden this large and complex, an irrigation system is necessary. The first year, while learning the plants, a few were lost to overwatering. After the first winter, thirty of the six hundred drip emitters were not working, but the next spring only three were plugged. The site has become more stable. The drip schedule varies as plants need it, but one four-hour cycle per week in summer and one three-hour cycle per month in winter is typical. Emitter outputs vary from a half-gallon per hour to six gallons per hour depending on plant needs. Fertilizing is also done on an as-needed basis. The lawns are top-dressed with compost in spring and mowed three times during the grow-ing season. Iron supplements were needed on many plants while they were being watered more heavily.

The Telekis spend a great deal of time in their garden "being aware, observing things." It is hard to separate time spent actively pulling a few tumbleweeds and squashing a few aphids, checking emitters, and snipping suckers off the young trees from time spent monitoring the development of seedings and gauging the need to water. Quiet time spent learning to read the landscape is personally rewarding and guarantees the long-term success of the garden. As the plant communities develop, the mainte-nance needs change. Tumbleweeds are the only seedlings to automatically go. Volunteer seedlings of blue spurge, chocolate flower, valerian, silver groundsel, Apache plume, blue flax, and ricegrass are beginning to colonize. The prairie sage, desert zinnia, and Mexican evening primrose are spreading by rhizomes. Spectacle pod, vetch, and purple aster have moved in from the surrounding desert. Can desert marigold and phlox heliotrope be far behind? For now, the volunteers are being left to find niches, but their enthusiasm may need to be controlled eventually. Hiring competent help who under-stand naturalized garden management is a challenge. Most landscape maintenance companies control growth by mowing and pruning, weed out everything not intentionally planted, and use poisons to control insects. Finding people willing to balance growth by adjusting emitter output and selectively thinning and deadheading, and balance pests with biological controls, reserving chemical pesticides only as a last resort, has been a sometimes frustrating, always enlightening challenge. Ideally, it has enlightened a few

EXPOSED AGGREGATE WALKWAYS DIVIDE THE GARDEN INTO LARGE PLANTING BEDS. SMALL NATIVE-GRASS LAWN AREAS EXTEND THE PORTAL SPACE. PLANTINGS CLOSEST TO THE GARDEN WALL ARE MOST DROUGHT TOLERANT AND NATIVE SPECIES PROVIDE A TRANSITION TO THE SURROUNDING DESERT. CM

of the maintenance people who didn't make the grade as well. Someday being on the cutting edge of horticulture may not involve sharp shears and a lawn mower. Sharp eyes and minds can be much easier on the ecosystem.

SHRUB-DESERT STRATEGIES: WILD, YET WELCOMING

My own garden is a laboratory. Ideas too outlandish or uncertain in outcome to expect anyone else to cooperate with find expression here. I wasn't always so adventuresome. Success has fed the fire. When my husband, Roland, and I settled on a plot of shrub desert miles from any city fifteen years ago, we relished the isolation, quite unaware of any ecological implications. We planted fruit trees and lilacs, spirea and honeysuckle, daylilies, delphiniums, ajuga, asters, and many other tried-and-true, "easy-to-grow" landscape ornamentals. Of the plants we brought with us initially, all but the Scot's pine and junipers, yucca, and crabapple failed within the first few years; most died the first summer. Considering that our intention was to develop a plant nursery, these initial losses were downright depressing. Defining disaster as a learning experience is an effective way of coping until time and discretion can numb the growing pains. I can't say exactly when blue-gray and sage green became my preferences in leaf color or when a bit of open space stopped demanding that I fill it in with something growing, but now I am at home in the desert, in harmony with this harsh and demanding environment. Visitors to our garden, too much an amalgam of experiments and evolving ideas to be a self-conscious showplace, have described it as peaceful, beautiful, and a great place to grow up. Horticulturally, this is where I came of age.

We were lucky not to have access to heavy equipment at the outset, so all our land clearing had to be done with a shovel, rake, and personal fortitude. We only removed the native cover where buildings, paths, and the driveway forced us to do so. New plants were planted in the gaps between broom dalea and threadleaf sage, plants I later learned were nitrogen-fixing assets in our sand. Drip tubing was likewise laid out in meandering fashion. Though many of those first plants died, they were replaced with better-adapted species that took root and, within the sweep of sage and dalea, have enriched the native plant community without displacing it. In retrospect, I now realize that we saved ourselves years of revegetation by opting to go with the flow.

The first stroke of enlightenment involved water. It quickly became apparent that no matter how much I poured onto the plants, more evaporated and was transpired than was absorbed by the plants. One afternoon I watched a dust devil lift my cold frame, the only protection my tender seedlings had, way up in the sky, where it blew apart, scattering bits of lumber and fiberglass a hundred yards in every direction. I felt like Dorothy on the way to Oz, only openness, heat, and wind were my nemeses. We began to plant windbreaks. Friends living along the river offered us Russian olives free for the digging. While we have come to regard them as our first big mistake, they have

ROCK SAGE, CHAMISA, PIÑON, AND PROSTRATE SUMAC DIVERSIFY THE SAGE, DALEA, AND DROPSEED THEME THAT IS DOMINANT IN THE DESERT ECOSYSTEM. CM

provided nectar for bees, fruit and nesting sites for many birds, and roosts for both brewer's blackbirds and the sharp-shinned hawk that has moved in to prey on them. As garden trees they are messy, always shedding leaves or flowers or fruit or twigs. As desert trees they are pathetic. Adapted to life on relatively moist floodplains, they are shallowly rooted and suffer from bacterial infections caused by heat stress and prolonged drought. Given enough water they are fast growing, but their weak young branches break up in windstorms. Benefitting from their protection, our first desert willows and New Mexico olives began to grow, followed by soapberries and hoptrees, rose locust (another mistake), several species and cultivars of juniper, Arizona cypress, and, just recently, Texas ash and red oaks, cork oaks, chitalpas, Afghan pines (still another mistake?), and incense cedar. We now have a few roses, species types, such as Lady Banks, on a trellis against a north-facing wall, and rugosas, as well as the native Apache plume, fernbush, and cliffrose. Our fruit trees are jujubes; our snapdragons are all penstemons. For spring-flowering shrubs we have fendlerbush and Utah serviceberry, in summer flamebush, blue mist, and vitex. For fragrance we kept the locally abundant broom dalea and sage that are the strong threads holding the ecological tapestry together.

Our second stroke of luck or enlightenment was in planting the trees in clusters so that groupings of trees and shrubs would create enclosed spaces to harbor nursery plants. Rather than one tall and wide windbreak, we have a honeycomb of outdoor

PLANTING GROVES OF SMALL TREES CREATES A HONEYCOMB OF CALMER OUTDOOR ROOMS ON THE WILDSWEPT NORTHERN CHIHUAHUAN PLAIN.

rooms, some shady, others more open. This gives local wildlife a host of niches to live in and hunt from. The need for pest control has steadily declined as the ease in establishing new plants has increased. Even the rabbits and quail have too much to choose from to do serious damage to anything. We haven't created a garden so much as become the respectful guardians of the native landscape. Who has tamed whom is debatable, but all of us who live here seem to be prospering from the experience.

GRASSLAND AND SHRUB-DESERT PLANTS

The common thread among shrub-desert and grassland plants is their threadiness. Their small and finely dissected leaves lose less moisture in the heat. Their narrow, supple stems are wind resilient. One of the amenities desert-grassland gardens need most is cooling shade, but few trees grace this ecosystem complex. The uplands are the best place to look for small trees that will adapt here. Trees that root deeply to gain a foothold on slopes will tap more soil area for moisture than will trees evolved along streams where water is shallow and plentiful. Still, you will find a few trees among the oasis natives (see chapter 6) that are modest in their demands and will root deeply in search of water if they are initially established by deep watering. Most of the drought-requiring plants, those that resent too much water too often, are desert-grassland natives. Sometimes slow to start because they spend their youth building a massive root system to support their flowering, over time these plants will command your utmost respect. Complete profiles are found in the companion volume, *Plants for Natural Gardens*, for the plants listed here.

Grassland and Shrub-Desert Plants

Upland

Desert/Grassland

Oasis

Not Rec. for Urban Gardens   S=Sun, PS=Part-shade, SH=Shade; DR=Drought requiring, DE=Drought enduring, DEV=Drought evading, DT=Drought tolerant

TREES

 Desert willow/*Chilopsis linearis* and cultivars **DE S**

Chitalpa/X *Chitalpa tashkentensis* and cultivars

Honey mesquite/*Prosopis juliflora* var. *glandulosa* **DE S**

Soaptree, Palmilla/*Yucca elata* **DR S**

Joshua tree/*Y. brevifolia*

Palm yucca/*Y. faxoniana*

SHRUBS

 Beebrush, Oreganillo/*Aloysia wrightii* **DE S**

 Leadplant/*Amorpha canescens* **DE S/PS**

Dwarf leadplant/*A. nana*

Desert honeysuckle/*Anisacanthus thurberii* **DE S**

Threadleaf sage, Sand sage/*Artemisia filifolia* **DR/DE S**

Silver spreader/*A. caucasica*

Fringed sage/*A. frigida*

Silvermound/*A. schmidtiana*

 Fourwing saltbush/*Atriplex canescens* **DR S**

Shadscale/*A. confertifolia*

Gardner saltbush/*A. gardneri*

Bird of paradise/*Caesalpinia gilliesii* **DR/DE S**

Sotol/*Dasylirion wheeleri* **DR S**

Red yucca/*Hesperaloe parviflora*

Narrowleaf yucca/*Yucca angustissima*

Spanish dagger/*Y. baccata*

Soapweed/*Y. glauca*

Beaked yucca/*Y. rostrata*

Thompson yucca/*Y. thompsoniana*

 Green joint fir/*Ephedra viridis* **DR/DE S**

Joint fir/*E. nevadensis, E. torryana,* and *E. trifurca*

Ocotillo/*Fouqueria splendens* **DR S**

Creosotebush/*Larrea tridentata* **DR/DE S**

 Christmas cholla, Pencil cactus/*Opuntia leptocaulis* **DR S**

Silver cholla/*O. echinocarpa*

Pencil cholla/*O. kleiniae*

Cow tongue/ *O. linguiformis*

Purple prickly pear/*O. macrocentra*

Dune broom/*Parryella filifolia* **DR S**

 Mariola/*Parthenium incanum* **DE S**

Bush penstemon, Sand penstemon/*Penstemon ambiguus* **DR S**

Thurber penstemon/*P. thurberi*

Mexican oregano, Bush mint/*Poliomintha incana* **DR/DE S**

 Western sand cherry/*Prunus besseyi* **DE S/PS**

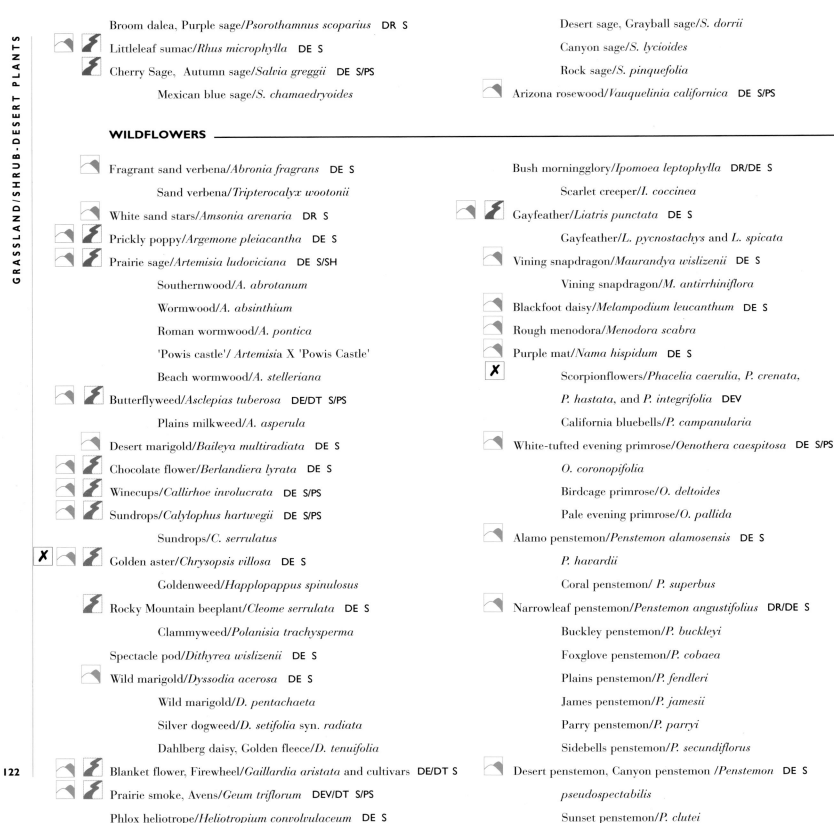

Broom dalea, Purple sage/*Psorothamnus scoparius* DR S

Littleleaf sumac/*Rhus microphylla* DE S

Cherry Sage, Autumn sage/*Salvia greggii* DE S/PS

Mexican blue sage/*S. chamaedryoides*

Desert sage, Grayball sage/*S. dorrii*

Canyon sage/*S. lycioides*

Rock sage/*S. pinquefolia*

Arizona rosewood/*Vauquelinia californica* DE S/PS

WILDFLOWERS

Fragrant sand verbena/*Abronia fragrans* DE S

Sand verbena/*Tripterocalyx wootonii*

White sand stars/*Amsonia arenaria* DR S

Prickly poppy/*Argemone pleiacantha* DE S

Prairie sage/*Artemisia ludoviciana* DE S/SH

Southernwood/*A. abrotanum*

Wormwood/*A. absinthium*

Roman wormwood/*A. pontica*

'Powis castle'/ *Artemisia* X 'Powis Castle'

Beach wormwood/*A. stelleriana*

Butterflyweed/*Asclepias tuberosa* DE/DT S/PS

Plains milkweed/*A. asperula*

Desert marigold/*Baileya multiradiata* DE S

Chocolate flower/*Berlandiera lyrata* DE S

Winecups/*Callirhoe involucrata* DE S/PS

Sundrops/*Calylophus hartwegii* DE S/PS

Sundrops/*C. serrulatus*

Golden aster/*Chrysopsis villosa* DE S

Goldenweed/*Happlopappus spinulosus*

Rocky Mountain beeplant/*Cleome serrulata* DE S

Clammyweed/*Polanisia trachysperma*

Spectacle pod/*Dithyrea wislizenii* DE S

Wild marigold/*Dyssodia acerosa* DE S

Wild marigold/*D. pentachaeta*

Silver dogweed/*D. setifolia* syn. *radiata*

Dahlberg daisy, Golden fleece/*D. tenuifolia*

Blanket flower, Firewheel/*Gaillardia aristata* and cultivars DE/DT S

Prairie smoke, Avens/*Geum triflorum* DEV/DT S/PS

Phlox heliotrope/*Heliotropium convolvulaceum* DE S

Bush morningglory/*Ipomoea leptophylla* DR/DE S

Scarlet creeper/*I. coccinea*

Gayfeather/*Liatris punctata* DE S

Gayfeather/*L. pycnostachys* and *L. spicata*

Vining snapdragon/*Maurandya wislizenii* DE S

Vining snapdragon/*M. antirrhiniflora*

Blackfoot daisy/*Melampodium leucanthum* DE S

Rough menodora/*Menodora scabra*

Purple mat/*Nama hispidum* DE S

Scorpionflowers/*Phacelia caerulia, P. crenata,*

P. hastata, and *P. integrifolia* DEV

California bluebells/*P. campanularia*

White-tufted evening primrose/*Oenothera caespitosa* DE S/PS

O. coronopifolia

Birdcage primrose/*O. deltoides*

Pale evening primrose/*O. pallida*

Alamo penstemon/*Penstemon alamosensis* DE S

P. havardii

Coral penstemon/ *P. superbus*

Narrowleaf penstemon/*Penstemon angustifolius* DR/DE S

Buckley penstemon/*P. buckleyi*

Foxglove penstemon/*P. cobaea*

Plains penstemon/*P. fendleri*

James penstemon/*P. jamesii*

Parry penstemon/*P. parryi*

Sidebells penstemon/*P. secundiflorus*

Desert penstemon, Canyon penstemon /*Penstemon* DE S

pseudospectabilis

Sunset penstemon/*P. clutei*

Palmer penstemon/*P. palmeri*

Purple prairieclover/*Petalostemum purpureum* **DE S/PS**

White prairieclover/*P. candidum*

Purple groundcherry/*Physalis lobata* syn. *Quincula lobata* **DE S/PS**

Paperflower/*Psilostrophe tagetina* **DR/DE S**

Coneflower, Mexican hat/*Ratibida columnifera* **DE S**

Pitcher sage/*Salvia azurea grandiflora* syn. *S. pitcheri* **DE S/SH**

Mealy sage/*S. farinacea*

Cedar sage/*S. roemeriana*

'Blue Queen' and 'Rose Queen'/*Salvia X superba*

Skullcap/*Scutellaria wrightii* syn. *S. resinosa* and *S. potosina* **DE S/PS**

Moonpod/*Selinocarpus diffusus* **DR/DE S**

Red umbrellawort/*Oxybaphus coccineus*

Desert four o'clock/*O. comatus*

Silver groundsel/*Senecio longilobus* **DR/DE S**

S. multicapitata

Scarlet globemallow/*Sphaeralcea coccinea* **DE S**

Desert mallow/*S. ambigua*

Gooseberry globemallow/*S. grossulariaefolia* and *S. munroana*

Globemallow/*S. angustifolia, S. fendleri, S. incana,* and *S. subhastata*

Flameflower/*Talinum calycinum* **DE/DT S/PS**

Flameflowers/*T. angustissimum, T. aurantiacum,* and *T. longipes*

Rayed cota, Hopi tea/*Thelesperma ambigua* **DE S/PS**

Rayed cota/*T. filifolium*

Greenthread/*T. megapotamica*

Western spiderwort/*Tradescantia occidentalis* **DE/DT PS/SH**

Dayflower/*Commelina erecta*

Fern verbena/*Verbena bipinnatifida* **DE S/PS**

Prairie verbena/*V. canadensis*

Desert verbena/*V. goodingii*

Vervain/*V. macdougalii*

Moss verbena/*V. tenuisecta*

Showy goldeneye/*Viguiera multiflora* **DE S**

Skeletonleaf goldeneye/*V. stenoloba*

Crownsbeard/*Verbesina enceloides*

Desert mule's ears/*Wyetia scabra* **DR/DE S**

Mountain mule's ear/*W. amplexicaulis* and *W. arizonica*

White mountain mule's ear/*W. helianthoides*

Desert zinnia/*Zinnia grandiflora* **DE S**

White desert zinnia/*Z. acerosa*

GRASSES

Sand bluestem/*Andropogon hallii* **DE S**

Cane beardgrass/*A. barbinoides*

Silver bluestem/*A. saccharoides*

Splitbeard bluestem/*A. ternarius*

Blue grama/*Bouteloua gracilis* **DE/DT S**

Black grama/ *B. eriopoda*

Hairy grama/*B. hirsuta*

Buffalograss/*Buchloe dactyloides* **DE/DT S**

Arizona cottontop/*Digitatia* syn. *Trichachne californica* **DE S**

Sand lovegrass/*Eragrostis tricodes* **DE S/PS**

Galleta/*Hilaria jamesii* **DE S**

Tobosa/*H. mutica*

Indian ricegrass/*Oryzopsis hymenoides* **DE S**

Little bluestem/*Schizachyrium* syn. *Andropogon scoparium* **DE S**

Giant sacaton/*Sporobolus wrightii* **DE S**

Sand dropseed/*S. cryptandrus*

Mesa dropseed/*S. flexuosus*

Fluffgrass/*Tridens pulchellum* **DE S**

Hairy tridens/*T. pilosus*

Burrograss/*Scleropogon brevifolius*

6 Oasis Gardens

IT IS THE SUDDEN CHANGE OF FOCUS, an abundance of water in the desert, that makes oases so special. In a general sense, oasis ecosystems are defined as places that are wetter than their surroundings. The streams running through the high country are oases in the forest, but the lusher vegetation that higher altitudes and greater rainfall produce make them less of a contrast to their surroundings. The further downslope we venture, the more striking the difference between the moisture-rich drainageways and the drier surrounding hills becomes. On the plains and in the desert, the runoff is infrequent but enough to mark arroyos as greenbelts. For gardening purposes, I define oasis ecosystems as the low-lying water collecting and distributing areas that border the rivers of the Southwest. Because of damming for flood control, irrigation, and recreation, the riverbeds themselves may be nearly dry for extended periods of time while water is diverted for human uses. Still, the subsurface drainage into these areas has kept the water tables relatively high and supports the ribbons of lush green forests.

THE OASIS MOSAIC

It is hard to find any truly natural bosque ecosystems to use as models because people have been drawn to, used, and abused these places for so long. The rivers themselves have only been restrained into controlled channels within the past fifty years. The Rio Grande in central New Mexico now occupies a channel usually less than fifty feet wide.

OASIS GARDENS ARE NATURALLY THE MOST VERDANT OF HIGH-DESERT ECOSYSTEMS. THIS VIEW FEATURES RIVER BIRCH, PITCHER SAGE, AND RED VALERIAN. (KINNEY GARDEN, PAGE 129).

MAJORS RIVERS IN THE SOUTHWEST
ARE BORDERED BY RIBBONS
OF LUSH VEGETATION.

ENOUGH WATER COLLECTS IN THIS
GRASSLAND BASIN TO SUPPORT A
COTTONWOOD.

Left to its own devices, it would still cut a braided pattern across a floodplain more than a mile wide in many places, washing away homes and silting over farmland. To protect people and property, the river has been tamed. New cottonwoods come as a result of seeds, viable for only a few days, lodging in the moisture-laden silt laid down during spring runoff. Channelizing the Rio Grande ended the seasonal flooding and has so restricted cottonwood regeneration that their future is in doubt. The trees and the river evolved, sustaining each other. Too much water flows under too many bridges to breach the levees and let the river have her way again. But if we value the beauty and the diversity of life that the bosque supports, we should play fair. Since we have interrupted the system, we might compensate by actively working to support reforestation. In several small ways the process has already begun. Through the cooperation of several agencies that manage the Rio Grande on public lands, controlled flooding is encouraging reseeding; cottonwood pole plantings are establishing new trees vegetatively in the meantime. Individual landowners are also planting young cottonwoods to renew the declining population. But channeling the river is not the only threat to the native cottonwood gallery. As old trees die they are replaced by Siberian elm, salt cedar, Russian olive, and tree of heaven, opportunists that can germinate and thrive in asphalt as long as they can suck up enough groundwater. Worse yet, these invading thugs are only part of the story. When the river valley flooded, groundwater was replenished at a rate that balanced what the native plant community used. As the valley was cleared and flood irrigated to raise chile and alfalfa, water was still recycled back into the ground. Now residential development is carpeting the valley with sprinkler-irrigated lawns. Groundwater is pumped, sprayed into the air, and evaporates before it can return to the water table. In Albuquerque, a city once thought to be floating on a vast underground lake, three times more groundwater is being pumped than is returned to the aquifer annually. The lake has shrunk to a series of big puddles and the pumping continues.

I used to avoid the river valley, preferring to admire the bosque from a distance, where the degradation is less obvious, than to walk this vandalized cathedral feeling sorrowful and angry. Several things have happened to make me hopeful. I keep meeting managers of public lands along the river who love their woods and wetlands and are individually and collectively working to turn things around. They are replacing invasive exotic plants with as diverse a community of native species as possible, managing wetlands with fewer chemicals by using natural means, such as manipulation of water levels and flow to enhance habitat, and trying to find some balance between thoughtful use and preservation. I am encouraged by homeowners who have bought acreage and want to develop a ground-nesting bird habitat or a butterfly garden and by teachers who want to create outdoor classrooms so their students learn to love and respect nature. Observing nature invariably leads us to realize we have a personal stake in the process, that we are part of nature. Her losses are our losses, her gains are ours as well. Knowledge comes one seed, one sprout at a time. Together we can keep oases green and vital.

River valley networks have tremendous value as corridors for the genetic exchange that keeps local ecosystems diverse and viable. Cottonwood bosque is a dominant riverine ecology, but Arizona sycamore and velvet ash woods, open grasslands and spottily treed savannas, willow thickets, ponds, *cienegas*, and marshes are all possible plant communities. Not all the ecological changes are due to human tinkering. Ponds naturally silt up and become marshes, then dry further into thickets or woodland. These lowland forests are multistoried. The tall tree canopy, majestic penthouses for riparian wildlife, overlook a tier of small trees such as alders, hackberry, soapberry, silver buffaloberry, and New Mexico olive which provide fruit for birds in summer and winter. Western virgin's bower and creeper twine their way through the gallery. Beneath the trees and in clearings coyote willow, wolfberry, currant, false indigo, threeleaf sumac, and wild roses bind the soil and yield still more cover and food for wildlife. On the ground floor, yerba mansa, creeping lippia, blue-eyed grass, statice, goldenrod, licorice, and many grasses make up the carpet. Birds and bats, beavers and muskrats, lizards and toads, porcupines and mule deer, rabbits and coyotes, and legions of insects

WINTER-BARE ALDERS AND PONDEROSA PINES LINE THE STREAM OF THIS UPLAND OASIS.

live throughout these layers of growth. In the soil, microrhizae and other bacteria and fungi, worms and nematodes, and still more insects convert decaying matter into new life. This web of interdependency is so fragile and complex I don't ever hope to be able to sort it all out. I'm just amazed that it exists in such marvelous balance. I want my grandchildren and their children to marvel, too.

When it comes to gardening, the wealth of shade is the most noticeable difference between oases and uplands, grassland, or shrub desert. Where there are trees there is water, not just in the ground but in the air. Trees act as huge evaporative coolers, deflecting drying winds over and around their canopies and making life easier for the plants in their protection. The years of disturbance by flood and plow have made weeds abundant and persistent. The wealth of weeds is another oasis hallmark. Just as the biotic community is layered, valley soils are the result of centuries of silt deposition. Dense clay is often layered on top of coarse sand. Sometimes clay is sandwiched between a surface layer of sandy loam and a base of coarse sand or gravel. Water moves between these layers unevenly, pooling up on top of each soil type before it gradually yields to gravity and continues its downward movement. After years of irrigating heavy soils, sodium sometimes crusts on the surface, limiting even the weeds that can grow on the resulting salt flats.

While the moderating effects of shade and moisture ought to make oasis gardening easier, the heavy soils and weed competition are limitations. It usually takes longer to stabilize a natural garden in the valley to the point that weeds no longer threaten new plantings. Learning to "read" silty clay soils—knowing when to water and how much water to apply—can be a frustratingly long process. First of all, silty valley clay is different from gritty foothills clay. Foothills clay dries like concrete, hard but oxygen and water permeable. Silty clay is finer. When it's wet you can become a foot taller walking across its gooey surface. Then it dries like pottery, may hold moisture in stagnant pools below the surface, and slows the movement of air to gasping plant roots. Water runs off its dry surface and finally penetrates slowly. Where a gallon of water permeates sand to a depth of a foot almost instantly, valley clay may absorb that same gallon only three or four inches deep and take several hours to do it. Drip irrigation is ideal in heavy soil because the gradual trickle application doesn't compact the soil and close the already limited pore space. As water filters through soil, a vacuum is formed in the open pores that draws oxygen into the soil, and since clay dries more slowly, oxygen is recharged more slowly. Heavy soil also compacts easily, further limiting both the water and air available to plant roots. Compared with drip systems designed for sandy soils, systems on clay should have smaller emitter output and should be run for longer cycles, or run in interrupted cycles, to prevent waterlogging and allow deep penetration. Plants carefully monitored to avoid overwatering will wilt in clay soil when the clay still seems moist. As the soil dries, the negatively charged clay particles draw and hold water so strongly that plants can't pull it away, leaving the clay damp and plants suffering. If the clay is laden with sodium, the salt pulls water out of plant tissues unless the plants are specially adapted with very high osmotic pressure in their cells to prevent moisture loss. Halophytes, plants adapted to salty soils, absorb water readily and give it up reluctantly. Plants adapted to clay soils often have lower oxygen requirements. When heavy or salty soil is a problem, choosing to grow plants adapted to such soils will make life much easier for everyone concerned.

Sometimes gypsum (calcium sulphate) or sulfur is used to correct saline conditions. The calcium in gypsum causes fine clay particles to clump up, increasing the potential air space in the soil. Sulfur also displaces sodium by reacting with the calcium in the soil, allowing the sodium to be leached below the root zone of plants. Both are radical solutions to extreme soil imbalance. Adding large amounts of organic matter to the soil is an excellent way to buffer salinity, provided that the plants used are adapted to humusy soil. Vegetable gardens, orchards, lawns, and some flower beds are best managed with liberal applications of compost. Deep and extensively rooted trees, shrubs, and wildflowers, especially those that require arid conditions, respond poorly to organically amended soil, probably because it doesn't dry out quickly enough to recharge the soil oxygen to levels needed by arid adaptives. It's better to avoid using plants that require well-drained highly oxygenated soils in valley clays, but some of us find life incomplete without a few penstemon. Gardeners are apt to rush in where angels fear to hoe, and there are a few ways to accommodate the wrong plant in the right place. Planting in raised beds of well-drained soil or excavating a bed area down to sandy subsoil and backfilling with permeable soil both involve replacing the problem soil. A lazier approach is planting the drainage-sensitive plants in a dense stand of a warm-season native grass such as buffalograss, blue grama, alkali grass, or vine mesquite. The grass roots will absorb excess moisture and help keep the soil profile open. Careful siting and watering finesse can make exceptions to nearly every rule.

OASIS STRATEGIES: PRESERVING MATURE TREES

Carol Kinney chose to make her home in the bosque. Located only four miles from downtown Albuquerque, but bordering a nature center state park preserve, her small patio home is dominated by large old cottonwoods. One corner of the southwestern-style home was sculpted to accommodate a large cottonwood, a screened porch was built around another. The front entrance and portal are bricked as an extension of the home's brick floors, while the driveway and all paths are paved with finely crushed rosy tan gravel to keep oxygen and water available to established tree roots. The gravel color complements the adobe architecture, blending into the plantings with no hard border

THE NARROW CORRIDOR BETWEEN THE HOUSE AND NATURE CENTER IS BORDERED WITH WILDFLOWERS, INCLUDING PITCHER SAGE (BLUE), 'GOLDSTRUM' RUDBECKIA (YELLOW), AND VALERIAN (PINK).

BEFORE ANY PLANTING COULD BE DONE, A FOREST OF SIBERIAN ELMS WAS REMOVED TO OPEN SPACE FOR THE FALSE INDIGO, SILVER BUFFALO-BERRY, AND NEW MEXICO OLIVES THAT ARE A TYPICAL UNDERSTORY PLANT COMMUNITY IN COTTON-WOOD FORESTS.

between them. The streetside garden is a mix of native arroyo shrubs, including Apache plume and chamisa in the sunny areas and redbuds and cotoneaster ground cover under the cottonwood canopy. There is only five feet of space from the north wall of the house to the property line shared with the nature preserve. Because of the potential fire hazard from the accumulation of years of deadwood and leaf litter, Carol asked for and was granted permission to install a single row of sprinklers at the property line to spray out into the open-space land to dampen the tinder. At the time, the area was overgrown with Siberian elms that would have blocked the sprinkler spray pattern. The nature center managers encouraged Carol to remove the invading elms and replant with native species. First the elms—more than one hundred plants, ranging from saplings to six-inch diameter trees—were cut down as close to the ground as possible and the stumps painted with herbicide. This course of action is actually less environmentally disruptive than stump removal would have been. The herbicide 2,4-D was used because, of the chemicals known to be effective, it biodegrades fairly quickly. Care was taken to only treat the freshly cut surfaces of the stumps, so that the results were obtained with the least amount of chemical use. The few trees that resprouted were recut and treated again.

The grade from the house to the property line had to be raised to cover elevated house foundations necessary because of the cottonwood roots and high water table. The narrow area between the house and the woods became a meandering gravel path bordered with a mix of garden perennials, such as 'Goldsturm' rudbeckia, 'Moonshine' yarrow, garlic chives, red valerian, and dwarf plumbago, and wildflowers, including blue flax, scarlet bugler, cherry sage, and yerba mansa. French drains under the path carry the runoff from the roof into plantings in the open space. To make the transition between garden and open space as seamless as possible, the original leaf litter was temporarily raked back into the bosque and the backfill tapered off into the open space. The litter was then raked back to the fence line. Some deadfall was removed, but most was distributed back away from the revegetation area. Large weathered logs were left for habitat, and the natural leaf litter was left as mulch. The utilitarian green steel fence posts and barbed wire were replaced with slender unpeeled cedar posts and smooth wire. Woods rose, false indigo, and desert willow were planted in clumps straddling the fence to partly obscure it. Young valley cottonwoods replaced some of the cleared elms, and New Mexico olive and silver buffaloberry were clustered in the background. Prairie sage, blanketflower, evening primrose, coneflower, and pitcher sage were among the wildflowers introduced as ground cover. Goldenrod, blue-eyed grass, and globemallow have moved in as well. A native patch of fine-textured alkali muhly is slowly spreading to form an attractive ground cover, and several coarser bunchgrasses fill the spaces between the flowers. Plants were chosen for their ecological fitness but also to provide as much seasonal color as possible, with a bonus of some interesting fruits and seed heads in winter.

Though no tilling was done, at times the planting took on aspects of an archeological dig. From the number of cans and bottles, dishes, rusted tools, and other artifacts uncovered, it became apparent that the area had a history of disturbance. In order to encourage blankets of wildflowers among the grasses, the bosque clearings have been watered three times weekly in twenty-minute cycles during warm weather. The aim is to gradually reduce the watering as a balance is established. Initially this generous addition of water to newly disturbed soil harboring centuries of dormant seeds resulted in weeds coming in waves. The first invader was yellow clover. A lacy scattering of seedlings in May became a solid three-foot-high blanket smothering the entire area by July. After a thorough soaking the clover was hand pulled. Herbicide was ruled out because of the extensive area involved. Even so, we worked carefully around the young plants that had been recently planted and left any benign "weeds" that might prove useful for wildlife. The following year kochia was the intruder, easier to eliminate by waiting until most of it began to flower and then cutting it off at the ground before it could reseed. "It took three years to learn to distinguish between weeds and desirables, and I still don't know many of the names!" says Carol, and it's no wonder since every season produced a new crop of interlopers. "If an unknown plant is attractive, more of

EVERY ROOM IN THE HOUSE OPENS
ONTO THE WOODS, AND THE
CHANGING SEASONS AND MOODS
OF NATURE ARE WOVEN INTO THE
LIFE INSIDE.

the time than not I leave it, removing any unwanted plants before they scatter seeds."
Pulling out perennial weeds, including new Siberian elms, from the millions of seeds left
in the soil and leaf litter opened up the soil for a new flush of weeds to germinate. The
disturbance also helped spread the pitcher sage and interesting seeds that arrive by
wind or bird each year, including goldenrod and wheat. The first three years were *work*,
but as the years pass, weed control becomes much less demanding. Selective thinning
is the ongoing management strategy that tempers the garden without compromising the
balance gradually being struck.

Each year, the trees are pruned up and some shrubs are thinned so the wildflowers
are more visible and receive more sunlight. Spring cleaning includes time spent removing
the cottonwood leaves that bury the drip-irrigated perennial border and streetscape
ground covers during the winter. The shallow layers of the leaves are added to the
bosque cover where the sprinklers help break them down. Cottonwood leaves have a
waxy cuticle that helps conserve moisture but makes the leaves slow to compost.
Another spring chore is trimming off the seed heads and dried grasses left for winter
interest. No fertilizer has been used, and only one insect control effort on the new
cottonwoods in four years has kept the garden safe for wildlife. Considerable time, an
estimated thirty-five hours of spring cleanup and approximately three hours a week
of monitoring and weeding during the growing season, has been spent establishing and

fine-tuning the landscape. While maintenance could be reduced considerably if the bosque clearing was watered less, it would be at the expense of the desired lushness. Establishing a garden balance includes weighing the investment in time and resources against the return in habitat and personal satisfaction. It also involves other forms of benign intervention. Recently, a beaver living in the adjacent clear ditch discovered the young cottonwoods. The remaining ones have been wrapped loosely at the base with thirty-inch-high chicken wire, an unnatural-looking but effective way to solve a very natural problem. As every room in the house opens onto the woods, the changing seasons and moods of the bosque are woven into the fabric of Carol's life. "One doesn't get used to and take for granted a mid-city bosque oasis. Through mostly uncurtained windows, constantly changing plants and the wildlife they bring are as much a part of my life as breathing. The tranquility and joy, the sense of belonging to this richness, sustain me."

OASIS STRATEGY: SPACES

Renovating and enlarging an old adobe home on a long narrow plot of retired farmland in the Rio Grande Valley gave Bob Levin a variety of outdoor spaces and interesting landscape situations. In considering how to deal with his new homestead, Bob's "over-riding purpose was to experience the Southwest, not import midwestern ecology." He

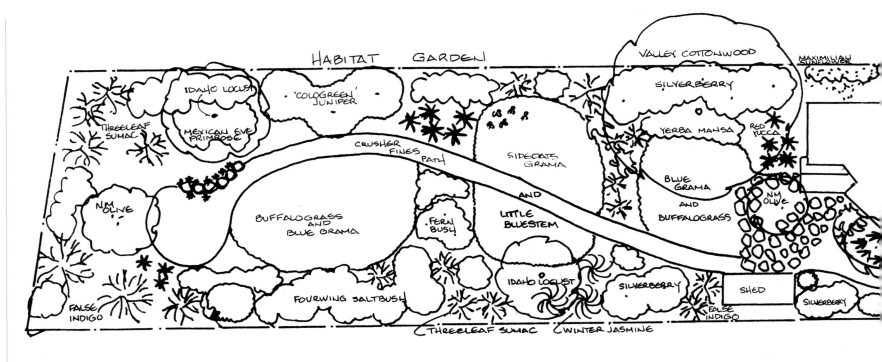

HABITAT GARDEN

THREELEAF SUMAC • IDAHO LOCUST • 'COLOGREEN' JUNIPER • VALLEY COTTONWOOD • MAXIMILLIAN SUNFLOWER • SILVERBERRY • MEXICAN EVE PRIMROSE • YERBA MANSA • RED YUCCA • N.M. OLIVE • CRUSHER FINES PATH • BLUE GRAMA AND • N.M. OLIVE • BUFFALOGRASS AND BLUE GRAMA • FERN BUSH • LITTLE BLUESTEM • SIDEOATS GRAMA • BLUE GRAMA AND BUFFALOGRASS • FALSE INDIGO • FOURWING SALTBUSH • IDAHO LOCUST • SILVERBERRY • SHED • SILVERBERRY • FALSE INDIGO • THREELEAF SUMAC • WINTER JASMINE

THE LEVIN SITE PRESENTED AN OPPORTUNITY TO DESIGN A SERIES OF OUTDOOR ROOMS. FROM RIGHT:

ENTRYWAY RUNOFF BASIN AND DRIVE-WAY BORDER PLANTING INCLUDE VALLEY COTTONWOOD, APACHE PLUME, CHAMISA, VITEX, TRUMPET VINE, BLUE MIST, CORALBERRY, WINTER JASMINE, THREADLEAF SAGE, BUSH PENSTEMON, GAYFEATHER, DESERT ZINNIA, BLUE SPURGE, 'AUTUMN JOY' SEDUM, AND PITCHER SAGE.

PATIO GARDEN PLANTS INCLUDE DESERT WILLOW, GRAYLEAF COTONEASTER, SPANISH BROOM, DWARF BUTTERFLYBUSH, CHERRY SAGE, ENGLISH LAVENDER, CATMINT, AND 'GOLDSTURM' RUDBECKIA.

had helped reconstruct a natural prairie on his farm in Wisconsin before retiring to the high desert and came to the Southwest with a love of native grassland. Having spent eighteen verdant summers in the upper midwestern countryside, the austere beauty of his new home was uncomfortable at first. Still he felt "it would be a terrible draw of water to use inappropriate plants in this climate." He didn't come here to garden, much less to waste water doing it.

The country lane fronting the property often floods during heavy rain, and storm drainage collects at the driveway entrance. The driveway surface is compacted crusher fines, a porous pavement that allows water to penetrate. Excess water drains under a wooden footbridge into a large cobblestone-lined basin where a young valley cotton-wood converts wastewater to shade and habitat. The main entrance to the house is through a south-facing courtyard. Large living room and dining room windows shaded by a portal bring that garden into the house. Generous planters catch the runoff from the roof and brick paving where desert willows, cherry sage, catmint, Spanish broom, and dwarf butterfly bush grown in gravel-lined basins perfume the air and bring hum-mingbirds and butterflies home to dinner. The kitchen opens onto a small vegetable garden in the most sheltered space in the compound. The soil is enriched and evapora-tion rate and daily temperature fluctuations minimized so that the small area is as productive as possible.

The single largest garden space is at the rear of the lot. The master bedroom and

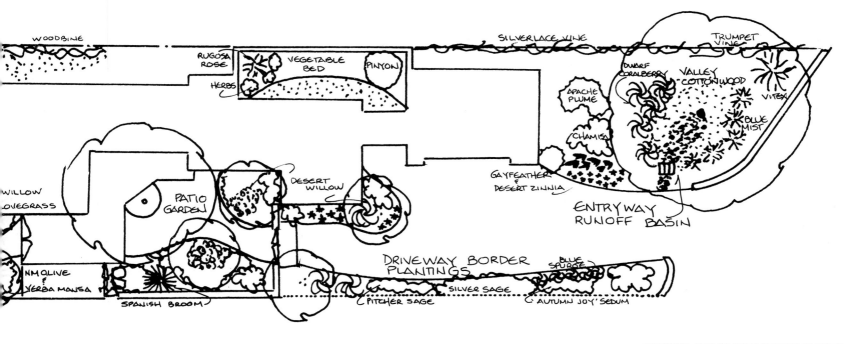

WOODBINE · SILVERLACE VINE · TRUMPET VINE · RUGOSA ROSE · VEGETABLE BED · PINYON · HERBS · DWARF CORALBERRY · VALLEY COTTONWOOD · VITEX · APACHE PLUME · BLUE MIST · CHAMISA · WILLOW LOVEGRASS · PATIO GARDEN · DESERT WILLOW · GAYFEATHER & DESERT ZINNIA · ENTRY WAY RUNOFF BASIN · NM OLIVE & YERBA MANSA · SPANISH BROOM · DRIVEWAY BORDER PLANTINGS · BLUE SPURGE · PITCHER SAGE · SILVER SAGE · 'AUTUMN JOY' SEDUM

center courtyard open onto a long narrow backyard exposed to the baking western sun. The section closest to the house had been an organic vegetable garden, and further back was the remains of an old alfalfa field. From a design standpoint, this fifty-five-foot-wide, one hundred fifty-foot-long space had both assets and liabilities. The west end of the house offers wonderful sunset views and has a built-in *banco* (bench) for enjoying the winter sun, but overheats on summer afternoons. The shade from a neighbor's trees cools the opposite end of the lot, which is also the only spot with a clear view of the distant mountains. Between these two living spaces was an alleyway of undetermined purpose. The long north border of the lot is adjacent to a park, and a dense planting was needed as a screen there but would further narrow the perspective.

A broad path of crusher fines now meanders from a flagstone patio and small buffalograss lawn next to the house to a sitting area at the far end of the lot. Only the flagstone right outside the door was set in mortar to keep dirt and dried grass from being carried into the house. The rest was set on soil with six-inch gaps between the flagstones. These spaces were planted with buffalograss that merges into a small lawn area. A cottonwood and a New Mexico olive were placed to shade the house and patio. While the trees develop, the grass helps minimize reflected heat.

Native grasses became the dominant element in the back garden. The path winds through a series of grass plots separated by clusters of midheight shrubs such as winter jasmine, threadleaf sage, and blue mist. Buffalograss and blue grama were used

HABITAT AND POCKET PRAIRIE PLANTS INCLUDE ROCKY MOUNTAIN JUNIPER AND 'HILLSPIRE' JUNIPER, NEW MEXICO OLIVE, VALLEY COTTONWOOD, WOODBINE, FALSE INDIGO, FERNBUSH, THREE-LEAF SUMAC, FOURWING SALTBUSH, SILVERBERRY, RED YUCCA, YERBA MANSA, PRAIRIE SAGE, MAXIMILIAN SUNFLOWER, BUFFALOGRASS, BLUE GRAMA, SIDEOATS GRAMA, LITTLE BLUESTEM, AND SAND LOVEGRASS.

DESERT WILLOW, CHERRY SAGE,
GRAYLEAF COTONEASTER, AND
CATMINT ARE AMONG THE PLANTS
THAT BRIGHTEN THE COURTYARD
WITH THEIR FLOWERS FROM APRIL
THROUGH OCTOBER. CM

closest to the living areas since they can be mowed occasionally as play space for Bob's grandchildren. Little bluestem and sideoats grama, two taller bunchgrasses, were used in the middle ground. The large open fields to the west may entice ground-nesting birds to find a safe haven in this modest prairie, though the surrounding area may have become too urbanized to support these early victims of development. A bit more protected from neighborhood cats, songbirds may find the juniper and silverberry border suitable for nesting as the plants develop more height and density. Hummingbirds found the desert willow the first season, and butterflies are drawn to the false indigo and fernbush. The grasses were seeded heavily and the shrub borders are deeply mulched to suppress weeds. The first year, three hours a week were spent from May through September tending to the new plants, cutting annual weeds, and fine-tuning the drip system. Two years after planting, a few rough spots still demand attention. The lovegrass planted under the desert willow near the south wall of the house grew more than four feet tall and fell across the path with the combination of drip irrigation and roof runoff. Most of the emitters have been plugged to keep the grass shorter, as intended. The grass plots are mowed three or four times a summer to keep the remaining annual weeds from reseeding. Bindweed, capitalizing on the drip irrigation, is an ongoing problem and is being weeded out by hand, rather than with

APACHE PLUME, PRICKLY PEAR, CHAMISA, GAYFEATHER, AND DESERT ZINNIA ADD COLOR AND TEXTURE. CM

herbicide, until the shrubs have gotten large enough to compete and be more self-sustaining. Glyphosate will only be used as a last resort if the weeds threaten a major resurgence. So far, that seems unlikely. Once the planting is established, an overall spring cleanup to remove seed stalks and invigorate the grasses, infrequent mowing of the play areas, and periodic deep watering are the only maintenance that will be needed.

OASIS STRATEGY: LEARNING TO PRESERVE AND DEVELOP

The outdoor classroom at Los Padillas Elementary School satisfies childhood curiosities, supports a diversity of wildlife, supplies a living laboratory for teaching life science, improves groundwater quality, and provides the community with a continuous supply of caring young citizens. That's a high level of achievement for a four and one-half acre fragment of bosque where a grove of cottonwoods, a few wolfberries and saltbush, a swale filled with yerba mansa, and a sweep of alkali sacaton and white aster have quietly held their ground since the Albuquerque school was founded nearly a century ago.

Teachers and their students had been using the space informally for nature studies and saw the value and the possibilities there. They set off on a mission of development and preservation that took five years of negotiating with the school system and lobbying the state legislature for funding to reach a design and construction stage. Besides vision

A WIDE PATH OF COMPACTED CRUSHER FINES MEANDERS THROUGH A SERIES OF NATIVE-GRASS PLOTS DIVIDED BY SHRUB AND FLOWER BORDERS MULCHED WITH BARK TO DIVIDE THE LONG NARROW LOT INTO A SERIES OF "POCKET PRAIRIES."

WITHIN TWO YEARS THE GRASSES (SIDEOATS GRAMA FOREGROUND, BLUE GRAMA TOWARD THE HOUSE) HAVE FILLED IN WELL. THE TREES WILL TAKE SEVERAL MORE YEARS TO MATURE AND FILL THEIR PLACES IN THE GARDEN. CM

and persistence, the core group of teachers, calling themselves Los Padillas Ecology Task Force, had the benefit of a practical problem to rally around. The school is located in an area where groundwater is only four feet below the surface in summer. The school's septic system was in need of reconstruction and the high water table complicated the job. Why not use a constructed wetland to treat the effluent and create a wildlife sanctuary in the process?

Nearly two-thirds of the area was undisturbed trees, native understory, and grassland, and from the onset it was decided that the existing ecosystem was to be protected during the development of the wetlands and remain the heart of the outdoor classroom. Craig Campbell of COPA and Southwest Wetlands Group, following the ideas set down by students and teachers, laid out a basic master plan. The plan included using the abandoned raised septic mounds as mesa biomes to flank the entrance to the preserve and developing representative piñon-juniper woodland, shrub desert grassland, and sandhills plant communities along the previously disturbed northwest borders in addition to the effluent treatment beds, clean water pond and marsh, and shade ramada study center.

A thousand-gallon septic tank collects the sewage; the effluent runs in sequence into two two-thousand-square-foot gravel beds, each plastic lined and two feet deep, planted with cattails, bulrushes, and reeds and bordered with yellow water iris. These beds are designed so that the effluent flows six inches beneath the surface and is treated by a combination of microorganism activity, adsorption, plant uptake, and metabolic processes. The plants pump oxygen into the root zone and create an environment for aerobic bacteria to thrive in an otherwise anaerobic zone. The combination of microorganisms accelerates denitrification and purification of the wastewater. Although the naturally treated water is clear and usually odorless, as added safeguard it passes through an ultraviolet, or UV, unit to disinfect it before it is piped into the pond. The two-thousand-square-foot, eighteen-inch-deep pond is also lined to retain water year-round and allow study of aquatic biological systems, but it is bordered by a shallow thousand-square-foot unlined marsh that absorbs any overflow and ultimately returns excess water to the ground. The pond is bordered by alders and coyote willows, and the marsh water is filtered through cattails, bulrushes, sedges, and duckweed. Mosquito fish (gambusia) eat mosquito larva. The pond was placed near the largest cottonwood grove, and screwbean mesquite, New Mexico olive, and threeleaf sumac were added to diversify the riparian ecosystem.

To show variations within a larger ecosystem, the piñon-juniper biome was planted as a long narrow band with piñon dominant at the east end mixed with mountain mahogany, giant four o'clock, and prairie sage. Gradually, Gambel oak replaced the mountain mahogany, one-seed juniper mixed with the piñon, and the understory includes penstemon and evening primrose. At the hotter, more exposed west end of the woodland ecosystem, the juniper replaced the piñons, with datil and cliffrose as companions.

The shrub-desert grassland and sandhills areas occupy the hottest, most open west exposure on the site. Fourwing saltbush, Apache plume, and winterfat on the north end gradually transitioned into true Chihuahuan desert indicators, including creosotebush, littleleaf sumac, desert willows, and threadleaf sage. The threadleaf makes the transition to the sandhills, where it mixes with broom dalea, dunebroom, bush penstemon, and desert mule's ears.

The abandoned septic mounds were seeded with a mix of native grasses, including sideoats grama, Indian ricegrass, giant sacaton, dropseed, and sand bluestem. The gap between the mounds became the main entryway, a path meandering between desert willows, Apache plume, chamisa, bush penstemon, and desert zinnia. The north mesa slopes are planted with cliffrose, fernbush, cliff fendlerbush, and a few alligator juniper. The southwest-facing slope has ocotillo, prickly pear, and pencil cholla, Mexican

LOS PADILLAS ELEMENTARY SCHOOL'S OUTDOOR CLASSROOM BEGAN WITH TEACHERS AND STUDENTS RECOGNIZING THE BEAUTY AND VALUE OF A FORGOTTEN FRAGMENT OF COTTONWOOD BOSQUE AND NATIVE GRASSLAND NEXT TO THE DEVELOPED SCHOOL GROUNDS.

A CRUSHER-FINES PATH WAS LAID OUT THROUGH THE WOODS ON EACH SIDE OF THE ALKALI SACATON PRAIRIE, AND BENCHES WERE PLACED FOR VISITORS TO LINGER AND ENJOY THE VIEWS.

THE POND STUDY AREA IS A PLACE TO OBSERVE THE WONDERS OF NATURE. SINCE THE CONSTRUCTED WETLAND DOES NOT REMOVE PHOSPHOROUS, THE NEW POND HAS A CYCLIC FLOATING MAT-ALGAE PROBLEM. ALGAE BLOOMS OCCASIONALLY MAKE THE POND RESEMBLE PEA SOUP, WHEN TEMPERATURES AND INPUT FROM THE WETLANDS ARE RIPE. WATER LILIES WERE PLANTED TO SHADE THE WATER'S SURFACE AND LIMIT ALGAE GROWTH, AND ELODEA, OR OXYGENATING PLANTS, WERE PLANTED ON THE POND BOTTOM TO COMPETE WITH THE ALGAE FOR MINERAL SALTS WHICH THE ALGAE REQUIRE TO FLOURISH. ALGAE-EATING MINNOWS AND MOSQUITO LARVAE-EATING GAMBUSIA FISH WERE ALSO ADDED TO THE POND. TADPOLES, ANOTHER ALGAE-CONSUMING PIECE OF THE ECOLOGICAL PUZZLE, CAN BE ADDED IN SPRING. AS A TENUOUS NATURAL BALANCE EVOLVES, THE POND WILL BE LESS LIKELY TO RESPOND TO MINOR CHANGES SO DRAMATICALLY.

oregano and bush morningglory. The southern mesa is planted with algerita, madrone, beargrass, sotol, soaptree yucca, and desert marigold.

The most difficult thing about developing the planting palette was limiting the selections to a reasonable number in terms of budget and availability at the time of planting. The plants used are some of the most beautiful, interesting to study, and attractive to a diversity of wildlife, but they are only the beginning. Once the initial planting has had time to become established and begins to build larger colonies, generations of students will have the opportunity to add new species as they learn the diversity of the surrounding ecosystems that their outdoor classroom represents. Already the outdoor classroom contains plants that support divers songbirds, butterflies, and hummingbirds. A class studying moths as pollinators might add hooker's evening primrose in the riparian zone across the path from the four o'clock and white-tufted evening primrose moth habitat in their upland ecosystem. Indian ricegrass might be added to the sandhills by students studying quail. Everyone involved in the project hopes that its success will breed other habitats in schoolyards and backyards across the city.

OASES PLANTS

Because oasis ecology is rare in the high desert, there are fewer native plants specifically adapted to its heavy, sometimes salty soils that are also attractive garden subjects.

LOS PADILLAS'S THIRD-GRADE CLASS ('94) RELEASES A TOAD IN THE POND STUDY AREA.

Where tall tree canopies create cooler microclimates and the soil is well drained, upland natives sometimes adapt well. Commonly planted shade trees such as sycamore, honey locust, and ash are more at home in bottomlands with shallow groundwater than anywhere else in the high desert. Many common landscape shrubs and garden flowers such as spirea, forsythia, peonies, and daylilies also find life in the oasis less stressful. Shrub-desert and grassland plants naturally extend into river valleys with little tree cover. The plants listed here are the unheralded southwestern natives with garden value. Plants from other ecosystems that will adapt to oases are indicated in their respective lists found in chapters 4, 5, 7, and 8. Complete profiles are found in volume two, *Plants for Natural Gardens*.

Oasis Plants

TREES

Alder/*Alnus tenuifolia*   DT S/SH

Alder/*A. oblongifolia*

River birch/*Betula nigra*   DT S/SH

Water birch/*B. fontinalis* and *B. occidentalis*

New Mexico olive, Desert olive, Mountain ash,

Desert privet/*Forestiera neomexicana*   DE S/SH

✗ Arizona sycamore/*Platanus wrightii*   DT S

Valley cottonwood/*Populus fremontii*   DE S

Lanceleaf, Mountain cottonwood/*P. acuminata*

Plains cottonwood/*P. sargentii*

Screwbean mesquite/*Prosopis pubescens*   DE S/PS

Mexican elder/*Sambucus mexicanus*   DE S/PS

Silver buffaloberry/*Shepherdia argentea*   DT S/PS

Roundleaf buffaloberry/*S. rotundifolia*   DE

SHRUBS AND VINES

False indigo/*Amorpha fruticosa*   DE S/SH

Broom baccharis/*Baccharis salicina*   DE S/PS

Coyotebush/*B. pilularis*

Desert broom/*B. sarothroides*

✗ Buttonbush/*Cephalanthus occidentalis*   S/SH

Western virgin's bower/*Clematis ligusticifolius*   DT S/SH

Wolfberry/*Lycium pallidum*   DE S/SH

Chinese wolfberry/*L. chinensis*

Woodbine/*Parthenocissus inserta*   DE S/SH

Boston ivy/*P. tricuspidata*

Golden currant/*Ribes aureum*   DT/DE S/SH

Wax currant/*R. cereum*

Woods rose/*Rosa woodsii*   DT/DE S/SH

Wonder rose/*R. mirifica*

Star rose/*R. stellata*

✗ Coyote willow/*Salix exigua*   DT S/SH

Peachleaf willow/*S. amygdaloides*

Bebb willow/*S. bebbiana*

Gooding willow/*S. goodingii*

WILDFLOWERS

Yerba mansa/*Anemopsis californica*   DE S/SH

White aster/*Aster ericoides*   DT S/PS

  Plains aster/*A. batesii*

Bundleflower/*Desmanthus illinoensis*   DE/DT S/PS

Purple coneflower/*Echinacea purpurea*   DT S/PS

  'Goldstrum' rudbeckia/*Rudbeckia fulgida* 'Goldstrum'

  Black-eyed susan/*R. hirta*

Tulip gentian/*Eustoma grandiflora*   DT S/PS

Gaura/*Gaura lindheimeri*   DT S/PS

  Scarlet gaura/*G. coccinea*   DE

X Wild licorice/*Glycyrrhiza lepidota*   DE/DT S/PS

Maximilian sunflower/*Helianthus maximiliani*   DE/DT S

Cardinal flower/*Lobelia cardinalis*   S/SH

Mexican evening primrose/*Oenothera berlandiera*   DE/DT S/SH

  Hooker evening primrose/*O. hookeri*

  Mexican evening primrose/*O. speciosa*

Creeping lippia, Frogfruit/*Phyla nodiflora*   DE S/SH

Blue-eyed grass/*Sisyrinchium demissum*   DT S/SH

  Blue-eyed grass/*S. campestre*

  Grass widow/*S. inflatum*

  Star iris/*S. longipes*

  Blue-eyed grass/*S. montanum* syn. *S. angustifolium*

Goldenrod/*Solidago canadensis*   DT S/PS

  Dwarf goldenrod/*S. spathulata*

Ironweed/*Vernonia marginata*   DE S/PS

GRASSES

Western wheat/*Andropyron smithii*   DT S/PS

X Western cane/*Arundo donax*   DT S

Saltgrass/*Distichlis stricta*   DE S/PS

Scratchgrass, Alkali muhly/*Muhlenbergia asperifolia*   S/PS

  Ear muhly/*M. arenacea*

Vine mesquite/*Panicum obtusum*   DE S/PS

  Switchgrass/*P. virgatum*   DT

Indiangrass/*Sorgastrum nutans*   DT S

Alkali sacaton/*Sporobolus airoides*   DE S/PS

Upland   Desert/Grassland   Oasis   **X** Not Rec. for Urban Gardens   S=Sun, PS=Part-shade, SH=Shade; DR=Drought requiring, DE=Drought enduring, DEV=Drought evading, DT=Drought tolerant

143

7 Urban Islands

THE PATTERNS OF NATURE—larger trees and denser growth in wetter areas, more sparsely scattered grasses or desert shrubs in hotter drier places—are ecological responses to local conditions. Cities have their own ecologies that often bear no resemblance to the natural ecosystems they have replaced. Urban patterns involving the layout of streets, their widths and axes, and the placement, proportions, and style of public buildings, businesses, and residences chronicle the human history of places. They are evidence of the cultural biases of the early settlers, what they brought with them to the place, and their respect or disregard for nature. No matter how beautiful the architecture or how grand the plan, the larger the city, the more its gardens are refuges, precious spaces that soften the hard edges, cool the glare, filter the grime, muffle the noise, and make cities livable. They are a critical link to the natural world.

How do we garden naturally in such artificial circumstances? Perhaps the only remnants of nature in an urban garden are the soil and the weed seeds it contains, and chances are that even the weeds are foreign imports, part of the human history of the place. Weeds, nature's response to disturbance, are the first step in ecological recovery and one we aim to minimize in garden ecology. Whether the soil is gravelly upland granite, the lighter sand of shrub desert, the silty loam of grassland, or valley clay, the soil and microclimates are key to rebuilding a sustainable plant community. Urban environments can be both more temperate and more extreme than their natural counterparts. In winter, the heat radiating off buildings and paving is often enough to

IN URBAN GARDENS, SPACE IS PRECIOUS. AN EXPOSED AGGREGATE SIDEWALK MEANDERS BETWEEN PLANTS CHOSEN FOR THEIR SEASONAL COLOR OR EVERGREEN CONSTANCY. LEFT OF PATH FROM FRONT TO BACK: GRAYLEAF COTONEASTER, 'BURGUNDY' BLANKET FLOWER, CHERRY TREE, DWARF PLUMBAGO, AND COMPACT MAHONIA. RIGHT OF PATH: 'EICHHOLZ' COTONEASTER, PINELEAF PENSTEMON, AND CHAMISA. (ERICSON GARDEN, PAGE 147).

make plants hardy a full zone north of their expected range. In summer, the added heat can make gardening in the naturally hot high desert even more challenging. Overall, temperatures may be increased more than ten degrees. Tall buildings channel winds, increasing their velocity, and, no matter what their size, create microclimates. North-facing walls provide cool shaded niches similar to those found in foothills canyons. Low spots where the runoff from roof surfaces and paving collects are oases in the making. Older neighborhoods may have a tall tree canopy similar to bosques, with a lower-than-average evapotranspiration rate but higher-than-average competition for water because of the network of established tree roots. South- and west-facing walls trap heat, creating environments as arid as any shrub desert. New neighborhoods amplify the most severe climatic conditions because the earth has been stripped of any vegetation that would otherwise buffer the wind-channeling and heat-reflecting effects of new construction. Prairie grassland is the hardest ecosystem to represent on a small city lot. The grasses and wildflowers may grow well enough, but the majestic sweep, the connection of earth and sky that is the essence of prairie, is missing. By grouping prairie plants to contrast their subtle textures and colors, it is possible to downplay the lack of grand proportions, emphasizing the immediate interplay between smaller-scale plant groupings.

This tighter focus distinguishes city gardens from suburban and rural landscapes. Space is at a premium. Each plant usually plays several roles in the garden, providing shade and color, texture and enclosure, carpeting and erosion or dust control. The same considerations given to moderating the harsh aspects of the climate and capitalizing on the resources at hand in the uplands, desert grasslands, and oases apply in the city with a few refinements. The smaller the space or the more purposes it serves, the more important each member of the plant community becomes. Because urban landscapes are heavily used year-round, they need to be inviting throughout the seasons. Botanical slackers need not apply.

Urban spaces are highly organized, defined by walls and fences and pavement. There are more hard surfaces and proportionately less permeable soil. Runoff from roof guttering and pavement has to be used or diverted in less space. Ideally, changes in grade should be gentle. The combination of large volumes of runoff water, steeps slopes, and confined spaces can be disastrous. Constructing channels to direct the flow of water with overflows into the storm drains, and terracing to retain the slopes, may be necessary. The hard-engineering solutions to site problems can be softened with plants that partly conceal them and benefit from the microclimates they create. Aesthetically, hard edges and tight spaces make city gardens more patterned and formal. Naturalized urban gardens need cultivated edges and trimmed borders along paths. Plants having more compact growth habits and sculptural forms bridge the gap between man-made and natural. One of the joys of living in the high-desert Southwest is that mountains usually dominate the horizon, but in the city these vistas are less immediate; privacy is more important. Providing close-up screening while framing a distant view can be complementary or conflicting aims depending on the situation. Trellised vines can accomplish both with greater height in less ground space. Overall plant selection for urban spaces usually includes plants that are more compact, refined in growth, smaller at maturity, and less apt to reseed abundantly or run rampant with invasive roots. Horticultural cultivars are less likely to be invasive than their wild ancestors, though, depending on the size of the space and the attitude of the gardener, what is an effective ground cover for one may be a space-grabbing menace to another.

Another impact of tighter quarters in city spaces is that the neighbors are closer, so what you do affects them more, and vice versa. It is almost a given that the city gardener will have some landscape concerns that are the result of neighbors' life-styles and horticultural biases: an eyesore that a neighbor sees as artful, useful, or otherwise indispensable; runoff that originates next door, often from poorly designed or maintained irrigation of lawns and flower beds; areas of deep shade from adjacent trees. In the spirit of making lemonade out of unsolicited lemons, plant a screen to hide the objectionable view and accept the runoff or shade as the gifts they really are in this climate. Find a way to use them. Visit your neighbors' property as part of your planning process so that you can see from their perspective how your choices might affect them.

URBAN STRATEGIES: TIME AND SPACE TO SMELL THE ROSES

Even before breaking ground for their new home, Pam Martin and Bob Ericson were thinking about the garden. Their attitude toward the landscaping mirrored their personal priorities: balancing family and careers, having beautiful and useful outdoor spaces to complement their new home, and being water conservative and limiting maintenance. Aware that having time and space to cherish themselves and each other makes them more effective and happier human beings, they view their garden as a place of companionable serenity. The challenge of good design is realizing the gardeners' vision within the limitations of the space. At Pam and Bob's, an already small west-facing backyard, one hundred twenty-five feet wide but only thirty-five feet deep, was set aside to accommodate a scaled-down swimming pool needed both for physical therapy and recreation. Across its width, the remaining space is an extension of the kitchen, study, and master bedrooms. On the south side of the house, a fifteen-foot-wide corridor allows access to the backyard. The north side tapers from fourteen feet wide at the back to three feet wide in the front yard. The neighborhood covenants require greenspace, interpreted as lawn by the majority of homeowners, although every street and cul-de-sac has landscapes that feature native or adaptive plants. Pam and Bob wanted to limit the water- and labor-intensive lawn to an area around the pool, where it would

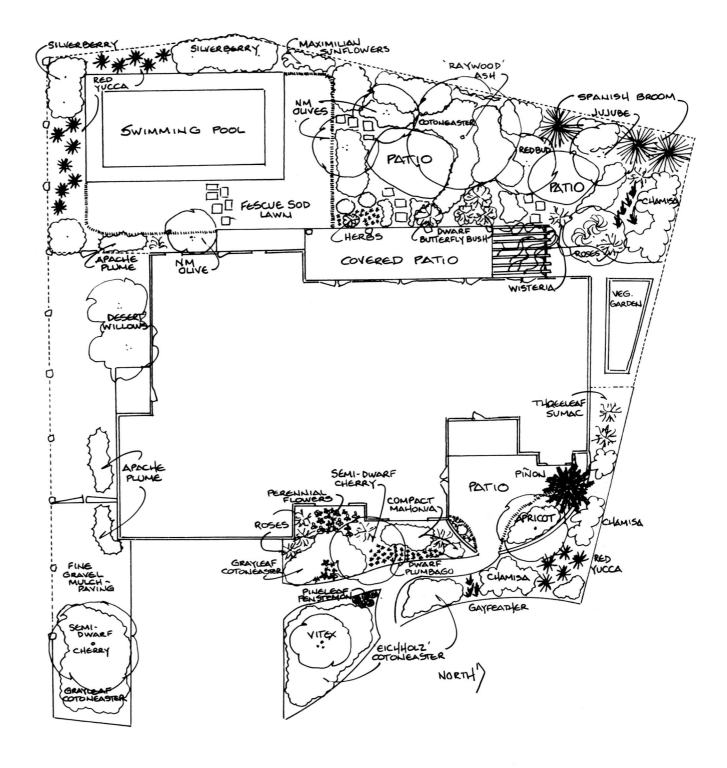

SILVERBERRY
SILVERBERRY
MAXIMILIAN SUNFLOWERS
'RAYWOOD' ASH
SPANISH BROOM
JUJUBE
RED YUCCA
NM OLIVES
COTONEASTER
REDBUD
CHAMISA
SWIMMING POOL
PATIO
PATIO
FESCUE SOD LAWN
HERBS
DWARF BUTTERFLY BUSH
ROSES
APACHE PLUME
NM OLIVE
COVERED PATIO
WISTERIA
VEG. GARDEN
DESERT WILLOWS
THREELEAF SUMAC
APACHE PLUME
SEMI-DWARF CHERRY
COMPACT MAHONIA
PATIO
PIÑON
PERENNIAL FLOWERS
APRICOT
CHAMISA
ROSES
GRAYLEAF COTONEASTER
DWARF PLUMBAGO
RED YUCCA
FINE GRAVEL MULCH PAVING
PINELEAF PENSTEMON
CHAMISA
GAYFEATHER
SEMI-DWARF CHERRY
VITEX
'EICHHOLZ' COTONEASTER
GRAYLEAF COTONEASTER
NORTH

PLANTS DISTANCE THE HOUSE FROM THE STREET AND PROVIDE YEAR-ROUND INTEREST WITH TREE AND SHRUB FORMS, FOLIAGE TEXTURES, AND FLOWER COLOR. 'EICHHOLZ' COTONEASTER REPLACES LAWN GRASS AS AN EVERGREEN GROUND COVER. COLOR FOCUS SHIFTS SEASONALLY. IN AUTUMN, GAY-FEATHER AND CHAMISA PROVIDE THE PUNCH.

be used for cooling the hot western exposure. The rest of the garden is devoted to evergreen or seasonal color and the fragrance enjoyed from sitting areas within the garden or from the indoor spaces they adjoin. There are four separate outdoor living rooms, each furnished with plants that enhance their intended purpose.

A walled courtyard serves as both the main entrance from the street and an extension of the dining room. The exposed aggregate patio, edged and accented with brickwork, is shaded and screened by a New Mexico olive and semidwarf apricot tree and bordered with cherry sage, English lavender, and spring bulbs for color and fragrance. The curbside landscape outside the entry courtyard is a mix of spring-blooming semidwarf fruit trees, a summer-flowering tree-form vitex, the changing seasonal interest of chamisa, mahonia, and woods rose, evergreen cotoneaster as ground cover, and pockets of perennials and wildflowers, including 'Moonshine' yarrow, blue flax, pineleaf and Rocky Mountain penstemons, purple coneflower, dwarf plumbago, and gayfeather, for a progression of color throughout the year. Plants are grouped according to their water requirements and growth preferences: the penstemon are clustered near the walkways, where the reflected heat keeps them drier, while the spring bulbs, yarrow, flax, and purple coneflower are clustered where they are shaded in the afternoon and provide a continuous display of color in front of the window of the informal dining area. The dwarf plumbago and cotoneaster are massed under the fruit trees to shade the soil and create moist pockets to support the trees' relatively shallow root systems. Bark mulch was used to suppress weeds and conserve moisture and is gradually being covered over as the plants fill in.

The hot southside corridor is unseen from both the house and the rest of the garden. Most of the runoff from the roof drains into this space, which needed to be kept open to allow occasional vehicle access to the pool equipment and backyard. It became a catchall utility space for a dog run and clothesline as well. A grove of desert willows cools the south wall and provides shade for Boomer, the sixty-five-pound golden retriever who presides there when no one else is home. The trees and a border of Apache plume use the runoff caught in drainage basins lined with coarse gravels. Finer gravel mulch is a serviceable and easy-to-maintain permeable pavement.

The backyard space is defined by the pool and the indoor spaces that adjoin it. To conserve water, the pool has a retractable solar cover, which helps heat the water, keeps it cleaner, and limits evaporation when the pool is not in use. An eight-foot border of turf-type fescue sod surrounds the pool on the two sides closest to the house. Silverberry and red yucca form the back border, selected for year-round interest and to minimize leaf litter near the pool. There is a generously proportioned portal that adjoins the family room and study, ending in an arbor planted with wisteria and climbing roses near the master bedroom. French doors and windows open out onto the portal and garden. Two small earth–tone–tinted concrete patios are surrounded by plantings chosen for shade, color, and fragrance. These borders are layered in height and leaf density to give the illusion of greater depth as they partly enclose and screen each small patio. After just two years the ground covers and shrubs provide the desired cover, but the slowly developing tree canopy still needs a few years to produce the desired shade.

The selection of shrubs and ground covers reflects the uses of the spaces. The herb garden is close to the kitchen portal and the patio, used for barbecuing and outdoor dining in summer. Pam says, "We've gotten into the habit of using the fresh rosemary, sage, and oregano. It's close at hand and attractive and fragrant as part of the land-scape." The garden spaces off the study and the master bedroom are used for reading and quiet conversation; these plantings are lush and colorful. "The romantic corner near our bedroom produces delicious breezes. The perfume of roses, wisteria, and desert willow wafts in the window."

On the north side around the corner from the patios, a forty-eight-square-foot vegetable garden is tucked away where it is highly productive during the growing season, close enough and small enough to tend easily, and out of sight when frost blackens the last tomato leaves. Eight cubic yards of composted soil were added to fill the drip-irrigated raised beds. "We've had much larger gardens in the past, but this seems a good balance between the amount of effort we put in and the amount of produce we actually use." The bounty from the vegetable bed includes several months of mixed

salad greens, tomatoes, peppers, radishes, chives, basil, and even miniature pumpkins for fall decorating. All the household vegetable matter and lawn clippings are composted to assure future productivity.

This lush and colorful garden is relatively conservative in its demands. The lawn is sprinkled three times a week for twelve minutes in the early morning in summer. The rest of the plantings are drip irrigated forty-five minutes per week in summer and twenty minutes in winter. The actual volume delivered per plant is adjusted by increasing the number of emitters on larger, more thirsty plants. Bindweed was particularly well entrenched in the backyard. Consistent spot spraying with glyphosate has just about eliminated it after three years. The search-and-spray operation was done almost every week from spring through fall in the first year and took about fifteen minutes each time. The lawn is fertilized four times a year, the roses twice a year, and the fruit trees have slow-release fertilizer stakes dug in below their emitters. The vegetable garden is supplemented with compost, and the rest of the plantings are not fertilized. The fruit trees and roses are pruned once each spring, and Bob and Pam spend a full six hours on a beautiful spring day dethatching the lawn and trimming and cleaning up the entire garden. The fruit trees are sprayed, but for the most part the garden is pest free.

Including weekly lawn mowing from April through September and tending the vegetable garden ("We visit the garden a lot from spring through fall, but I wouldn't call it work."), Pam and Bob estimate they spend forty-five minutes to an hour each week maintaining their landscape during the growing season and virtually no time except to occasionally sweep the paths and patio and pick up windblown litter in winter. Considering how much a part of each room in the house these garden spaces are, their caretakers feel there is ample return for the time spent. They observe that "one of the most pleasing aspects of the yard is the view from the rooms inside the house. There is

THE BACKYARD SPACE IS DEFINED BY THE POOL AND THE ADJOINING INDOOR SPACES. AN HERB GARDEN DISPLAYS A TAPESTRY OF LEAF TEXTURES AND AROMAS NEAREST THE KITCHEN, WHILE AT THE FAR REACHES OF THE GARDEN ROSES AND WISTERIA PERFUME THE MASTER BEDROOM.

always something interesting, something colorful blooming. We start picking bouquets when the daffodils bloom in March and we have cut flowers right through fall."

URBAN STRATEGIES: ISLAND IN A SEA OF ASPHALT

Landscaped street medians provide much needed relief from the heat and hustle of city traffic. From a planting perspective, they are harsher and more forbidding than any natural ecosystem, including Death Valley in July. In addition to being open, hot, and windy exposures, most medians are raised as a safety device to separate traffic lanes, with no opportunity to harvest the runoff from the surrounding pavement. Depending on the legal speed of the traffic, types of plantings are restricted. Large trees that might provide welcome shade have to be set back a safe distance from the curb to reduce the impact on motorists if a vehicle runs into a tree. The faster the speed limit, the greater the required recovery zone and subsequent setback. Often medians are not wide enough to safely accommodate trees. While part of the value of median plantings is buffering, unobstructed line of sight is critical near turn lanes. Maximum plant heights of thirty inches or tree canopies above eight feet are mandated in many cases. Limitations of space also affect both plant tolerances and aesthetics. The average life span of a street tree in the United States is seven to fourteen years. Large trees adapted to streamside ecosystems are poor choices for planting in traffic islands in more temperate climates. In the high desert it is cruel and unusual punishment. While a sixty-four-square-foot opening in pavement is the rule of thumb for minimum recommended open soil space for street tree planters, most large shade trees have a minimum root run of at least nine-hundred square feet. Seven years seems a merciful release from a terrible life sentence. Median plantings should be diverse enough to provide year-round flower or foliage color and still be grouped in masses dense enough to be visually impressive at thirty-five miles per hour. Mowed turf grass, while refreshingly green, is probably the worst median ground cover in this climate. Access for maintenance poses traffic hazards. Spray irrigation of narrow strips bordered by hard paving always generates runoff that eventually undermines the pavement and also creates hazards of unexpectedly icy driving surfaces. This can leave the median designer gridlocked, in search of low-maintenance, heat-loving, pollution-tolerant, drought-requiring, low-growing plants or small trees that can take occasional tread wear, prefer a mulch of beer cans and cigarette butts, and are limber enough not to trap blowing papers and other litter.

The Layton Avenue median in Albuquerque posed all these problems plus a peculiar hydrological condition known as collapsible soil. Watering to establish new transplants had to be minimized since irrigation of nearby medians and neighborhood landscapes planted with cool-season turf grasses had resulted in sinkholes opening up beneath the pavement and building foundations. Plants evolved to cope with the heat and aridity of shrub-desert ecosystems were logical choices for this and most high-desert streetscapes. Desert shrubs are deeply rooted and able to survive harsh exposures with minimal

GAYFEATHER, BLUE SPURGE, PURPLE THREEAWN, AND APACHE PLUME ARE AMONG THE RESILIENT PLANTS THAT BEAUTIFY THIS URBAN ISLAND—THE LAYTON AVENUE MEDIAN.

supplemental irrigation. Their compact forms are well suited to the restricted growing space. With the exception of cactus and other thorny plants, their limber-stemmed adaptation to wind tends to help shed blowing trash, and their small leaves reduce the litter they themselves generate. Plant selection can include impressive seasonal flower displays with maintenance limited to periodic cleanup and litter removal. The Layton median was wide enough to accommodate desert willows for light shade. Their pink flowers add color in summer, and in winter their sculptural shape is attractive. Threadleaf sage was used for its lacy texture and silver color contrast. Red yucca was used for its long flowering season and winter foliage. Blue spurge provides year-round foliage color and yellow flower color in March. Narrowleaf penstemon, occasionally mistaken for hyacinths in spring, was also used for early season color. Bush penstemon was included for summer color and longevity and gayfeather for reliable fall color. Clumps of Indian ricegrass were included as a filler with textural interest, and clumps of purple threeawn have grown from seeds blown down the avenue. Plants are clustered for visual impact, and groupings are repeated along the length of the median with a naturalized rhythm that reduces the impact of plant disappearances due to horticultural or vehicular accidents.

The Layton Avenue median was planted and is maintained by volunteers from the local neighborhood association. Although they may never have to deal with planting a city median, many urban gardeners have comparably hot and arid growing conditions to contend with. The parking strip between the street and sidewalk in front of many homes offers the same grim prospects for plant growth. Medians, however, are islands that stand alone. Designwise, residential parking strips should have some connection to the rest of the landscape. The same way an uplands or oasis garden might merge into grasslands or shrub desert, the city landscape might become progressively more arid as it moves from the house toward the street.

URBAN ISLAND PLANTS

As garden styles evolve throughout the United States, smaller flowering trees and shrubs, perennial flowers, and ornamental grasses are gaining ground. Many old garden favorites and newly introduced plants from other arid regions are available to use in high-desert urban gardens. Locally native upland, desert grassland, and oasis plants can make starting a garden in a newly developed area easier. Once the locals have tempered the conditions a bit, these other plants will thrive as well. In older neighborhoods, the growing conditions may be so changed by traditional gardening practices and plantings that it may be difficult to grow plants adapted to harsher conditions. As always, plants will perform best if they are chosen to fit specific niches in the garden. The following list of adaptive plants is intended to round out the plant selection offered in this book. More complete information about these plants is found in the second volume, *Plants for Natural Gardens*.

Adaptive Plants

TREES

Smoketree/*Cotinus coggygria*

Leland cypress/*Cuppressocyparis leylandi*

Claret ash/*Fraxinus oxycarpa*

Kentucky coffee tree/*Gymnocladus dioica*

Chinese juniper/*Juniperus chinensis* 'Hetzi', 'Hetzi Columnaris',
 'Keteeler's', 'Robusta', 'Spartan', 'Spearmint'

Eastern red cedar/*Juniperus virginiana* 'Canaerti' and 'Hillspire'

Golden raintree/*Koelreuteria paniculata*

Osage orange/*Maclura pomifera*

Crabapple/*Malus* species and cultivars

Chinaberry/*Melia azederach*

Chinese pistache/*Pistacia chinensis*

Cork oak/*Quercus suber*

Idaho locust/*Robinia* X *ambigua*

Black locust/*Robinia pseudoacacia*

Chinese lacebark elm/*Ulmus parvifolia*

Vitex/*Vitex agnus-castus*

Jujube/*Zizyphus jujuba*

DECIDUOUS SHRUBS

Dwarf butterflybush/*Buddleia davidii* var. *nanhoensis*

Trumpet vine/*Campsis radicans*

Blue mist/*Caryopteris* X *clandonensis*

Cranberry cotoneaster/*Cotoneaster apiculatus*

Grayleaf cotoneaster/*Cotoneaster buxifolius*
 syn. *glaucophyllus*

Pyrenees cotoneaster/*Cotoneaster congestus*

Bearberry cotoneaster/*Cotoneaster dammeri*

Rockspray/ *Cotoneaster horizontalis*

Red clusterberry/*Cotoneaster lacteus* syn. *parneyi*

Silverberry/*Elaeagnus pungens*

Curry plant/*Helichrysum angustifolium*

Winter jasmine/*Jasminum nudiflorum*

Chinese juniper/*Juniperus chinensis* 'Ames', 'Hetzi',
 Mint Julep', 'Sea Green', 'Spearmint'

Spreading juniper/*Juniperus horizontalis*
 'Gray Carpet', 'Wilton Carpet',

Sabina juniper/*Juniperus sabina* 'Arcadia', 'Buffalo', 'Scandia'

Crapemyrtle/*Lagerstroemia indica* X *faurieri* 'Pecos' or 'Zuni'

English Lavender/*Lavandula angustifolia*

Coral Honeysuckle/*Lonicera sempervirens*

Compact mahonia/*Mahonia aquifolia* 'Compacta'

Silver lace vine/*Polygonum aubertii*

Lady Bank's rose/*Rosa banksiae* 'Lutea' and 'Alba'

Shrub roses/*Rosa floribunda, B. polyantha*, hybrid musks and
     perpetuals

Austrian copper/*Rosa foetida* 'Bicolor'

Rugosa rose/*Rosa rugosa*

'Arp' rosemary/*Rosmarinus officianalis* 'Arp'

Santolina/*Santolina chamaecyparissus* and *S. virens*

Spanish broom/*Spartium junceum*

Chinese lilac/*Syringa rothomagensis*

WILDFLOWERS

Mat daisy/*Anacyclus depressus*

Mountain bluet/*Centaurea montana*

Red Valerian/*Centranthus ruber*

Snow in summer/*Cerastium tomentosum*

Dwarf plumbago/*Ceratostigma plumbaginoides*

'Bowles Mauve' wallflower/*Cheiranthus* syn. *Erysimum linifolium*

Purple iceplant/*Delosperma cooperi*

Yellow iceplant/*Delosperma nubigenum*

'Blue Butterflies' dwarf delphinium/*Delphinium chinensis* hybrid

Pinks/*Dianthus* species and cultivars

Blue spurge/*Euphorbia myrsinites*

Creeping baby's breath/*Gypsophila repens*

Sunrose/*Helianthemum nummularium*

Daylilies/*Hemerocallis* hybrids

Candytuft/*Iberis sempervirens*

Starflower/*Ipheion uniflorum*

Bearded iris/*Iris* hybrids

Siberian iris/*Iris siberica*

Torch lily/*Kniphofia uvaria*

Grape hyacinth/*Muscari armeniacum*

Catmint/*Nepeta mussini* syn. *N. faassenii*

Oregano/*Origanum* species

Russian sage/*Perovskia atriplicifolia*

Rue/*Ruta graveolens*

'Autumn Joy' sedum/*Sedum telephium*

Partridge feather/*Tanacetum densum-amani*

Wooly and Creeping thymes/*Thymus* species

Silver speedwell/*Veronica incana*

Turkish speedwell/*Veronica liwanensis*

Wooly veronica/*Veronica pectinata*

GRASSES

Blue avena/*Helictotrichon sempervirens*

Hardy fountaingrass/*Pennisetum aloepecuroides*

Dwarf fountaingrass/*Pennisetum villosum*

8 A Garden Party

BACKYARD HABITATS ENHANCE THE DIVERSITY of wildlife locally while forming links with larger natural areas. Habitat gardening is a personal commitment to a better world that starts with a new perspective on the spaces we individually maintain. Habitats satisfy needs beyond our personal comfort. The shade trees that cool our summer afternoons provide perching and nesting sites for hawks and owls. The windbreaks that provide the human amenities of reduced wind, dust, and noise also shelter and feed orioles, towhees, finches, quail, woodpeckers, and raccoons. Ground covers that reduce weed invasion and prevent erosion also shelter ground-nesting species such as pheasant and meadowlarks. With plant diversity comes a bounty of insect activity to support bats, swallows, nighthawks, lizards, and turtles. Seeing ourselves as threads in this fabric of life allows us to participate in the process of weaving a stronger, more beautiful cloth.

THE ATTITUDE

Natural gardening involves developing a vision of beauty based on local ecology. Habitat gardening goes a step further in opening the gates to wildlife, a guest list often overlooked in landscape planning. Books and articles on habitat gardening suggest making lists of the wildlife species you'd like to attract and the plants that those species are likely to use. While there is no harm in developing wish lists, those lists need to be based on what is locally possible. A laissez-faire policy is an easy and productive way

A ROADRUNNER NEST IN A ROCKY MOUNTAIN JUNIPER. ROADRUNNERS ARE OPPORTUNISTS WHO BUILD NESTS, SOMETIMES WITHIN FIVE FEET OF THE GROUND, IN SUCH DENSE OR THORNY VEGETATION AS SALTBUSH, CHOLLA, MESQUITE, PINES, AND JUNIPERS.

to start. Provide the basic needs of water, shelter, and food, create inviting spaces, and include plants that will invite birds and butterflies into the garden. Provide seeds, herbage, and berries that mature over a range of seasons and provide cover in a range of sizes and densities. Then watch and wait. Wildlife is opportunistic. The more diverse the flora, the more diverse the fauna will be. Some of the visitors will be easier to live with than others. Insects, as numerous and beneficial as they are, rarely appear on habitat garden wish lists. Yet many birds, including hummingbirds, feed on insects. Waging a successful war on bugs will also harm the charismatic wildlife on the wish list. Nature is messy and habitat gardens glory in the mess, but there's also an innate order in the natural world. Animals are creatures of habit and we can establish a balance in the garden by learning to use habitual behaviors and natural adaptations to limit the impact of nuisance species. It all starts with developing a more informed and flexible attitude toward nature and gardening. The wildest of habitats isn't an appropriate alternative to the front lawn, but bordered by a tended shrub and wildflower border a habitat garden can be a very engrossing low-maintenance addition to the backyard.

THE PROCESS

The first step in developing a habitat is to consider the opportunities and limitations of the site. The more disturbed and unnatural your present site is, the longer it will take to reestablish healthy diversity. If pesticides have been used extensively, insect pests will probably be more prolific than their predators for the time it takes to rid the food chain of toxins. If the soil has been greatly disturbed, weed and erosion problems will figure in initial planting plans. Tender new plants being cultivated to provide food and shelter for wildlife will need protection until they are established enough to survive seasonal browsing. Use local ecosystems as models for selecting compatible plants that will naturalize and provide a sustainable plant community.

THE BASIC NEEDS OF WILDLIFE: WATER, SHELTER, AND FOOD

Providing a consistent source of water is critical in our southwestern climate. The water source can be as simple as a frostproof basin or as grand as a man-made lake. Regardless of the size of the reservoir, it should contain some water year-round and be large enough and sited to remain partially ice free in winter.

Protection from predators and cover from which to stalk prey and for resting and nesting are also important to provide. The number of breeding pairs of songbirds is strongly influenced by shrub density. A layered canopy with a mix of evergreen and deciduous trees and shrubs providing sixty to seventy percent cover, and open areas of wildflowers and grasses, is most effective in attracting and maintaining a diverse wildlife community. This balance of evergreen and deciduous plants, shade canopy, shrub masses, and ground cover is the hallmark both of good landscape design and

sound habitat. Habitat gardening departs from traditional landscaping in the omission of expansive lawn monocultures as understory since closely mowed turf has little wildlife value.

The list of appropriate plants useful as food sources varies with the ecology and potential inhabitants of the site. As always, diversity is the best approach, providing plants for herbage, seed, fruit, nectar, and insects. Just as the size of the site influences the type and number of animal species it can accommodate, it similarly dictates the diversity of appropriate plants. On a small site, using plants that are naturally compact in growth habit will help to expand the available space. On a large site it makes sense to zone plants according to the amount of water they require and mass species in dense thickets. This will not only provide cover for wildlife but also limit weed competition, make it easier for the plantings to become established, and have greater visual impact.

EVERGREENS

Of the conifers, juniper and pine provide excellent winter shelter and nesting opportunities as well as nutritious seeds. Fruits of algerita, a native barberry, are relished by many birds, and the barbed leaves and dense growth habit provide a haven from predators. Mountain mahogany and cliffrose are important seed sources in summer and

FRUITS OF ALGERITA, A NATIVE BARBERRY, ARE RELISHED BY MANY BIRDS, AND THE DENSE GROWTH AND PRICKLY LEAVES PROVIDE PROTECTION FROM PREDATORS.

NEW MEXICO OLIVE HAS PERSISTENT FRUITS THAT BECOME MORE PALATABLE WITH FREEZING, MAKING IT A VALUABLE WINTER FOOD SOURCE.

fall and provide year-round browsing and cover. Oaks may be either evergreen or deciduous, tall canopy or shrubby, depending upon the species, but their acorns are the mainstay of woodpeckers, turkeys, raccoons, deer, and bear in winter when food is scarce. Oaks are also valuable because of their long life span. Where adapted, they provide habitat for centuries. On the hottest, driest sites fourwing saltbush survives the harsh conditions of salty soils and drought fatal to most evergreens and reliably produces high-protein forage and seeds. Because of its tenacity and the fact that seeds of saltbush dispersed by wildlife germinate readily, it is best reserved for the more severe sites where it can provide cover and shelter but will not overwhelm less aggressive plants.

SUMMER- AND FALL-FRUITING DECIDUOUS PLANTS

Although deciduous plants do not provide winter shelter, their dense growth habit and, in some species, thorny branches offer nesting sites for a variety of birds. It is important to include both summer- and fall-fruiting plants in the habitat. The starchy pods of mesquite are a summertime staple of many animals. From a gardener's perspective, serviceberry, golden currant, and western sand cherry are beautiful spring-flowering shrubs with red fall foliage. To dozens of summer migratory birds, they are four-star resorts. The flowers of threeleaf and littleleaf sumac are less conspicuous than those of serviceberry and sand cherry, but their red fruit and autumn foliage are attractive to songbirds and gardeners alike. Moreover, they are better adapted to hot, dry sites than either serviceberry or currants. False indigo, native to riparian ecosystems in the Southwest, is an attractive tall screen, hedge, or shelterbelt component with spikes of dark blue flowers in May and fine-textured foliage that turns golden in autumn. Its seeds are relished by quail and mourning doves.

LARGE, GRASSY, OPEN AREAS ARE IMPOR-
TANT TO GROUND-NESTING SPECIES
AND TO HUNTING PREDATORS. CM

New Mexico olive, smooth sumac, and woods rose have persistent fruits that become more palatable after freezing. They fill an important niche in the food chain, providing winter forage for year-round residents and winter migrants. Woods rose is also valuable as a thicket-forming shrub with potential as erosion control as well as dense thorny cover for wildlife.

WILDFLOWERS AND GRASSES

Open areas in the tree-and-shrub canopy are important as cover for ground-nesting birds such as pheasant, meadowlarks, and, in drier ecosystems, doves and quail. Such breaks in dense cover also serve as hunting sites for foxes, coyotes, skunks, hawks, and owls. Midsummer-flowering prairieclover is another deeply rooted perennial with limited maintenance requirements that persists in grasslands, adding a grace note of seasonal color. Maximilian sunflower and gayfeather are long-lived perennials that flower and produce seeds year after year on undisturbed soil, thus reducing the likelihood of invasion by annual weeds. The striking purple spikes of gayfeather in late summer and the columns of yellow flowers produced by the Maximilian sunflower at the end of each growing season earn their acceptance horticulturally, providing an abundance of seeds in fall and early winter for habitat. While their beauty is certainly an asset, their bounty of seeds and contribution to ecosystem stability are equally valuable.

The national focus on grasses as ornamentals is very convenient for habitat gardeners living in high-plains grassland communities. Many of our common native grasses provide subtle color and textural interest. Indian ricegrass grows well and seeds on sites having less than eight inches annual precipitation, reliably providing food for wildlife where only the strong and flexible persist. The russet winter color of little bluestem gives it garden appeal. Combined with gayfeather, prairieclover, and sideoats grama, it creates a carefree, colorful meadow habitat for ground nesters. An annual mowing in early spring before nesting begins and periodic deep watering in summer are all the care required in areas that are naturally semiarid grasslands.

Hummingbirds and butterflies are among the most irresistible guests at any garden party. Hummers are easy to accommodate with just a few small snags as perches and tubular red-spectrum flowers as lunch. Because they are aggressively territorial, hummers require a series of "rooms" separated by tall shrub-border nesting areas for protection from the thugs of their species. Desert willow, cherry sage, giant four o'clock, the red and purple-blue penstemons, and century plants are all good hummingbird attractants, with a range of exposure and water requirements adapted to many types of habitat.

Butterflies are favored guests for the animation and color they bring to the garden. They favor nectar-producing flowers that offer them a platform on which to perch and sip. Evening primroses, false indigo, and roses provide early season nectar. Butterflyweed, blanketflower, coneflowers, and yarrow carry butterflies through summer. Gayfeather and chamisa end the butterfly season with a flash of purple and gold. Further, the foliage of butterflyweed, roses, many composites, penstemon, legumes, and evening primroses is an excellent food source for butterfly larvae. Once established, most plants will outgrow the caterpillars' voracious foraging. Those that don't survive can hardly be viewed as losses, having fueled the change from worm to wonder.

MANAGEMENT STRATEGIES

Developing a backyard habitat is an attempt to shortcut hundreds of years of evolution by using natural models as road maps. Flexibility is a sound basis for managing a habitat area. Choose a diversity of plants that is environmentally appropriate to the site. In the initial stage when a habitat area is being established, the extra water and fertilizer needed to get transplants off to a strong start will also make the soft new growth more attractive to insects and palatable to browsing wildlife. Strange as it may seem, the insect pests are a plus, helping to establish a predator population of beneficial insects, birds, and mammals. If the plants are well sited, as they become established they will progress from needing protection for survival to providing shelter and forage as intended. Introduced species, on the other hand, may never become self-sustaining. Such plants that are likely to remain vulnerable should be protected in a walled or fenced part of the garden apart from the habitat area. Temporarily enclosing in wire tents new transplants that will eventually naturalize helps ease the frustrations inherent in the process of restoring balance to a disturbed ecosystem.

The use of pesticides of any kind should be carefully considered in establishing a natural system and probably eliminated in the management stages. Even "safe" biological controls can upset fragile balances in a habitat. Learning the players, and the complex interrelatedness that is revealed in the drama of nature, is the best management tool you can acquire.

With wildlife comes the dispersal of seeds. To support this activity you will want to provide small areas of bare soil for dust baths and digestive grit. Inevitably, weeds will be among the seeds that sprout in a habitat garden, and selective weeding to balance the planting will be required, at least initially.

Leaf litter and dead snags are useful for animals and their prey both. The insects that feed on decaying vegetation and wood are no threat to healthy plants and are dietary essentials for many animals. The snags provide perching and resting places. On a large lot, deadwood can be screened from unappreciative neighbors; in more urban areas, birdhouses are an appropriate substitute. Pets can cause problems in a wildlife habitat. Although most cats can learn to walk so they don't ring bells intended to warn their prey, collaring cats with iridescent tags that reflect sun and moonlight can make them less effective predators. Maintaining open spaces around water sources and feeders also gives wildlife the advantage. A few well-cared-for pets will usually have little impact on an ecosystem in dynamic balance.

There are two organizational resources in developing and, if necessary, defending habitat gardens. The National Wildlife Federation, 1400 16th Street NW, Washington, D.C. 20036-2266, has a "Backyard Habitat Program" to provide information about and lend legitimacy to wildlife projects. The Institute for Urban Wildlife, 10921 Trotting Ridge Way, Columbia, Md 21044, advertises similar services. Because these programs originate in the mid-Atlantic area, some of the information provided may not be appropriate in the Southwest. Explore local resources, such as the Audubon chapter in your area, local botanic gardens, nature centers, zoological parks, natural history museum staff members, and university ecologists and wildlife biologists.

As we work toward reestablishing the connection with natural areas in behalf of the wildlife that human development is displacing, we reconnect ourselves with the richness of nature. We establish a balance in our own lives and perspectives that serve us well in all our endeavors. Balance, the ability to absorb change and benefit from it, is the ultimate measure of success.

BOSQUE DEL APACHE HABITAT GARDEN

The landscape for the visitors' center at Bosque del Apache National Wildlife Refuge south of Socorro, New Mexico, caters to visitors who travel by wing and hoof, as well as those who arrive by car and bus. The landscape project began in 1988 as a cooper-

AN INAUSPICIOUS BEGINNING FOR THE HABITAT GARDEN: THE ONLY GREEN IS TUMBLEWEED AND KOCHIA.

ative effort with the Native Plant Society of New Mexico, which provided funding for planning and volunteer help for planting. The design focuses on locally native plants to reflect a sense of place, to provide habitat for wildlife in the headquarters area, to identify plants found elsewhere on the refuge and in surrounding natural areas, and to minimize the water and other maintenance needed. Hosting tens of thousands of birds and an even greater number of visitors that the birds attract doesn't allow staff much time to perform routine maintenance duties.

Located in south-central New Mexico, where the Chihuahuan desert merges with high-plains grassland, the refuge is well positioned to be a proving ground for a garden based on native plants from piñon-juniper uplands to shrub-desert grassland. The refuge is itself an oasis. Bosque, the riverine forest for which the refuge is named, is dominated by the great valley cottonwoods. An understory of New Mexico olives, silver buffaloberries, and false indigo provides lower tiers for perching, nesting, and foraging spaces. Wolfberry forms dense thorny thickets alongside a stand of fourwing saltbush that keeps quail fat and happy and close in for viewing year-round.

What the arid woodland plant communities lack in stature, they compensate for in understory diversity. Piñon pines, one-seed juniper, and Gambel oak are the dominant trees, although deer browsing keeps the oaks more shrubby. Mountain mahogany, sumac, cliffrose, yucca, fringed sage, cliff fendlerbush, algerita, rock sage, and winter-

fat add middlestory cover and forage. Giant four o'clock, pitcher sage, blanketflower, globemallow, scarlet bugler and pineleaf penstemon, prairie sage, blue grama, and little bluestem contribute seasonal color and seeds.

Confirming its position in the northern Chihuahuan desert, the Bosque habitat garden features the aromatic evergreen creosotebush sharing space with ocotillo, honey mesquite, and littleleaf sumac. Broom dalea and threadleaf sage that stabilize blow sands over hundreds of square miles just north of the refuge occupy some of the driest niches in the garden. Hummingbirds seek out the rose-pink desert penstemon while blackfoot daisy, wild marigold, spectacle pod, desert zinnia, Indian ricegrass, grama, and sand lovegrass lure songbirds, doves, and quail. Desert willows, Apache plume, chamisa, chocolate flower, and bush penstemon border an open area representing an arroyo ecosystem, where the dense plant cover allows wildlife to observe tourists at their leisure.

Grasslands merge into all the other ecosystems, sharing characteristics of each where they meet, anchoring the arid soils and providing cover for ground-nesting birds such as meadowlarks, dove, and killdeer. In order to persist here, wildflowers must be deeply rooted and drought enduring. Bush morningglory, gayfeather, and prairieclover are among the most resilient. Indian ricegrass, blue grama, little bluestem, and galleta were reintroduced here by mulching with hay. Sideoats grama and lovegrass arrived by wind or wing.

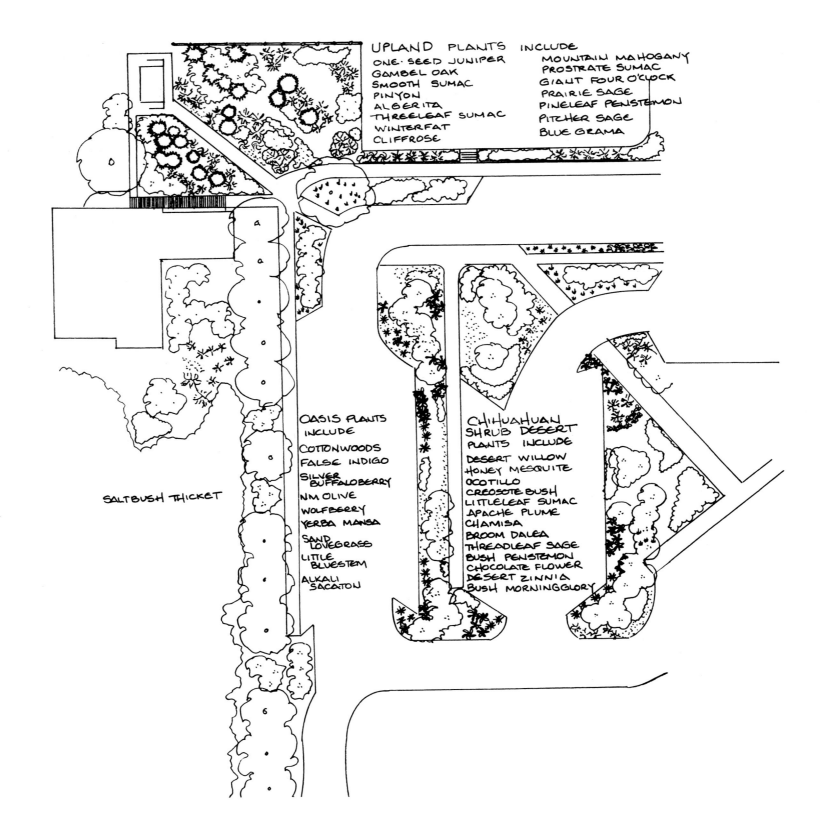

UPLAND PLANTS INCLUDE

ONE-SEED JUNIPER   MOUNTAIN MAHOGANY
GAMBEL OAK   PROSTRATE SUMAC
SMOOTH SUMAC   GIANT FOUR O'CLOCK
PINYON   PRAIRIE SAGE
ALGERITA   PINELEAF PENSTEMON
THREELEAF SUMAC   PITCHER SAGE
WINTERFAT   BLUE GRAMA
CLIFFROSE

OASIS PLANTS
INCLUDE

COTTONWOODS
FALSE INDIGO
SILVER
BUFFALOBERRY
NM OLIVE
WOLFBERRY
YERBA MANSA
SAND
LOVEGRASS
LITTLE
BLUESTEM
ALKALI
SACATON

CHIHUAHUAN
SHRUB DESERT
PLANTS INCLUDE

DESERT WILLOW
HONEY MESQUITE
OCOTILLO
CREOSOTE BUSH
LITTLELEAF SUMAC
APACHE PLUME
CHAMISA
BROOM DALEA
THREADLEAF SAGE
BUSH PENSTEMON
CHOCOLATE FLOWER
DESERT ZINNIA
BUSH MORNINGGLORY

SALTBUSH THICKET

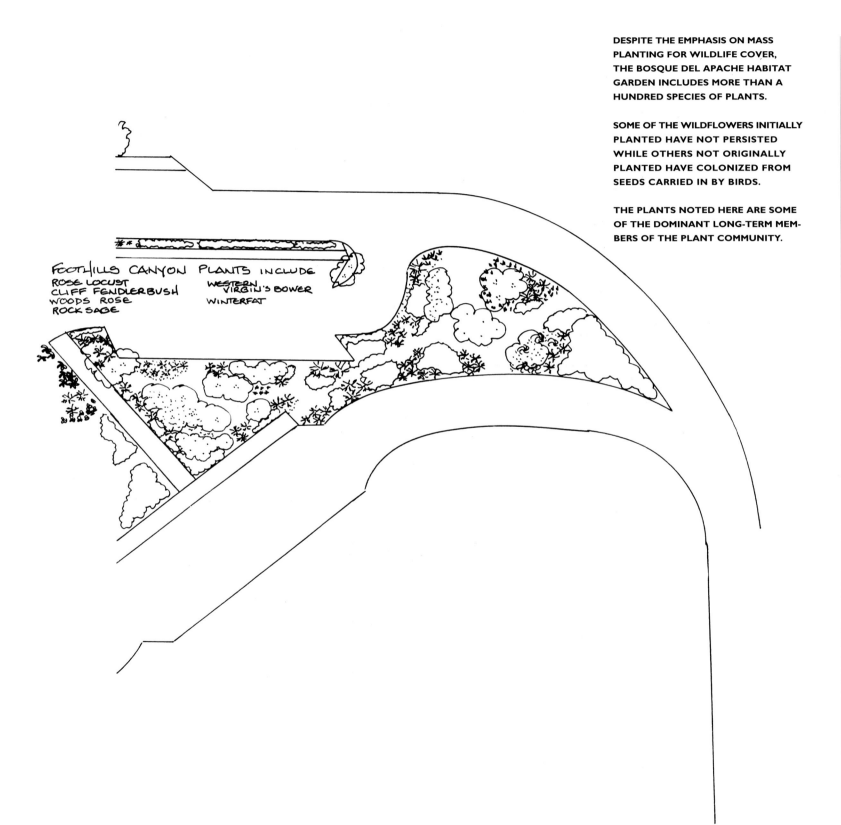

DESPITE THE EMPHASIS ON MASS
PLANTING FOR WILDLIFE COVER,
THE BOSQUE DEL APACHE HABITAT
GARDEN INCLUDES MORE THAN A
HUNDRED SPECIES OF PLANTS.

SOME OF THE WILDFLOWERS INITIALLY
PLANTED HAVE NOT PERSISTED
WHILE OTHERS NOT ORIGINALLY
PLANTED HAVE COLONIZED FROM
SEEDS CARRIED IN BY BIRDS.

THE PLANTS NOTED HERE ARE SOME
OF THE DOMINANT LONG-TERM MEM-
BERS OF THE PLANT COMMUNITY.

FOOTHILLS CANYON PLANTS INCLUDE
ROSE LOCUST
CLIFF FENDLERBUSH
WOODS ROSE
ROCK SAGE
WESTERN VIRGIN'S BOWER
WINTERFAT

Most of the refuge's human visitors come in winter when the numbers of migrating waterfowl reach a peak. Most high-desert vegetation is least impressive then. Drying winds and relatively mild day temperatures that plunge overnight make life and leaves risky for evergreens. Landscape interest is maintained in the dormant garden by emphasizing textures and featuring plants with interesting seed heads. Coincidentally, those seed heads are even more interesting to wildlife.

The transformation of nearly five acres of fill dirt and tumbleweeds divided by curbs and sidewalks into suitable habitat for the killdeer and mule deer, hummingbirds, quail, doves, rabbits, coyote, and an occasional vermillion flycatcher in summer took three years to reach a plateau of establishment. The planting of more than two thousand container-grown plants representing sixty species was done in stages from November through June. Due to budget cutbacks, the installation of the drip irrigation system was delayed a season, and all the watering and weeding was done by a dedicated refuge staff member and a group of summer youth-program teenagers. Despite a record-breaking hot summer, very few plants were lost, and most of those were eaten by rabbits or deer. The end of the heat wave and budget freeze allowed the drip system to be installed and a generous mulch distributed; the weed problem consequently subsided. By the third year, supplemental watering was limited to one deep soaking monthly. As the garden matured, the grasses increased quickly the second season, then stabilized. A few of the shorter-lived wildflowers, such as blanketflower, blue flax, and some of the penstemon, disappeared. Pocket gophers consumed most of the succulent roots of the initial planting of gayfeather and four o'clock. The four o'clock responded by making new plants of every small section of root left behind, and the stand has tripled in as many years. The gayfeather, with its single tapering taproot, disappeared. We responded by planting new roots in cylinders of hardware cloth for protection, and so far the greedy gophers have been thwarted. In spring and fall, a team of volunteers spends a morning trimming off empty seed stalks, clearing grass thatch, and transplanting seedlings that come up in awkward places. Throughout the year, a few volunteers weed and clean up litter on an occasional basis. No fertilizers or pesticides are used.

We knew from the woods rose and Gambel oak having been chewed to stubs the first winter that deer and rabbits had been visiting, but the real sign that the garden was succeeding as habitat came the spring after the mulches were laid down. When we arrived for the seasonal cleanup, we were greeted by the diversionary tactic of a squawking killdeer dragging her wing across the parking lot away from one of the planting islands. It took awhile to find her clutch of three eggs, the color of coffee with cream overlaid with dark brown blotches. They were nestled in the bark mulch along-

EGGS DEPOSITED IN MULCH.

THE SEEDS OF CREOSOTEBUSH (RIGHT CENTER), A DOMINANT PLANT IN THE CHIHUAHUAN DESERT, ATTRACT HUNGRY QUAIL. THE ROSE-PINK FLOWERS OF DESERT PENSTE-MON PROVIDE NECTAR FOR THE FIRST HUMMINGBIRD MIGRANTS IN SPRING.

side one of the drip lines. She returns each year, nesting in different places but always in the bark. As a designer, it is tremendously gratifying to have clients, bursting with enthusiasm for their new garden, describe their favorite plant grouping or color scheme. When a client lays eggs in your mulch, you have really accomplished something!

A listing of plants that will attract and sustain wildlife follows.

Plants for Habitat

Most of the plants recommended in the previous plant lists have some wildlife value: all evergreens provide winter shelter; all trees provide nesting and roosting; all seldom-mowed grasses provide cover. The following plants are exceptionally valuable for the reasons noted.

UPLAND TREES

Redbuds/*Cercis* species	Nesting/Early spring bee nectar
Hawthorns/*Crataegus* species	Nesting/Fall fruit
Walnuts/*Juglans* species	Cover and nesting/Fall nuts
Junipers/*Juniperus* species	Cover and nesting/Several seasons of seeds
Oaks/*Quercus* species	Cover and nesting/Summer and fall acorns
Staghorn-type sumacs/*Rhus lanceolata, R. glabra*	Cover and nesting/Winter seeds

UPLAND SHRUBS AND VINES

Serviceberries/*Amelanchier* species	Summer fruit
Manzanitas/*Arctostaphylos* species	Summer fruit
Algerita/*Berberis* haematocarpa	Cover and nesting/Summer fruit
Winterfat/*Ceratoides lanata* syn. *Eurotia lanata*	Winter seeds and browse
Mountain mahoganies/*Cercocarpus* species	Cover and nesting/Fall seeds
Fernbush/*Chamaebatieria millefolium*	Summer butterfly nectar
Cholla/*Opuntia imbricata*	Cover/Butterfly and hummingbird nectar/Summer fruit
Squawapple/*Periphyllum ramosissimus*	Summer and fall fruit
Threeleaf sumac/*Rhus trilobata*	Summer fruit

UPLAND WILDFLOWERS

Giant hyssop/*Agastache cana*	Hummingbird nectar
Indian paintbrushes/*Castilleja* species	Hummingbird nectar

Buckwheats/*Eriogonum* species	Bee, butterfly, and predatory insect nectar
Red rocket/*Ipomopsis aggregata*	Hummingbird nectar
Standing cypress/*Ipomopsis rubra*	Hummingbird nectar
syn. *Gilia coronopifolia*	
Peppergrass/*Lepidium montanum*	Bee, butterfly, and predatory insect nectar
Giant four o'clock/*Mirabilis multiflora*	Hummingbird and hawkmoth nectar
Evening primroses/*Oenothera* species	Hawkmoth nectar/Caterpillar food
Penstemons (Red, pink and purple)	Hummingbird nectar
/*Penstemon* species	
Scarlet mint/*Stachys coccinea*	Hummingbird nectar
California fuschia/*Zauschneria californica*	Hummingbird nectar
syn. *Z. latifolia*	

GRASSLAND AND SHRUB-DESERT TREES

Desert willow/*Chilopsis linearis*	Hummingbird nectar
Honey mesquite/*Prosopis glandulosa*	Bee, butterfly, and predatory insect nectar
Yuccas/*Yucca* species	Nesting/Pronuba moth food

GRASSLAND AND SHRUB-DESERT SHRUBS

Beebrush/*Aloysia wrightii*	Bee, butterfly, and predatory insect nectar
Leadplants/*Amorpha* species	Bee, butterfly, and predatory insect nectar
Desert honeysuckle/*Anisacanthus thurberii*	Hummingbird nectar
Saltbushes/*Artiplex* species	Cover and nesting/Winter seeds
Bird of paradise/*Caesalpinia gilliesii*	Hummingbird nectar
Ocotillo/*Fouqueria splendens*	Hummingbird and bat nectar
Cholla/*Opuntia leptocaulis*	Cover and nesting/Nectar, fruit, and seeds
Prickly pear cactus/*Opuntia macrocentra*	Cover and nesting/Nectar, fruit, and seeds
Western sand cherry/*Prunus besseyi*	Summer fruit
Broom dalea/*Psorothamnus scoparius*	Bee nectar
Littleleaf sumac/*Rhus microphylla*	Summer fruit
Cherry, Autumn sage/*Salvia greggii*	Hummingbird nectar

GRASSLAND AND SHRUB-DESERT WILDFLOWERS

Fragrant sand verbena/*Abronia fragrans*	Bee, butterfly, and predatory insect nectar
Sand verbena/*Tripterocalyx wootonii*	Bee, butterfly, and predatory insect nectar
Prickly poppy/*Argemone pleiacantha*	Summer and fall seeds
Butterflyweeds/*Asclepias* species	Butterfly nectar/Caterpillar food

Rocky Mountain beeplant/*Cleome serrulata*	Bee, butterfly, and predatory insect nectar
Spectacle pod/*Dithyrea wislizenii*	Bee, butterfly, and predatory insect nectar
Bush morningglory/*Ipomoea leptophylla*	Hummingbird nectar
Gayfeathers/*Liatris* species	Bee, butterfly, and predatory insect nectar
Evening primroses/*Oenothera* species	Hawkmoth nectar/Caterpillar food
Penstemons (Red, pink, and purple) /*Penstemon* species	Hummingbird nectar
Purple prairieclover/*Petalostemum purpureum*	Bee, butterfly, and predatory insect nectar/seed
Pitcher sage/*Salvia azurea grandiflora* syn. *S. Pitcheri*	Bee nectar/Fall seeds

OASIS TREES

New Mexico olive/*Forestiera neomexicana*	Early spring bee nectar/Late summer to winter seeds
Cottonwoods/*Populus* species	Nesting cavities
Mexican elder/*Sambucus mexicanus*	Butterfly nectar/Summer fruit
Silver buffaloberry/*Shepherdia argentea*	Summer fruit

OASIS SHRUBS AND VINES

False indigo/*Amorpha fruticosa*	Bee, butterfly, and predatory insect nectar
Buttonbush/*Cephalanthus occidentalis*	Butterfly nectar
Wolfberry/*Lycium pallidum*	Cover/Summer fruit
Woodbine/*Parthenocissus inserta*	Cover/Summer and fall fruits
Golden currant/*Ribes aureum*	Summer fruits
Woods rose/*Rosa woodsii*	Bee, butterfly nectar
Willows/*Salix* species	Bee, butterfly, and predatory insect nectar

OASIS WILDFLOWERS

White aster/*Aster ericoides*	Bee, butterfly, and predatory insect nectar
Purple coneflower/*Echinacea purpurea*	Bee, butterfly nectar
Black-eyed susan/*Rudbeckia hirta*	Bee, butterfly nectar
Maximilian sunflower/*Helianthus maximiliani*	Fall seeds
Cardinal flower/*Lobelia cardinalis*	Hummingbird nectar
Evening primroses/*Oenothera* species	Hawkmoth nectar/Caterpillar food
Goldenrods/*Solidago* species	Butterfly nectar
Ironweed/*Vernonia marginata*	Butterfly nectar

ADAPTIVE TREES

Crabapple/*Malus* species	Fall and winter fruits
Jujube/*Zizyphus jujuba*	Thorny cover/Fall fruit

ADAPTIVE SHRUBS

Dwarf butterflybush/*Buddleia davidii* var. *nanhoensis*	Butterfly nectar/Caterpillar food
Trumpet vine/*Campsis radicans*	Hummingbird nectar
Blue mist/*Caryopteris* X *clandonensis*	Bee, butterfly and predatory insect nectar
Cotoneasters/*Cotoneaster* species	Late summer to winter fruits
Winter jasmine/*Jasminum nudiflorum*	Early spring bee nectar
Lavender/*Lavandula angustifolia*	Bee, butterfly nectar
Coral honeysuckle/*Lonicera sempervirens*	Hummingbird nectar
Silver lace vine/*Polygonum aubertii*	Bee, butterfly, and predatory insect nectar
Shrub roses/*Rosa* species	Bee, butterfly nectar

ADAPTIVE FLOWERS

Valerian/*Centranthus ruber*	Hummingbird nectar
Torch lily/*Kniphofia uvaria*	Hummingbird nectar
Catmint/*Nepeta mussini* syn. *N. faassenii*	Spring to fall bee nectar
Russian sage/*Perovskia atriplicifolia*	Bee nectar
Rue/*Ruta graveolens*	Predatory insect nectar/Caterpillar food

9 Maintaining the Balance

THE THIRD YEAR IN THE EVOLUTION of a natural garden usually marks an obvious turning point. The garden's infancy and adolescence (previously discussed chapter 3) yield to full maturity. Individual plants begin to fill their assigned spaces; wildflowers bloom, set seeds, and expand into impressive colonies; groups of plants counter each other in color, texture, or form. Layers of cover emerge and give spaces depth and shadow. Patterns of shade begin to expand. Plant communities knit together against weed intrusion. The gardener's focus changes to meet the new circumstances. Less attention needs to be given to each plant separately. The big picture—how successfully the plants work together as a composition and a community—is the long-term concern. Developing a management plan is an exercise in critical thinking: Do we feel at home as we walk through the garden? Have our original priorities been met? Are wind-scoured corners and slopes more stable? Is the garden engaging year-round? Is there enough color in summer? Is there such a thing as "enough color"? Do songbirds, butterflies, and hummingbirds animate the borders? And finally, does the garden meet our expectations? If not, why not?

Natural gardens are reciprocal endeavors. Their management, like their design, aims to balance appearance and utility. Leaving a garden untended erases the human

CHOCOLATE FLOWER OFFERS NECTAR FOR BUTTERFLIES, SEEDS FOR MANY SONGBIRDS, AND A DELICIOUS CHOCOLATE FRAGRANCE FOR THE HUMAN PASSERBY.

175

element at its heart, but too much pruning and prodding belabors the human component at the expense of the plants themselves. The purpose of a garden determines its management plan. Outdoor living spaces usually need the most ongoing maintenance since they receive the greatest use and are most visible. Habitat gardens should receive the least interference. Between these poles, and even within the tame and wild areas, personal taste dictates. In the end, gardens are a rewarding means of self-expression. It is the personal style of the caretaker that makes the garden look neat and tailored, lush and exuberant, serene, welcoming, starkly dramatic, or charming.

Water Management

After two growing seasons, it is time to make adjustments in the garden. Overall, our aim is to wean the garden of its excessive need of care, limiting watering, weeding, spraying, fertilizing, pruning, and mowing to only what is needed for plant health and our personal satisfaction. The drought-requiring plants, those that could survive on natural rainfall, will grow too quickly and develop loose, floppy shapes unless we gradually sever the irrigation umbilical cord. Their weaning process often starts the year after planting. The third year, we test the limits of the drought-enduring plants, those that will remain somewhat dependent, by slowing the flow of supplemental water. Instead of increasing the irrigation to twice a month as spring temperatures become consistently mild, we might continue monthly deep watering until the beginning of summer. As summer heats up, instead of increasing to a weekly schedule, we may opt for the bimonthly schedule, lengthening the watering cycle somewhat to compensate for the longer time between irrigations. Along the way observe the response of the plants, watching for any loss of vigor, and make adjustments toward finding an irrigation schedule that gives the desired leaf density, abundance of flowers, and growth rate with the least amount of water. It may be necessary to increase the volume of water with additional drip emitters for some of the drought-tolerant plants, especially the shade trees and shrubs used for wind protection and privacy screening. As they become larger, they may require more water to support their mass. Some of the annuals and short-lived perennials that were planted for immediate gratification may begin to decline or disappear due to two factors: lacking deep root systems, they are unable to persist with less frequent watering; or, they no longer have the disturbed soil they need to reproduce. We have come to a fork in the management road. Do we miss them enough to turn up the water volume and scratch up the soil surface, even though weeds will also benefit from our efforts, or has the color and texture of the flowering shrubs and long-lived perennials made the annuals superfluous? The answer may be yes to both. We might maintain a more intensive watering schedule in the garden spaces we see and use most often and let the rest of the garden settle into its mature climax vegetation. Water management will vary from season to season and year to year to compensate for variations in rainfall, heat, and wind. An established native-grass lawn in the shrub desert that averages eight inches of precipitation annually could be maintained on a sixteen-inch annual irrigation schedule, programmed to receive one inch of water a month from September through April and one inch every two weeks from May through August. If summer rains are especially generous, the July and August watering may be reduced by half. If winter rain and snow are abundant, we might not water at all from mid-November to mid-February. If spring is especially warm and windy, we might need to increase watering in April, and if summer brings several weeks of temperatures near or above one hundred degrees F, we may find ourselves watering twice as often as usual to keep the grass green and the wildflowers in bloom. We might just as well decide to stay the course: keep supplemental watering to a minimum and let the garden sink into heat dormancy. For a month or two it may look ragged, but when the rains finally come the burst of growth and resurgence of flowers will be exciting. If the plants are well adapted and well established, they will remain healthy whichever management route we take.

Regardless of the weather, there is general upkeep of the irrigation system to consider. Clean drip-irrigation filters will keep the system working properly and prevent emitter clogging. How often the filters need flushing depends on the water source. Well water is apt to have more fine sand particles to muddy the filter. In the city, repairs to water mains can foul filters unexpectedly. Emitter clogs are sometimes a problem if the system hasn't been used for an extended period of time, such as over winter. Mineral salts will crystalize in the tiny emitter orifices and seal them off. Sometimes the back pressure from running the system will dissolve or dislodge the salts. Syphoning a weak acid, a strong vinegar, or a very dilute sulfuric acid solution through the lines can sometimes remedy alkali clogging. Some emitters are designed so they can be gently squeezed with pliers to expand the pores and free grit or salts. Occasionally you may need simply to replace them. Experience gained during the early establishment of the garden helps determine how often to clean filters and check emitters.

Sometimes our perspective changes as the garden develops, and this attitude shift may require that we modify the irrigation system to accommodate departures from the original plan. Native-grass lawns have a way of turning into infrequently mowed ground covers. We might have put off mowing because the grass didn't really need it or because we had other things to do. One day we notice how soft and lush it looks. The thought of replacing the wavy texture with a crewcut stubble seems a shame, and soon the eyebrow seed heads of blue grama, dancing eighteen inches above what was supposed to be the lawn, have added a graceful fringe to the grassy shawl. Since the sprinkler heads we installed only pop up six inches, the elegant surprise of unmowed grama in the places the sprinkler reaches is contrasted by brittle dry patches where the tall grass blocks the spray pattern. We have come to another fork in the management road. We can choose to mow regularly as we originally intended or replace the sprinkler nozzles with ones that can spray over the tall grass and limit our mowing to once each winter or early spring.

Weed Management

Major recurrences of weeds in an established natural garden are an indication that something is out of balance. Sometimes the problem lies with the amount or frequency of watering. Excess watering too early in spring can favor the development both of the winter weeds such as mustard and unwanted cool-season grasses at the expense of heat-loving plants such as broom dalea and desert willow. Keeping warm-season lawns so dry in summer that they begin to thin out to mimic the open spacing characteristic of shrub-desert and grassland ecosystems can result in a flush of weed invasion when rain or irrigation brings a resurgence of growth.

Weed problems in an established habitat garden may be the dubious gift of guests. Bird droppings contain seeds, primed by passage through their gullets and ready to sprout. Rodents and ants leave seed caches that may become clumps of sunflowers, giant four o'clocks, or odious bindweed. Since we have no control over what wildlife brings to the potluck, we may need to sort through the buffet occasionally and discard weeds that might threaten the balance.

There are likely to be weed "hot spots" both in terms of the level of weeds we can tolerate and the likelihood that weeds will invade. Weeds in the flower beds next to the patio or along the walk to the front door are more noticeable and will nag at us until we remove them. It will be easier to eliminate them sooner rather than later. Behind the garage where water runs off the roof, the dog scratches and digs, and the vacant lot next door is a tumbleweed farm, weeds are more likely to invade and less likely to matter. In the focal areas, a few minutes of weeding can be a contemplative start to a hectic day or a way to unwind in the cool of the evening and will keep the high-priority spaces in good order. Seasonal weeding of less focal areas is usually enough to keep the rest of a naturalized landscape looking tended and the ecosystem balanced.

MULCHING

The effectiveness of mulches will gradually diminish over time, either due to the material breaking down or because enough blowing sand has accumulated in the mulch to allow weeds to gain ground. Whether replenishing is called for depends on the kind of mulch, how lavishly it was first applied, and its purpose.

Gravel pathways and driveways that take constant wear will need top-dressing every three to ten years depending on the amount of wear, whether filter fabric was used underneath, and the desired appearance. Sometimes the original four or six inches

WHERE PLANTS ARE WIDELY SPACED, MULCHES NEED REPLACING PERIODI-CALLY. CM

will be gone within a few years. In dry sand or wet clay, gravel mulch sinks into the surface under foot and tire pressure. Filter fabric/weed barrier or base course keeps gravel from being compressed into the soil and generally lengthens the time before top-dressing is needed. Gravels used to line drainage channels may need replenishing more often if flow rates are higher and plantings aren't used to slow the flow and filter silt.

Bark, pine needles, native-grass hay, and other materials that gradually decompose—when used on densely planted areas to moderate soil temperatures, retain moisture, and limit weed competition initially—often don't need replenishing. By the time the mulch has deteriorated, the plants have covered enough space and stabilized the soil enough to make the mulch unnecessary. If plant groupings are more widely spaced, the gaps between plants may need to be recovered. How often renewal is needed depends partly on how much moisture is available to speed the mulch composting and whether weeds are invading. Since the uplands and oases are wetter than shrub-desert grassland, mulches will decompose faster there. The tall trees in the river valley can yield a wealth of leaf mulch. Finer-textured, smaller-sized mulches also deteriorate faster and need supplementing more frequently. After spring or fall cleanups, shredding tree and shrub prunings and recycling leaves and mowed prairie grass as mulch for recovering worn areas make waste products into resources within the garden ecosystem.

Pest Management

As an equilibrium develops in the garden, much of the effort required by the caretaker is limited to thoughtful observation. Refining irrigation to sustenance levels usually helps balance insect activity and rabbit browsing since there is a decrease in the succulent new growth that prompts feeding frenzies. As the garden ecosystem evolves, native populations of insect predators begin to balance the pest population. As hosts of the garden party, we only need to circulate among the guests and keep the buffet supplied. In the few instances when our intervention is warranted, we should try to mediate flare-ups with the least disruption to the party as a whole. The plant profiles in the companion volume note potential trouble areas to monitor and suggest possible controls. Since many of the plants are new to cultivation, the information is by no means complete. Your local county extension entomologist can help you to identify the pest and recommend an integrated management process for dealing with it if necessary. Recurrent problems with insects or disease on specific plants are usually strong signals that the plants don't belong in the place or company they're in. Sometimes moving or removing the host plants is the best long-term solution.

Growth Management

FERTILIZING

Once a natural garden is established, little fertilizing is necessary except where the landscape departs from local ecological models. Lawns need fertilizing because of the competition between plants and the uniformity desired. Native-grass lawns usually thrive on an annual application of one to one and one-half pounds of nitrogen per thousand square feet of area in late spring. Timing is important. In a test done in northeastern Colorado by the Central Plains Experiment Range, annual fall fertilizing with one-half pound of ammonium nitrate per thousand square feet of blue grama weakened the stand of grass. Warm-season grasses should not be stimulated to produce top growth when the soil is too cold to allow for corresponding root growth. Likewise, when native grasses are watered excessively, at the same time the plants are stimulated to grow rapidly, nutrients are washed out of the soil and the soil microorganisms that normally help make nutrients available suffer from loss of oxygen in their environment. The grasses turn yellow because they can't absorb the nutrients they need. More fertilizer will correct the nutrient deficiency, but the real solution is to reduce the water applied over the long term. When summer temperatures near one hundred degrees F for more than a few days at a time, lawns have to be watered more to balance the increased evapotranspiration rate. Heat also hinders the absorption of iron, turning lawns yellow. Chelated iron, which is buffered to remain absorbable, or acidified iron,

HIGH-DESERT TREES MAY BE LEFT
UNPRUNED FOR SEVERAL YEARS TO
ALLOW THEM THE MAXIMUM LEAF
MASS TO PRODUCE STRONG ROOT
AND BRANCH SYSTEMS.

ONCE TREES DEVELOP SOME PERSONALITY,
REMOVING SUCKERS FROM THE BASE
OF THE TRUNKS AND THINNING OUT
SUPERFLUOUS LOWER BRANCHES TO
REVEAL INTERESTING TRUNK CONTOURS
AND BRANCHING PATTERNS IS A WAY
TO ENHANCE THE NATURAL FORMS
AND CREATE GARDEN SCULPTURE, AS
WITH THIS NEW MEXICO OLIVE.

such as iron sulfate, will regreen the grasses without stimulating new growth that will require more water. Because they are less adapted to the high desert, cool-season grasses require more water and fertilizer to grow well. Turf-type fescues should be fertilized in early spring and late fall with a balanced blend of nitrogen, phosphorous, potassium, and iron. In summer, iron supplements will keep a fescue lawn green and help to conserve water by not stimulating growth.

Chlorosis, heat- and alkali-induced nutrient deficiencies, sometimes occur in trees and shrubs that are out of balance in the garden. Arizona ash suffers iron and zinc deficiencies when used out of the streambank bosque ecosystem where it is native. Aspen develops scorched leaf margins when moved to hotter, drier settings than it is adapted to. Yellowing ash leaves can be corrected with chelated iron or zinc, but fertilizing a heat-stressed aspen will only speed its decline. In the human body, vitamins are food supplements, not remedies for an ill-considered life-style. The same is true in the garden.

PRUNING

Why prune? From the plant's perspective, pruning can make an individual healthier, stronger, and more wind resilient. Gently shaped plants imply order and suggest a bit of control in a wild setting. As has already been suggested, pruning is not a means of making oversized plants fit small spaces. Rather, pruning enhances the character of plants by clearing away extraneous growth so that their natural forms are more evident.

Understanding how plants grow and respond to cutting helps in deciding where and when to cut. Making a few cuts and watching the results is the best way to learn. The buds are the growing points for shoot elongation. Removing the terminal buds, the dominant growing tips on primary branches, activates the lateral buds that produce the side shoots. When terminal buds are cut off, after a growth pause while the plant adjusts to the change in direction, several side shoots will replace each single terminal. Since several shoots now share the sap that once pushed the stout solo bud, they will be shorter and thinner than the shoot removed. Pruning cuts don't heal. Plants have branch collars that form boundaries limiting the access of diseases and insects. Cuts should be made just outside the collars, an eighth to a quarter inch above a bud angled in the direction you want the new growth to take.

Timing has a great effect on subsequent growth. In the leafing-out stage, plants use up a considerable portion of their energy reserves. Once the leaves expand and begin photosynthesizing, plants begin to rapidly regain their reserves. Hence, pruning a plant at budbreak in spring will weaken it by delaying its ability to recharge. Similarly, in fall as leaves begin to drop, root growth accelerates. Any wood removed at this time decreases the reserves available for root expansion. Additionally, woody plants should not be heavily pruned (or fertilized with nitrogen) in late summer because this may stimulate tender new growth vulnerable to frost. Spring-flowering trees and shrubs are best pruned right after they flower; summer- and fall-blooming plants early in spring or summer. Plants near their limit of cold hardiness should be pruned late in spring to clean up any winter damage. Shade trees should be shaped in early summer. Conifers with thready foliage, such as junipers, look best unpruned, but if you must cut, from April to early August is best. Pines can be dwarfed somewhat and forced to grow more densely by breaking their candles in half as they start expanding in spring. If timed right, they'll snap cleanly like asparagus shoots. Evergreens rarely regrow new leaves when cut back to old wood, so any trimming should be confined to the newest growth.

High-desert trees are naturally shaped as single or multiple trunks, their forms influenced by exposure to light and wind. Plants grow more slowly and stronger in windy places and, to reduce their evaporative surfaces, tend to be rounded and squat the more intense the sunlight. For the first few years it is better to leave woody plants unpruned and to observe their growth patterns. This waiting period also allows young plants to produce more leaves, which increases their food production and, in turn, provides for more extensive root and stem production. Once trees are large enough to have developed some personality, a bit of skillful cutting to remove suckers and water sprouts that sap the plants' energy and thinning out of some of the smaller branches so that the trunks are exposed will strengthen trees physically and aesthetically. Another advantage to delaying pruning until a tree is older is that with age the bark will begin

BEFORE:
PERENNIALS SUCH AS SCARLET BUGLER HAVE GROUND-HUGGING ROSETTES OF LEAVES AND TALL FLOWER SPIKES WHICH LATER BEAR WOODY SEED CAPSULES.

AFTER:
TO INVIGORATE THE CLUMP OF BASAL LEAVES AND TIDY THE GARDEN, THE FLOWER OR SEED STALKS CAN BE REMOVED WHEN THE LAST FLOWERS FADE OR THE SEEDPODS RIPEN.

to thicken and the expanding canopy shade the trunk. In the high desert, the exposed southwest surface of thin-barked saplings is vulnerable to sunscald, especially in fall or early spring when leaves no longer shade the bark and temperatures fluctuate wildly. During the day, trees are warmed by the sun and sap begins to flow. When temperatures plunge at night, sap freezes and expands, creating cracks that provide access for insects and disease. The damaged tissue no longer transports fluids between top growth and roots, and young trees are irreparably weakened. If we remove the protective lower shoots too early, or remove too much growth on older trees at one time, we expose tender growth unnecessarily. Oaks respond especially poorly to drastic pruning, particularly limbing up to tree standards. Pruning is best done in small increments and with a clear end in mind.

Shrubs and vines usually are pruned either to enhance an open, airy form or to induce denser growth. Thinning for openness is similar to shaping multitrunk trees, except that fewer large branches are removed near the base of the plant and more of the small, twiggy stems in the canopy are trimmed away. Early summer is the time for thinning since to prune earlier in the spring will stimulate plants to immediately replace what has been removed. Broomy plants with graceful arching stems respond better to thinning than to cutting back at the tips. Tip pruning forces branching near the ends of the stems, which will distort the natural character of such plants.

When fast-growing shrubs such as chamisa and vines such as clematis or silverlace have become overgrown, radical surgery is the best revitalizer. Depending upon its size and density, chamisa can either be trimmed back fairly uniformly to a foot or two from the ground or have the oldest stems removed at ground level and the rest of the branches cut back to two or three feet from the ground. Done in early spring, just before active growth resumes, the plant will produce abundant new growth to hide the stubs left by pruning and will develop a denser form. Vines that produce many twiggy stems are best grown on an open support, such as a post and crossbar fence or large timbered shade structure, so that they can be pruned back to the ground every three to five years to remove the inevitable buildup of old growth.

BEFORE:
PERENNIALS SUCH AS CONEFLOWER PRODUCE FLOWERS ON BRANCHED STALKS OVER AN EXTENDED BLOOM SEASON.

AFTER:
REMOVING THE SPENT FLOWERS EARLY IN THE SEASON, BEFORE THEY PRODUCE SEEDS, KEEPS PLANTS VIGOROUS AND MORE COLORFUL. TOWARD SUMMER'S END, LET SEEDHEADS DEVELOP TO ENCOURAGE RESEEDING AND FEED WILDLIFE.

GROOMING

Removing the old flower stems from shrubs and wildflowers is a hybrid of pruning and mowing. What we want to accomplish determines when to deadhead. To prolong blooming or limit self-seeding, snip off spent flower stems immediately so the plants don't expend energy producing seeds instead of blossoms. To encourage self-sowing or to feed wildlife, wait until seeds ripen and scatter or trim off mature seed stalks and use them for mulch. Sometimes the seed heads are attractive and provide winter interest in the dormant landscape. It's easiest to trim back the dried seed stalks of fernbush, blue mist, 'Autumn Joy' sedum, and garlic chives to where leaves begin to emerge in spring, just as new growth starts. Once new shoots begin expanding, it takes longer to sort the deadwood from soft new growth. Other plants, such as cherry sage and bush penstemon, aren't particularly attractive when dormant and should be trimmed back in fall.

The difference between grooming and mowing is the degree of finesse and the tools used. In flower beds along patios and paths and outside windows, where the focus is tighter, carefully trimming with hand shears leaves the most refined impression. Where less emphasis is placed on the individual plants and in spaces too large to manicure, a weed-eater or mower with a high blade setting can impose a veneer of order.

MOWING

In nature, a combination of fire and foraging creatures from grasshoppers to quail to bison rejuvenates prairie grasses and wildflowers. Under cultivation we both increase the herbage produced and exclude some of its consumers. Mowing is the management strategy that compensates for this imbalance. Again, timing is important. Occasional high mowing in summer forces side shoots to develop and increases plant density. Scalping close to the soil in summer weakens plants especially at flowering times because too much of the food-producing ability is lost and the remaining stubble bakes in the hot sun. Late fall or winter mowing has little impact on warm-season plants, except to remove excess thatch. When to mow during cold dormancy depends on the appearance of the field. The weight of snow flattens tall grasses, and winter moisture fades and grays the subtle blond, pink, and russet foliage; during dry winters grasses remain colorful and graceful. Whenever the prairie begins to look messy, trimming is in order. If the grass was tall enough to make hay, it can be collected to use as mulch or recycled as compost.

Manipulating the mowing can give up to an extra month of green lawn. More often than not, the first frost in autumn is followed by another month of mild weather. If we let the warm-season grasses grow taller toward the end of summer, after the first hard freeze in fall, we can mow off the frost-browned tops and reveal the green undergrowth.

BURNING

Fire is a fast, exciting way to remove old growth and tinder before they build up to either a major chore or hazardous proportions. Who would have thought that pyromania could be an asset in the garden? There are limits, of course, and it's best to refer back to nature for cues. Naturally, grasslands and chaparral have a twenty- to thirty-year burn cycle when litter accumulates and lightning sets off a blaze. In grasslands, fire checks the invasion of shrub and tree seedlings. In savannas, the large fire-resistant trees survive. In woodlands and chaparral, fire stimulates the germination of dormant seeds. In all ecosystems fire removes debris that stifles plant vigor and releases nutrients to support the resurgence of growth that follows. The kind of fire unleashed determines its potential for renewal or destruction. Where fuel, accumulated over decades, burns hot and long, most woody plants will be consumed. The intensity of fire is linked to the

BEFORE:
PERENNIALS SUCH AS FLAMEFLOWER PRODUCE TUFTS OF LEAVES CLOSE TO THE GROUND AND BRANCHED FLOWER STEMS THAT BLOOM CONTINUOUSLY THROUGH SUMMER UNTIL FROST.

AFTER:
FROSTED PLANT TOPS CAN BE REMOVED OR LEFT TO DECOMPOSE OVER WINTER. THE LIVE PORTION OF THE PLANT IS THE TUBEROUS ROOT IN THE GROUND.

amount of tinder available, but wind can push the flames and topography can create updrafts that make fire more powerful and unpredictable still. With only a few years' accumulation of litter, and level ground and still air, fire can be controllable. Cool fires clear smothering debris and can prevent destructive hot fires. They also create habitat edges where woody plants remain untouched. Fire is only an option when no plastic irrigation equipment has been used in the area and either no woody plants are desired within the burn area or trees are old enough for the bark to insulate the cambium layer from the heat.

Dormant vegetation tolerates fire better than actively growing plants do, so fire can be used to minimize the invasion of cool-season grasses and bindweed in warm-season grasslands if the burns are timed for spring before warm-season grasses begin to grow. Burning inhibits weeds better in dry soils since fire consumes soil moisture. In cooler upland prairies, spring fires can warm the soil and open soil space for new seedlings. In arid shrub-desert grasslands, fire can damage fragile plant communities, drying the soil and leaving more soil exposed to erosion. Many communities have fire restrictions, defining whether and when burning is an option. Your local fire department should have guidelines.

A GENTLE PLEA FOR DIVERSITY

It seems to be a quirk of human nature that we are happiest when we are stretching, absorbed in something larger than ourselves. We may not be comfortable out on the edge, but we are engaged, and there's both anticipation and satisfaction in the process. Still, some people consider the move toward native planting and making ecology a partner in horticulture to be "antigardening," an apocalypse sending us back to the dawn of gardening civilization. As one veteran gardener put it, it is "the uglification of the landscape." Is nature ugly or are we so used to foreign models for beauty that we fail to recognize the potential of our own high-desert landscape? Certainly, not all dryland native plants make good garden subjects. A few are ugly by almost any standard. Many actually are weeds in the garden. Being selective is what gardening is all about, but we need to expand our horizons. When it comes to redesigning our landscapes to more sustainable models, I fervently hope that diversity becomes the rallying cry of the changing century. As long as we follow natural patterns, the more diverse our selection of plants, the greater our chances are of developing gardens that achieve an ecological balance. The resource efficiency of natural gardens ensures that our grandchildren and their children will know the joy of birds squabbling over nesting space in the springtime and butterflies drifting through the garden in summer; that future generations will feel the melancholy bounty of a prairie gone to seed in autumn and the surging energy of an eagle hunting in winter. Natural gardening is a way to touch the future.

IN A WORLD WHERE THE HUMAN POPULATION IS INCREASING AS OTHER RESOURCES ARE DIMINISHING, NATURAL GARDENING IS A WAY TO TOUCH THE FUTURE. PETROGLYPH AT THREE RIVERS, NEAR ALAMOGORDO.

APPENDIX A:
Design Glossary/
Spatial Requirements

Outdoor activities need more generous proportions than do indoor activities.

SOCIAL SPACES

Standing room: 8 sq. ft. per person in groups
(7 sq. ft. is the minimum tolerable in large gatherings)

Sitting areas: 48 sq. ft. for 2 chairs
80 sq. ft. for 4 chairs clustered
2 ½ ft. per person on benches (benches should be 16" to 18"
high, at least 15" deep, preferably with a backrest)

Dining areas: 90 sq. ft. for a table and two chairs
100 sq. ft. for a table and four chairs
125 sq. ft. for a table and benches or chairs
seating eight
25 sq. ft. minimum for grill and counter space

RECREATIONAL SPACES

Lawns: frisbee, baseball, or football: 15' × 40'
volleyball: 45'× 80' overall/30'× 60' play space

badminton: 20'× 44' overall/17'× 39' play space
croquet: 50'× 95' overall/38'× 85' play space

Porous or hard-paved surfaces:

sandbox: 4'× 4' minimum (covered when not in use to keep cats out)
swingset: 10'× 15' minimum (play structures of amazing dimensions
and complexity are available. Remember to allow for safe
walking space around the swings.)
horseshoes: 10'× 50' overall/40' between stakes
basketball: 42'× 40' halfcourt/25'× 25' minimum
swimming pools: 24'× 42' including 3' surrounding deck (average pool)

lap pool: 10'× 60' plus 3' deck on at least two sides
spa: 5'× 5' minimum
tennis: 60'× 120' overall/36'× 78' play area
parking spaces: 8' or 9'× 18' or 20' per vehicle
miscellaneous storage: 2'× 3' per trash or recycling bin
4'× 4'× 8' for a cord of firewood

APPENDIX B: Grading

Grading concept to live by: Water runs downhill. Slopes should always run away from structures. The angle of repose—the equilibrium point that soil naturally builds up or slumps down to—varies with the soil type and moisture content. Consistently damp soil is more stable than soil that is subject to periodic flooding and drought. As water percolates into soil, the surface becomes heavier. The more extreme the slope, the more likely the surface will slump when wet.

SLOPES ARE MEASURED AND DESCRIBED AS RATIOS AND PERCENTAGES:

- a 1:1 slope, or 100% slope, rises 1 foot for each foot of horizontal space covered.
- a 2:1 slope, or 50% slope, rises 1 foot in 2 feet of horizontal space.

THERE ARE MINIMUM AND MAXIMUM GRADES FOR SPECIFIC FUNCTIONS:

- ½% slope (1" rise in 16') is the minimum allowable for paved surfaces and best only for very smooth finishes because such nearly flat surfaces shed water poorly.
- 1% slope (1" rise in 8') is the minimum ideal for concrete, brick, and tile.
- 1½% slope (3" rise in 16') is the minimum ideal for rougher surfaces such as asphalt, flag stone, or stabilized soil/soil cement.
- 2% slope (2" rise in 8') is the minimum ideal for lawns, especially in clay soil; also the minimum recommended for drainage swales.
- 3% slope (3" rise in 8') is a noticeable incline.
- 5% slope (6" rise in 10') is the maximum ideal for driveways (doesn't require changing gears) and maximum recommended for walkways.
- 10% slope (1' rise in 10') is the maximum recommended for driveways and drainage swales.
- 25% slope (1' rise in 4') is the maximum practical for mowed ground covers.
- 50% slope (1' rise in 2') is easily eroded; shrubby vegetation provides better stability.
- Stairs: maximum rise 8"/typical rise 6"/minimum tread 12"; all steps in a series should be the same so the walker can develop a comfortable rhythm.

APPENDIX C:
Plants for Windbreaks

Growth rate: Fast growing: 2 or more feet a year after the first year. Moderate growing: 1 to 2 feet a year. Slow growing: less than 1 foot a year once well established.

Water use: High: either large volumes or frequent application of water is needed. Medium: deep watering twice monthly in summer once established. Low: will survive without supplemental watering in its given ecosystem but will function better if deep watered monthly once established. Upland and Adaptive Plants: 14" rainfall; Grassland and Shrub-Desert Plants: 8" rainfall; Oasis Plants: 8" plus runoff or shallow groundwater.

COMMON NAME/BOTANICAL NAME	HEIGHT/SPACING	TYPE	GROWTH RATE	WATER REQUIREMENT
UPLAND TREES				
Incense cedar/*Calocedrus decurrens*	40'/10'	evergreen	moderate	medium
Oklahoma redbud/*Cercis reniformis*	20'/15'	deciduous	moderate	medium
Russian hawthorn/*Crataegus ambigua*	20'/10'	deciduous	moderate	medium
Thornless cockspur hawthorn /*Crataegus crus-galli* 'Inermis'	25'/12'	deciduous	moderate	medium
Washington hawthorn/*Crataegus phaenopyrum*	20'/10'	deciduous	moderate	high
Arizona cypress/*Cupressus arizonica*	25'/12'	evergreen	fast	medium to low
Singleleaf ash/*Fraxinus anomala*	20'/12'	deciduous	moderate	medium
Fragrant ash/*Fraxinus cuspidata*	20'/12'	deciduous	slow to moderate	low to medium
Rocky Mountain juniper/*Juniperus scopulorum* 'Blue Heaven', 'Cologreen', and 'Welchii'	20'/8–12'	evergreen	moderate	low to medium
Piñon/*Pinus edulis*	20'/12–15'	evergreen	slow	low to medium
Hoptree/*Ptelea trifoliata*	15'/9'	deciduous	moderate	low to medium
Gambel oak/*Quercus gambelii*	15'/12'–15'	deciduous	moderate to fast	low to medium
Texas red oak/*Quercus texana*	25'/12'–15'	deciduous	moderate to fast	medium
Shrub live oak/*Quercus turbinella*	12'/12'	evergreen	slow	low to medium
Prairie flameleaf sumac/*Rhus lanceolata*	15'/10'	deciduous	moderate to fast	low to medium
Soapberry/*Sapindus drummondii*	15'/10'	deciduous	moderate	low to medium
UPLAND SHRUBS				
Algerita/*Berberis haematocarpa*	8'/8'	evergreen	moderate	low to medium
Mountain mahogany/*Cercocarpus montanus*	12'/8'	evergreen or deciduous	moderate	low to medium

COMMON NAME/BOTANICAL NAME	HEIGHT/SPACING	TYPE	GROWTH RATE	WATER REQUIREMENT
Curlleaf mountain mahogany/*Cercocarpus ledifolius*	20'/8–12'	evergreen	moderate	low to medium
Squawapple/*Periphyllum ramosissimus*	8'/8'	deciduous	slow to moderate	low to medium
Cliffrose/*Cowania mexicana*	10'/7'	evergreen	moderate to fast	low
California buckthorn/*Rhamnus californica*	10'/6'	evergreen	slow	medium
Tallhedge/*Rhamnus frangula* 'Columnaris'	10'/4'	deciduous	moderate	medium to high

GRASSLAND AND SHRUB-DESERT TREES

Desert willow/*Chilopsis linearis*	15'/12'	deciduous	fast	low
Chitalpa/*Chitalpa* X *tashkentensis*	20'/12'	deciduous	fast	low

GRASSLAND AND SHRUB-DESERT SHRUBS

Littleleaf sumac/*Rhus microphylla*	8'/8'	deciduous	moderate	low to medium
Arizona rosewood/*Vauquelinia californica*	10'/8'	evergreen	moderate	low to medium

OASIS TREES

Alder/*Alnus tenuifolia*	20'/12'	deciduous	moderate	high
River birch/*Betula nigra*	25'/12–15'	deciduous	moderate	high
New Mexico olive/*Forestiera neomexicana*	15'/10'	deciduous	moderate	low to medium
Screwbean mesquite/*Prosopis pubescens*	15'/8'	deciduous	moderate to fast	low to medium
Mexican elder/*Sambucus mexicanus*	12'/12'	semievergreen	fast	medium
Silver buffaloberry/*Shepherdia argentea*	12'/8'	deciduous	moderate	medium to high

OASIS SHRUBS

False indigo/*Amorpha fruticosa*	8–12'/8'	deciduous	fast	medium
Broom baccheris/*Baccharis salicina*	8'/6'	deciduous	fast	low to medium
Buttonbush/*Cephalanthus occidentalis*	15'/12'	deciduous	moderate	high

ADAPTIVE TREES

Smoketree/*Cotinus coggygria*	15'/10'	deciduous	moderate	medium
Leland cypress/*Cuppressocyparis leylandi*	30'/10'	evergreen	moderate to fast	medium to high
Chinese juniper/*Juniperus chinensis* 'Hetzi Columnaris', Keteeler's, Robusta, 'Spartan', and 'Spearmint'	12–20'/5–10'	evergreen	moderate	low to medium
Eastern red cedar/*Juniperus virginiana* 'Canaerti' and 'Hillspire'	12–20'/5–10'	evergreen	moderate to fast	low to medium
Golden raintree/*Koelreuteria paniculata*	20'/12'	deciduous	slow	medium
Osage orange/*Maclura pomifera*	20'/12'	deciduous	moderate	medium
Cork oak/*Quercus suber*	30'/15'	evergreen	moderate to fast	medium
Idaho locust/*Robinia* X *ambigua*	30'/15'	deciduous	fast	medium to high
Black locust/*Robinia pseudoacacia*	30'/15'	deciduous	fast	medium to high
Vitex/*Vitex agnus-castus*	15'/10'	deciduous	moderate	medium
Jujube/*Ziziphus jujuba*	20'/10'	deciduous	moderate	medium

ADAPTIVE SHRUBS

Red clusterberry/*Cotoneaster lacteus*	8'/8'	evergreen	moderate	medium to high
Silverberry/*Elaeagnus pungens*	8'/8'	evergreen	moderate to fast	medium
Spanish broom/*Spartium junceum*	8'/8'	deciduous	moderate to fast	medium to low
Chinese lilac/*Syringa rothomagensis*	8'/6'	deciduous	moderate	medium to high

APPENDIX D:
Plants for Prairies

These are deeply rooted small shrubs and perennial wildflowers that persist in stands of prairie grasses.

SHRUBS

Leadplant/*Amorpha canescens*

Dwarf leadplant/*Amorpha nana*

Fringed sage/*Artemisia frigida*

Winterfat/*Ceratoides lanata* syn. *Eurotia lanata*

Dwarf chamisa/*Chrysothamnus* var. *nauseosus nauseosus*

Bush or Sand penstemon/*Penstemon ambiguus*

Spanish dagger/*Yucca baccata*

UPLAND WILDFLOWERS

Nodding onion/*Allium cernuum*

Indian paintbrush/*Castilleja integra*

Giant Four O'Clock/*Mirabilis multiflora*

Milkwort/*Polygala alba*

GRASSLAND AND SHRUB-DESERT WILDFLOWERS

Prickly poppy/*Argemone pleiacantha*

Prairie sage/*Artemisia ludoviciana*

Butterflyweed/*Asclepias tuberosa*

Chocolate flower/*Berlandiera lyrata*

Winecups/*Callirhoe involucrata*

Golden aster/*Chrysopsis villosa*

Bush morningglory/*Ipomoea leptophylla*

Gayfeather/*Liatris punctata*

Blackfoot daisy/*Melampodium leucanthum*

Rough menodora/*Menodora scabra*

White-tufted evening primrose/*Oenothera caespitosa*

Purple prairieclover/*Petalostemum purpureum*

White prairieclover/*Petalostemum candidum*

Pitcher sage/*Salvia azurea grandiflora* syn. *S. pitcheri*

Globemallow/*Sphaeralcea species*

Flameflower/*Talinum calycinum*

Showy goldeneye/*Viguiera multiflora*

Desert mule's ear/*Wyethia scabra*

Desert zinnia/*Zinnia grandiflora*

OASIS WILDFLOWERS

White aster/*Aster ericoides*

Bundleflower/*Desmanthus illinoensis*

Tulip gentian/*Eustoma grandiflora*

Wild licorice/*Glycyrrhiza lepidota*

Maximilian sunflower/*Helianthus maximiliani*

Goldenrod/*Solidago canadensis*

Ironweed/*Vernonia marginata*

APPENDIX E:
Prairie Grasses

These grasses can be combined, based on their growth preferences, to create prairie grasslands. (*) Indicates grasses that tend to dominate their plant community and should make up about half of the seed mix in order to simulate natural patterns. Warm-season grasses should be sown May to August, cool-season grasses February-April or September-October for best germination. Sod formers tend to exclude weeds and wildflowers as they develop. Heights listed are averages: grasses receiving extra water may grow substantially larger. Rainfall amounts are noted for basic survival. Deep watering once or twice a month from May through September to supplement listed rainfall will keep a planting attractive. Seeding rates given are for relatively small areas and are much higher than those typically given for revegetation to minimize weed competition and establish cover quickly. All seeding rates are for pure live seed (PLS), the tested germination percentage plus viable dormant seed minus impurities such as chaff or weed seed.

COMMON NAME / BOTANICAL NAME	GROWTH HABIT	HEIGHT	MIN. WATER NEEDS	SEEDING RATE (PER 1000 SQUARE FEET)
UPLAND				
(*) Purple threeawn/*Aristida purpurea*	Cool-season bunchgrass	12"	10" rainfall	½ lb.
(*) Sideoats grama/*Bouteloua curtipendula*	Warm-season bunch/sodgrass	24"	8" rainfall	2 to 3 lbs.
(*) Sheep's fescue/*Festuca ovina*	Cool-season bunchgrasses	12"	10–14" rainfall	2 to 4 lbs.
Mountain muhly/*Muhlenbergia montana*	Warm-season bunchgrass	12"	14" rainfall	¼ lb.
(*) Bush muhly/*Muhlenbergia porteri*	Warm-season bunchgrass	12"	8" rainfall	¼ lb.
(*) Spike muhly/*Muhlenbergia wrightii*	Cool-season bunchgrass	18"	15" rainfall	¼ lb.
Needle-and-thread/*Stipa comata*	Cool-season bunchgrass	24"	10" rainfall	¼ lb.

COMMON NAME / BOTANICAL NAME	GROWTH HABIT	HEIGHT	WATER NEEDS	SEEDING RATE (PER 1000 SQUARE FEET)
GRASSLAND AND SHRUB DESERT				
(*) Sand bluestem/*Andropogon hallii*	Warm-season sodgrass	30"	10" rainfall	½ lb.
Cane beardgrass/*Andropogon barbinoides*	Warm-season bunchgrass	30"	10" rainfall	2 lbs.
Silver bluestem/*Andropogon saccharoides*	Warm-season bunchgrass	30"	10" rainfall	½ lb.
(*) Black grama/*Bouteloua eriopoda*	Warm-season bunch/sodgrass	12"	6" rainfall	3 lbs.
(*) Blue grama/*Bouteloua gracilis*	Warm-season bunch/sodgrass	18"	10" rainfall	2 lbs.
(*) Buffalograss/*Buchloe dactyloides*	Warm-season sodgrass	6"	12" rainfall	2 to 3 lbs.
(*) Arizona cottontop/*Digitatia* syn. *Trichachne californica*	Warm-season bunchgrass	36"	12" rainfall	½ lb.
(*) Sand lovegrass/*Eragrostis tricodes*	Warm-season bunchgrass	30"	12" rainfall	½ lb.
Galleta/*Hilaria jamesii*	Warm-season bunch/sodgrass	12"	8" rainfall	3 lbs.
Indian ricegrass/*Oryzopsis hymenoides*	Cool-season bunchgrass	12"	6" rainfall	1 lb.
Burrograss/*Scleropogon brevifolius*	Warm-season sodgrass	8"	6" rainfall	3 lbs.
Little bluestem/*Schizachyrium* syn. *Andropogon scoparium*	Warm-season bunchgrass	18"	14" rainfall	½ lb.
Sand dropseed/*Sporobolus cryptandrus*	Warm-season bunchgrass	24"	10" rainfall	¼ lb.
Mesa dropseed/*Sporobolus flexuosus*	Warm-season bunchgrass	24"	6" rainfall	¼ lb.
Giant sacaton/*Sporobolus wrightii*	Warm-season bunchgrass	36"	12" rainfall	⅛ lb.
OASIS				
(*) Western wheat/*Andropyron smithii*	Cool-season sodgrass	30"	10" rainfall	3 lbs.
(*) Saltgrass/*Distichlis stricta*	Warm-season sodgrass	6"	8" rainfall	½ lb.
Scratchgrass/*Muhlenbergia asperifolia*	Warm-season sodgrass	8"	8" rainfall	1 lb.
Vine mesquite/*Panicum obtusum*	Warm-season sodgrass	12"	8" rainfall	2 lbs.
Switchgrass/*Panicum virgatum*	Warm-season sodgrass	36"	18" rainfall	1 lb.
Indiangrass/*Sorgastrum nutans*	Warm-season bunchgrass	36"	18" rainfall	2 lbs.
(*) Alkali sacaton/*Sporobolus airoides*	Warm-season bunchgrass	24"	8" rainfall	¼ lb.

Recommended Reading

ATTITUDES

Bowers, Janice Emily. *A Full Life in a Small Space and Other Essays from a Desert Garden*. Tucson: University of Arizona Press, 1993.

Cornell, Joseph. *Sharing Nature with Children*. Nevada City, Calif.: Dawn Publications, 1979.

Jensen, Jens. *Siftings*. Baltimore: The Johns Hopkins University Press, 1990.

Pollan, Michael. *Second Nature: A Gardener's Education*. New York: The Atlantic Monthly Press, 1991.

Stein, Sara. *Noah's Garden: Restoring the Ecology of Our Own Backyards*. Boston: Houghton-Mifflin Co., 1993.

Wasowski, Sally, and Andy Wasowski. *Requiem for a Lawnmower*. Dallas: Taylor Publishing Co., 1992.

SENSE OF PLACE

Brown, David E., ed. *Biotic Communities of the American Southwest: United States and Mexico*. Superior, Ariz.: Boyce Thompson Southwest Arboretum, 1982.

Cushman, Ruth Carol, and Steven R. Jones. *The Shortgrass Prairie*. Boulder: Pruett Publishing Co., 1989.

Dick-Peddie, William A. *New Mexico Vegetation: Past, Present and Future*. Albuquerque: University of New Mexico Press, 1993.

MacMahon, James A., ed. *Deserts: The Audubon Society Nature Series*. New York: Chanticleer Press, Inc., 1985.

Reisner, Marc. *Cadillac Desert: The American West and Its Disappearing Water*. New York: Penguin Books, 1987.

DESIGN/PLANNING

Hammer, Donald A. ed. *Constructed Wetlands for Waste Treatment*. Chelsea, Mich.: Lewis Publishers, 1989.

Knopf, Jim. *The Xeriscape Flower Gardener*. Boulder: Johnson Publishing Co., 1991.

Little, Charles E. *Greenways for America*. Baltimore: The Johns Hopkins University Press, 1990.

Mollison, Bill. *Permaculture: A Designers' Manual*. Tyalgum, Australia: Tagari Publications, 1988.

Moshiri, Gerald A., ed. *Constructed Wetlands for Water Quality Improvement*. Boca Raton, Fla.: CRC Press, Inc., 1993.

Simonds, John Ormsbee. *Landscape Architecture: A Manual of Site Planning and Design*. New York: McGraw-Hill Book Co., 1983.

Springer, Lauren. *The Undaunted Garden: Planting for Weather-Resilient Beauty*. Golden, Colo.: Fulcrum Publishing, 1994.

PLANTING AND MANAGING/ESTABLISHING A BALANCE

Brooklyn Botanic Garden. *Natural Insect Control: The Ecological Gardener's Guide to Foiling Pests*. Brooklyn, N.Y.: Brooklyn Botanic Garden Publications, 1994.

Dupriez, Hugues and Philippe DeLeener. *Ways of Water: Run-off, Irrigation and Drainage*. New York: Macmillan Publishing Co., 1990.

Olkowski, William and Helga and Sheila Daar. *Common-Sense Pest Control: Least-toxic Solutions for Your Home, Garden, Pets and Community*. Newtown, Conn.: The Taunton Press, 1991.

University of California Integrated Pest Management Project. *Pests of Landscape Trees and Shrubs: An Integrated Pest Management Guide*. ANR Publications, 6 701 San Pablo Avenue, Oakland, CA 94608-1239. Publication 3359, 1994.

Western Society of Weed Science and Cooperative Extension Service. *Weeds of the West*. Jackson, Wyoming: University of Wyo., 1991.

Wittrock, Gustave L. *The Pruning Book*. Emmaus, Pa.: Rodale Press, Inc., 1971.

HABITAT GARDENING

Benyus, Janine M. *The Field Guide to Wildlife Habitats of the Western United States*. New York: Simon and Schuster, Inc., 1989.

Guisti, Gregory A. *Protecting Your Garden from Animal Damage*. San Ramon, Calif.: Ortho Books, 1994.

Henderson, Carroll L. *Landscaping for Wildlife*. Saint Paul, Minn.: Minnesota Department of Natural Resources, 1981.

PROPAGATION

Deno, Norman C. *Seed Germination, Theory and Practice*. Norman Deno, 139 Leno Drive, State College, Pa. 16801, 1993.

Dirr, Michael A., and Charles W. Heuser, Jr. *The Reference Manual of Woody Plant Propagation: From Seed to Tissue Culture*. Athens, Ga.: Varsity Press, 1987.

Nokes, Jill. *How to Grow Native Plants of Texas and the Southwest*. Austin, Tex.: Texas Monthly Press, 1986.

USDA Yearbook of Agriculture. *Seeds of Woody Plants in the United States*. Washington, D.C.: U.S. Government Printing Office, Superintendent of Documents, 1961.

Young, James A. and Cheryl G. *Collecting, Processing and Germinating Seeds of Wildland Plants*. Portland, Oreg.: Timber Press, 1986.

PLANT PROFILES

Barr, Claude A. *Jewels of the Plains: Wildflowers of the Great Plains Grasslands and Hills*. Minneapolis: University of Minnesota Press, 1983.

Benson, Lyman. *Trees and Shrubs of the Southwestern Deserts*. Tucson: University of Arizona Press, 1981.

Heflin, Jean, and Erma Pilz. *The Beautiful Beardtongues of New Mexico: A Field Guide to New Mexico Penstemons*. Albuquerque, N.M.: Jack Rabbit Press, 1990.

Gould, Frank C. *Grasses of the Southwestern United States*. Tucson: University of Arizona Press, 1951.

Hickman, James C. *The Jepson Manual: Higher Plants of California*. Berkeley: University of California Press, 1993.

Lodewick, Kenneth, and Robin Lodewick. *Penstemon Field Identifier*. K & R Lodewick, 2526 University Street, Eugene, Oreg. 97403.

Mielke, Judy. *Native Plants for Southwestern Landscapes*. Austin: University of Texas Press, 1993.

Miller, George O. *Landscaping with Native Plants of Texas and the Southwest*. Stillwater, Minn.: Voyageur Press, 1991.

Simpson, Benny J. *A Field Guide to Texas Trees*. Austin: Texas Monthly Press, 1988.

Springer, Lauren. *The Undaunted Garden: Planting for Weather-Resilient Beauty*. Golden, Colo.: Fulcrum Publishing, 1994.

Vines, Robert A. *Trees, Shrubs and Woody Vines of the Southwest*. Austin: University of Texas Press, 1976.

Wasowski, Sally, and Andy Wasowski. *Native Texas Plants: Landscaping Region by Region*. Austin: Texas Monthly Press, 1988.

Index

Boldface indicates pages with illustrations.

About the Author

Photo courtesy of Nancy Hemry Botts

Judith Phillips has been a professional plant grower and landscape designer for the past twenty-five years. The past fifteen years have been devoted to growing and designing for plants native to high-desert climates. When not tending plants or drawing garden plans, she lectures and writes on the subject. Among her principal publications are *Southwestern Landscaping with Native Plants* (1987), also published by the Museum of New Mexico Press, and essays in *Taylor's Guide to Natural Gardening* and *Taylor's Master Guide to Gardening*. She lives and works in central New Mexico, where nature commands respect and wilderness is just beyond the garden wall.